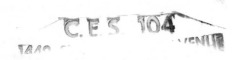

ScottForesman Science

Discover the Wonder

Series Consulting Author

David Heil
Associate Director,
Oregon Museum of Science & Industry
Portland, Oregon

Consulting Authors

Maureen Allen
Science Resource Teacher/Specialist
Irvine Unified School District
Irvine, California

Dr. Timothy Cooney
Professor of Earth Science & Science Education
Earth Science Department
University of Northern Iowa
Cedar Falls, Iowa

Angie Matamoros
Lead Science Supervisor
Broward County Schools
Ft. Lauderdale, Florida

Dr. Manuel Perry
Manager, Educational Programs
Lawrence Livermore National Laboratory
Livermore, California

Dr. Irwin Slesnick
Professor of Biology
Biology Department
Western Washington University
Bellingham, Washington

 ScottForesman

A Division of HarperCollins*Publishers*

Editorial Offices: Glenview, Illinois
Regional Offices: Sunnyvale, California • Tucker, Georgia
Glenview, Illinois • Oakland, New Jersey • Dallas, Texas

Content Consultants

Dr. Linda Berne
University of North Carolina
Charlotte, North Carolina

Dr. Kurt Brorson
Laboratory of Cellular and Molecular
Immunology
National Institutes of Health
Bethesda, Maryland

Dr. Bonnie Buratti
Jet Propulsion Laboratory
California Institute of Technology
Pasadena, California

Dr. Michael Garcia
Department of Geology and Geophysics
University of Hawaii
Honolulu, Hawaii

Dr. Norman Gelfand
Fermi National Accelerator Laboratory
Accelerator Division
Batavia, Illinois

Dr. Roger Pielke
Department of Atmospheric Science
Colorado State University
Fort Collins, Colorado

Dr. Harrison H. Schmitt
*Former Astronaut (Apollo 17) and
    United States Senator*
*Geologist and Science and Technology
    Consultant*
Albuquerque, New Mexico

Dr. Richard Shippee
Department of Biology
Vincennes University
Vincennes, Indiana

Dr. David Stronck
Department of Teacher Education
California State University at Hayward
Hayward, California

Dr. Merita Thompson
Department of Health Education
Eastern Kentucky University
Richmond, Kentucky

Dr. Antonio Garcia Trejo
Arizona Department of Environmental
    Quality
Chandler, Arizona

Dr. Lisa Wagner
Department of Biology
Georgia Southern University
Statesboro, Georgia

Multicultural Consultants

Dr. Thomas Crosby
Department of Biology
Morgan State University
Baltimore, Maryland

Dr. Frank Dukepoo
Department of Biology
Northern Arizona University
Flagstaff, Arizona

Dr. Amram Gamliel (Ben-Teman)
*Educational Consultant/Professional
    Writer*
Newton Center, Massachusetts

Dr. Hilda Hernandez
Department of Education
California State University at Chico
Chico, California

Dr. Luis A. Martinez-Perez
College of Education
Florida International University
Miami, Florida

Safety Consultant

Dr. Jack A. Gerlovich
*Science Education Safety
    Consultant/Author*
Waukee, Iowa

Reading Consultant

Dr. Robert A. Pavlik
Professor of Reading/Language Arts
Reading/Language Arts Department
Cardinal Stritch College
Milwaukee, Wisconsin

Activity Consultant

Mary Jo Diem
Science/Educational Consultant
Croton-on-Hudson, New York

Acknowledgments

Photographs Unless otherwise acknowledged, all photographs are the property of
ScottForesman. Page abbreviations are as follows: (T)top, (C)center, (B)bottom, (L)left,
(R)right, (INS)inset.
Cover Design Sheldon Cotler + Design
Cover Background: Gary Braasch/WOODFIN CAMP & ASSOC., Inc.   Inset: H.G. Ross/
FPG INTERNATIONAL   Magnifying Glass: Richard Chesnut
Page iv-v(T), v(BR) NASA   **vi(TL)** E.R. Degginger   **vi(BL)** Hermann Eisenbeiss/
Photo Researchers   **ix(R)** David Olson/Black Star   **xii** Warren Faidley/Weatherstock
x(B) Kim Taylor/Bruce Coleman, Inc.   **xi(BL)** John Covant/Photri, Inc.   **xiv(T)** Knut Bry
xiv(B) Michael & Patricia Fogden   **xv(T), xv(R-INS), xvi** Victor Englebert

Illustrations Unless otherwise acknowledged, all computer graphics by Ligature, Inc.
Page iv Roberta Polfus   **vi** George Kelvin   **viii-ix** Ebet Dudley   **xiv-xv** John Burgoyne

Acknowledgments continue on page 43.

ISBN: 0-673-42754-4
Copyright ©1993, Scott, Foresman and Company, Glenview, Illinois
All Rights Reserved. Printed in the United States of America.

About the Cover

The name of this beautiful bird describes it
very well. It's a red-and-green macaw.
These birds live in rainforests of Central
America and South America. The
background photograph was taken in Costa
Rica, in Central America.

Reviewers

Earth and Other Planets

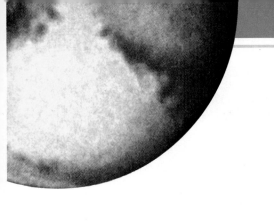

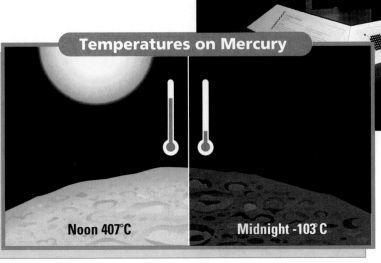

Temperatures on Mercury

Noon 407°C   Midnight -103°C

Water

CHAPTER

3 Water and Life

Volcanoes and Earthquakes

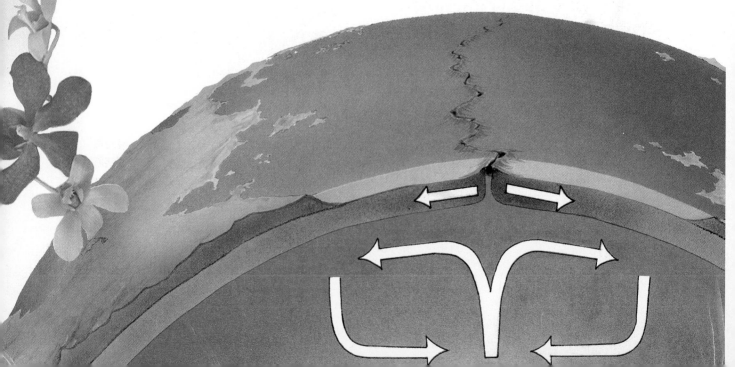

CHAPTER 3 Faults and Quakes

Flying

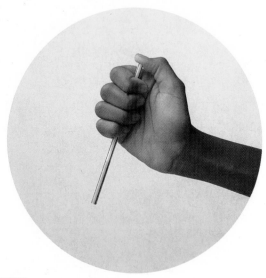

CHAPTER

3 Learning to Fly

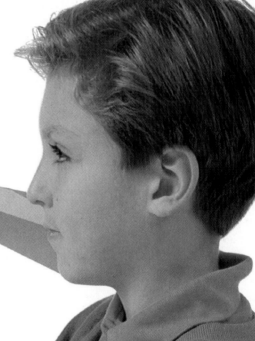

The Weather Report

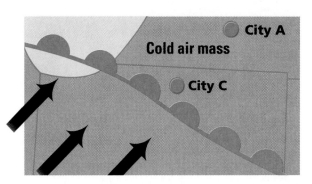

CHAPTER

3 Predicting Weather

Rainforests

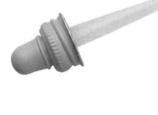

Earth and Other Planets

Earth and Other Planets

How can you be in two places at once? By taking an armchair tour. In this module, you'll observe Earth from outer space, visit the other planets, and get a new look at your beautiful home. So sit back, relax, and prepare yourself for the trip of a lifetime.

CHAPTER

1 Moving in Space

Can you spin around and around without ever stopping? No way! Yet spinning is just one of the constant movements that Earth makes as it travels through space.

CHAPTER

2 The Solar System

You can't beat this system! The solar system offers an amazing collection of planets, asteroids, and comets, along with lots of extra space.

Effects of Gravity

Moon — Path with no gravity

Moon — Path with gravity

3 The Blue Planet

We're happy to have the blues.
Unlike the other planets of the solar system, Earth is home to blue sky, blue water, and the many colors of life.

1 Moving in Space

Where did it go? I can't find it! How'd it get way over there?

How do shadows change?

Tape a black paper shape on a sunny window. Look for its shadow. Think of a way to keep track of the shape and position of this shadow. Look for this shadow every 15 minutes for two hours.

For Discussion

1. How would you explain any changes that occur?
2. How will the shadow look in three hours?

1.1 *The Moving Earth*

▶ *Is Earth moving?*

Imagine you're in space. Through the windows of your spaceship you can see millions of distant stars and other points of light. One of the stars looks much larger and brighter because that star is much closer to your spaceship. That star is the sun.

Suddenly you notice that one of the points of light seems to be getting larger. But, it's not really getting larger. It's getting closer. As the point of light gets closer and closer, you can see that it's a solid ball of matter—a planet. And, according to the spaceship's computer, the planet is hurtling through space toward you at more than 100,000 kilometers per hour.

The planet is called Earth. It's big, it's blue, it's beautiful, and it's headed straight for your spaceship! On and on Earth rushes. Then, just when you think that Earth will slam right into you, it zooms by, curving away into the distance. Where is this planet, shown in the picture below, going? Read on and find out!

▼ *Earth moving through space*

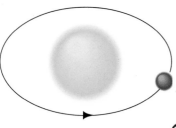

▲ *Earth's orbit around the sun is an ellipse.*

Orbiting the Sun

Earth is going around and around the sun just as a runner goes around and around a track.

The path Earth takes as it moves around the sun is called its orbit. The diagram at the left shows Earth's orbit around the sun. Notice in this diagram that Earth's orbit looks like a slightly flattened circle, called an ellipse (i lips′).

Remember how Earth zoomed by your spaceship? Now, imagine you're in the same spot in space one year later. Earth will zoom by you once again. Earth will have traveled almost 1 billion kilometers since the last time you saw it. During that one year, Earth will have made one **revolution** (rev′ ə lü′ shən) around the sun. One full orbit around another object is called one revolution.

Spinning Around an Axis

Revolving around the sun is not the only way Earth is moving. Earth is also spinning. Have you ever spun a toy top? You can learn a lot about Earth's spinning by looking at a toy top. The simplest top looks like a little ball, with a stem on the top side and a sharp point on the bottom. To spin the top you first rest the point on the floor and hold the stem with your fingers. Then you quickly twist the stem and let go. The top spins around and around until it stops.

Now imagine a straight line that starts at the stem of the top, passes through the ball, and ends at the sharp point. That imaginary line is called an axis. The top spins around and around its axis. One full spin around the axis is called a **rotation** (rō tā′ shən). The top makes hundreds of rotations in less than a minute.

Just like a top, Earth spins around and around an imaginary axis. Earth's axis starts at the north pole, passes through the center of the earth, and stops at the south pole. Unlike a top, however, Earth isn't spinning on a solid floor. You can see in the pictures that Earth is spinning in space as it orbits the sun. And unlike a top, Earth never stops spinning. Year after year Earth keeps spinning around its axis.

In the Discover Activity you saw how a shadow moves in a curved path in daylight. The shadow moves because of Earth's rotation. The amount of time for one rotation is called a day. On Earth, one rotation takes 24 hours. Every day of your life, Earth rotates once around its axis. In just over 365 days, Earth makes one revolution around the sun. During all that time, Earth keeps rotating as it orbits the sun.

◄ As Earth revolves around the sun, it also rotates around its axis.

Checkpoint

1. Describe Earth's movement around the sun. What name is given to this pattern of movement?
2. How does Earth move like a toy top?
3. Take Action! Have a friend represent the sun and you represent Earth. Show how Earth rotates around its axis while it revolves around the sun.

Exploring Motion Near the Earth's Surface

When objects fall, they move toward the earth's surface. In this activity, you use marbles to observe how objects move as they get close to the earth's surface.

Picture A

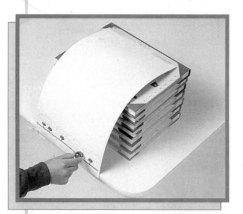

Picture B

Picture C

Gather These Materials

marker

long piece of
   posterboard, about
   40 cm x 25 cm

stack of books, about
   30 cm high

masking tape

marble

Follow This Procedure

1 Make a chart like the one on the next page. Record your observations in your chart.

2 Use a marker to draw the earth's horizon and some clouds near the bottom of one of the narrow edges of the posterboard. This will represent the area near the earth's surface.

3 Place the stack of books on the table behind the posterboard. Bend the posterboard so that it makes a smooth curve. Tape the top end of the posterboard to the top book in the pile. Tape the bottom end of the posterboard to the table. (Picture A)

Predict: Where along the cardboard will the marble take the longest time to fall?

4 Hold the marble against the posterboard where you have drawn clouds. (Picture B) Release it. Observe how the marble moves. Record what you observe.

5 Hold the marble against the center of the posterboard. Release it and observe how it moves. Record your observations.

6 Hold the marble near the top of the posterboard and then release it. (Picture C) Record your observations.

Distance from Earth	Effect of Gravity
Earth's horizon	
Above the horizon	
In space	

State Your Conclusions

1. From what point along the posterboard does the marble's speed seem to be the fastest?

2. From what point along the posterboard does the marble's speed seem to be the slowest?

Let's Experiment

How difficult is it to launch a rocket from the earth's surface? Use the cardboard model to show what happens when you launch a "marble rocket" upward, away from the earth's surface. Use what you know about scientific methods to find out.

1.2 *The Force of Gravity*

Why does the moon orbit Earth?

In the year 1665, a young man named Isaac Newton asked a simple question: Why does the moon orbit Earth? Newton knew that the moon goes around and around Earth. But he couldn't explain why. All year long Newton kept asking why the moon orbits Earth. He finally discovered the answer right under his feet.

Newton discovered the answer to his question by thinking about apples. He wondered why ripe apples fall down from apple trees. There must be a force that pulls the apples down to Earth, he thought. And if a force pulls the apples down to Earth, maybe a force also pulls the moon around and around Earth. Are those two forces the same, or are they different?

Newton kept thinking about apples, orbits, and forces. At last he came up with the answer. The two forces are the same! The force that pulls apples to the ground is the same as the force that pulls the moon around Earth. That force is called gravity. In this lesson, you will find out how gravity works. But first you will read about systems.

Systems in Space

Systems are all around you. For example, a rider and a bicycle form a system. The rider starts the bicycle by turning the pedals. The pedals turn the chain; the chain turns the gears; the gears turn the wheels. All those parts work together. As long as the rider keeps pedaling, the system keeps working.

A system you know quite well is your body. Blood carries oxygen and nutrients to your cells. Cells release energy so muscles, like your heart, can do their work. As long as these parts work together, you stay active and healthy.

The sun and Earth always work together. Year after year Earth orbits the sun. Year after year the sun shines on Earth. Because they work together, the sun and Earth can be called a **system**—a set of parts that affect each other.

The moon and Earth are also very different from one another. And they too form a system. Notice in the picture how the Earth and moon system is similar to the sun and Earth system. The moon is smaller than Earth, and it orbits Earth. Month after month the moon keeps orbiting Earth, even as Earth is orbiting the sun. Why does the moon orbit Earth? Why does Earth orbit the sun? The answer to both of those questions is gravity.

▲ The sun and Earth form a system, and Earth and the moon form another system.

How Gravity Behaves

You can't see gravity, and you can't touch it, but gravity is always present. **Gravity** (grav′ ə tē) is a force of attraction between objects. An apple and Earth are both objects. Gravity pulls them together. Because of gravity, the apple falls to Earth.

The force of gravity between two objects depends on how far apart those objects are. An apple grows on a branch just a few meters above Earth. Because the apple and Earth are so close together, the force of gravity between them is strong. But if the apple were 150 million kilometers from Earth, the force of gravity between them would be weak. The greater the distance between two objects, the weaker the force of gravity is between them.

Gravity is not only affected by the distance between objects. Gravity is also affected by mass. What is **mass**? It's the amount of matter an object contains. Earth has much more matter than an apple, so Earth has much more mass than an apple. Likewise, the sun has more matter than Earth, so the sun has much more mass than Earth.

The more mass two objects have, the greater the force of gravity is between them. Taken together, the sun and Earth have much more mass than the apple and Earth. So even though the sun is 150 million kilometers from Earth, the force of gravity between the sun and Earth is strong, because of their large combined mass. But if the apple were 150 million kilometers from Earth, the force of gravity between the apple and Earth would be weak. Not only would the apple and Earth be far apart, but their combined mass would be small.

Effects of Gravity

Moon

Path with no gravity

Moon Path with gravity

▲ *The moon orbits Earth because of the pull of gravity between them.*

Gravity and Orbits

Gravity pulls Earth and the moon together. But the moon doesn't fall to Earth like an apple. In the picture on page 12 you can see that the moon is always moving. What if the moon wasn't pulled by Earth's gravity? Then it would move in a straight path away from Earth. Notice in the picture that gravity pulls the moon out of its straight path. Because of the pull of gravity, the moon keeps falling in a path that curves around Earth. That curved path is the moon's orbit.

But why doesn't Earth orbit the moon? Because when two objects attract each other, the object with less mass will move more easily. The moon has much less mass than Earth. Therefore, the moon orbits around Earth instead of Earth orbiting around the moon.

By using what you have learned about gravity and mass, you can explain why an apple falls to Earth. To begin with, the force of gravity between the apple and Earth is strong because they are so close together. And because the apple has less mass than Earth, it moves more easily than Earth. Therefore the apple always falls to Earth.

Checkpoint

1. What is a system?
2. What happens to the force of gravity between two objects that are moving farther apart?
3. What path would the moon take if it weren't pulled by Earth's gravity?
4. **Take Action!** Select two objects. Show how you can decrease the pull of gravity between them. Also show which one would revolve around the other if they were in space.

Activity

The Path of Light

Instruments like binoculars and periscopes work because of the way light travels. Try this activity to find out how light travels.

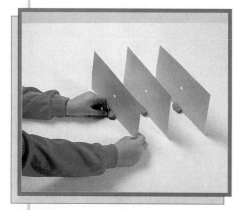

Picture A

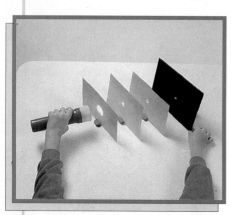

Picture B

Picture C

Gather These Materials

3 file cards
hole punch
clay

black construction paper
flashlight

Follow This Procedure

1 Make a chart like the one on the next page. Record your observations in your chart.

2 Place 3 file cards on top of each other so the corners are lined up. Punch a hole in the center of all 3 cards at once.

3 Place a lump of clay at the bottom of each card to hold the cards upright.

4 Place the 3 file cards with their holes lined up. They should be about 5 cm apart. (Picture A)

5 Hold the black construction paper in back of the last file card. (Picture B)

Predict: **Will light be able to travel through the cards onto the black paper?**

6 Turn on the flashlight. Shine the flashlight through the hole in the first card. Observe what happens to the light and record the results in the chart.

Record Your Results

Position of holes	Observations
When holes are lined up	
When holes aren't lined up	

Predict: *What would happen to the light if the holes were not lined up?*

7 Move the middle card so that the holes no longer line up. (Picture C)

8 Shine the flashlight through the holes again. What happens? Record your observations on your chart.

State Your Conclusions

1. Describe how light travels.
2. Why can't you see around corners?

Let's Experiment

Now that you've seen how light travels, can you use mirrors to direct light around corners? Use what you know about scientific methods to find out.

In a partial eclipse the moon moves between Earth and the sun. This blocks most of the sun's light from reaching Earth.

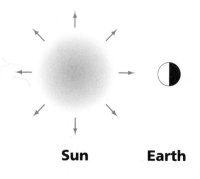

Sunlight travels away from the sun in straight line paths.

Sun   Earth

Half of Earth is always in darkness while the other half is always in light.

LESSON

1.3 Light and Shadows

How can the moon cover the sun?

In Baja California, Mexico, the morning of July 11, 1991, began like any other. The sun came up in the east and slowly rose in the sky. Not long after sunrise, however, something unusual happened. A large, dark object started to creep across the sun.

Over the next hour and a half the object covered more and more of the sun. The sky turned darker. Finally, at 10:24 A.M., day seemed to turn into night.

During the next five minutes, the morning of July 11 was like the night before. Then the object that blocked the sun began to move away. One and a half hours later the sun shone as brightly as ever.

Did a giant cloud block the sun? The object was giant, but it wasn't a cloud. It was the moon. In this lesson, you will learn how the moon's movement can keep the sun's light from reaching Earth. You will also learn about how Earth's movements cause day and night.

Catching the Rays

A baseball can help you understand day and night on Earth. When you look at a baseball you can see only half of it. The other half faces away from you. No matter how fast you spin the baseball, you can see only one half at a time. In the same way, one half of Earth is always facing the sun. The other half is always facing away from the sun. That side is dark because no sunlight can reach it. As Earth rotates, one part is always spinning into darkness. Another part of Earth, on the other side, is always spinning into sunlight.

Notice in the picture on page 16 that sunlight travels in rays that move away from the sun. Light moves incredibly fast—faster than any other speed we know. In just over eight short minutes, light can zoom across the 150 million kilometers of dark space that separates the sun and Earth. The sun's rays don't light up this space. They light up only Earth, the moon, and other solid objects that they hit. The rays can't pass through these solid objects. Therefore, as Earth rotates, the half facing the sun is light. The other half of Earth is dark, as shown in the picture below.

MATH

Traveling Time

Sunlight has a long way to go to reach the planets in our solar system. Each planet is a different distance from the sun, so sunlight reaches each one at a different time.

The graphs show how far sunlight travels in minutes and hours.

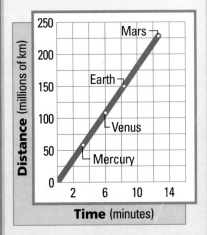

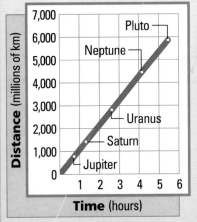

What Did You Find Out?
1. *How many kilometers away from the sun is Mercury? Pluto?*
2. *How long does sunlight take to reach Mercury? Pluto?*

Moonlight: Reflections on Sections

As the moon orbits Earth, it seems to change shape.

The moon, our closest neighbor in space, is shaped like a ball. Yet from day to day, its shape seems to change. Sometimes the moon appears as a round circle. At other times only thin slivers can be seen.

These changes are called phases of the moon. The phases appear in a pattern that repeats every 29⅓ days. This period is the time the moon takes to orbit Earth.

But the moon only seems to change shape. The shape of the moon that we see depends on how much of the sunlit half of the moon is facing Earth. And that depends on the position of the moon in its orbit around Earth.

1 New Moon Moon is between Earth and sun; sunlit side of moon faces away.

3 First Quarter One week later, half the moon's sunlit side faces Earth.

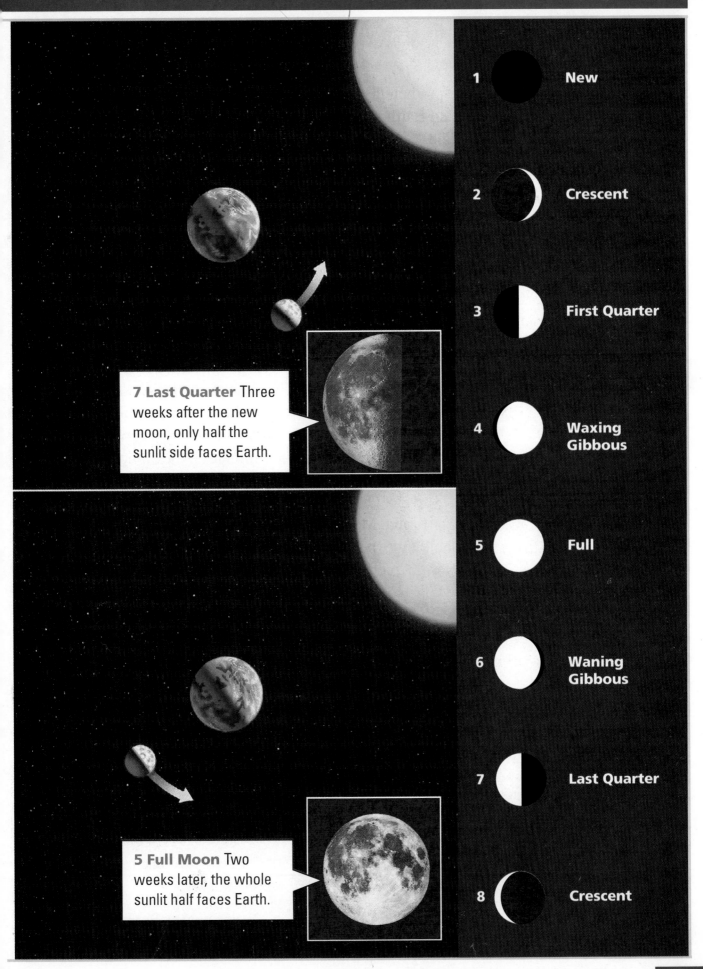

7 Last Quarter Three weeks after the new moon, only half the sunlit side faces Earth.

5 Full Moon Two weeks later, the whole sunlit half faces Earth.

1		New
2		Crescent
3		First Quarter
4		Waxing Gibbous
5		Full
6		Waning Gibbous
7		Last Quarter
8		Crescent

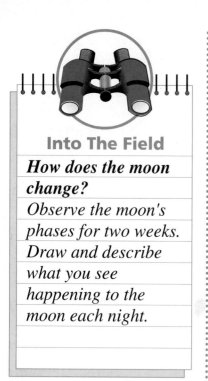

Into The Field

How does the moon change?

Observe the moon's phases for two weeks. Draw and describe what you see happening to the moon each night.

▼ The sun's light is blocked by the moon in a solar eclipse.

Making a Shadow

When the moon moves directly between the sun and Earth so that all three are lined up in a straight line, a **solar eclipse** (sō′ lər i klips′) begins. During a solar eclipse, the moon blocks sunlight from reaching Earth, making a shadow of the moon on Earth.

Find the moon's shadow on Earth in the picture below. The center of the moon's shadow is dark. Anyone in this part of the shadow sees a total solar eclipse. The moon totally blocks the sun. Only a bright ring around the sun can be seen. When the moon blocks only part of the sun from your view, you see a partial solar eclipse. The people in the outer rim of the moon's shadow see a partial solar eclipse. The moon moves quickly, so a total solar eclipse is brief. It can last anywhere from a few seconds to seven and a half minutes. An example of a total and of a partial solar eclipse is shown on the next page. On July 11, 1991, people in Baja California, Mexico, saw a total solar eclipse. At the same time, people in most of the other parts of North America saw a partial solar eclipse.

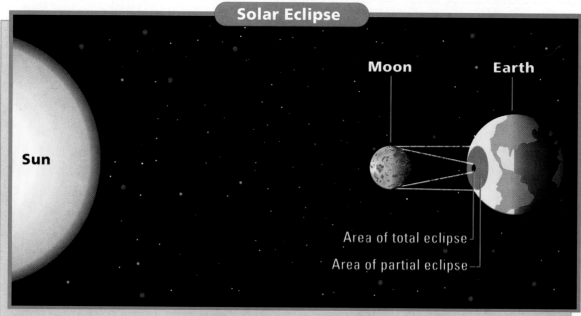

Solar Eclipse

Moon · Earth

Sun

Area of total eclipse

Area of partial eclipse

◄ *During a total solar eclipse, the sun is completely blocked from view on Earth. During a partial solar eclipse, only part of the sun is blocked from view.*

Notice in the diagram at the right that sometimes Earth passes between the sun and the moon. When that happens, Earth casts a shadow on the moon. That's called a lunar eclipse. Lunar eclipses are more common than solar eclipses.

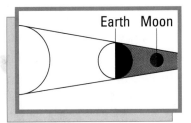

Earth Moon

▲ *When Earth moves directly between the moon and the sun, a lunar eclipse occurs.*

Joining the System

In the last lesson, you learned that the sun and Earth form a system. You also learned that Earth and the moon form a system. Both of those systems combined form a larger system. It is made up of the sun, Earth, and the moon. This system is part of a still larger system. It is called the solar system. You'll learn more about the solar system in the next chapter.

Checkpoint

1. Why is Earth always half dark?
2. What determines how much of the moon is visible to us here on Earth?
3. How are Earth, the sun, and the moon lined up during a solar eclipse?
4. Name four systems to which Earth belongs.
5. Take Action! Make a calendar that shows the phases of the moon each night for a month. Try to predict the phases that will occur next.

Inferring

When you use the information you have to make a guess about what is likely to be true, you are inferring. Scientists often make inferences. They may need to study something too far away in time or space to observe directly. Scientists might make inferences based on the data they gather. Or they might use what they already know about a similar event to infer facts.

Thinking It Through

What causes an eclipse of the moon? Use these questions to help you find out.

What do I know for sure about an eclipse of the moon?

I know that in an eclipse of the moon, the moon becomes dark at a time when it would usually shine. I also know that the moon shines by reflecting sunlight.

What event do I know that is like an eclipse of the moon?

I know about an eclipse of the sun.

What information about a solar eclipse helps explain an eclipse of the moon?

The moon causes a solar eclipse when it passes between the earth and the sun, casting a shadow on the earth's surface.

Can I make an inference?

Maybe something casts a shadow during an eclipse of the moon. But what makes the shadow? Maybe the earth comes between the sun and the moon and casts a shadow on the moon.

When you need to make an inference, keep these steps in mind:

1. Figure out what you know for sure.

2. Think of a similar event.

3. What do you know about the similar event that could fill in a gap in your information about this event?

4. Make an inference based on the similar event.

Your Turn

Imagine you are living on the moon. Would you be able to see an eclipse of the sun there? Use data from the chapter to help you find a likely answer.

Chapter Review

Thinking Back

1. Explain the difference between a **revolution** and a **rotation** of Earth.
2. What is **gravity** and how does it affect a system?
3. Explain why **mass** causes Earth to revolve around the sun rather than the sun around Earth.
4. Name a **system** and explain why it is a system.
5. When does a **solar eclipse** occur?
6. A planet has two moons of equal mass, one at a distance of 100,000 kilometers and another at 1,000,000 kilometers. Which moon would have a stronger force of gravity between it and the planet? Why?
7. Explain why half of Earth is always dark.
8. Describe the changes the moon goes through as it orbits Earth once.

Connecting Ideas

1. Copy the concept map. Use the terms at the right to complete the map about revolving.

moon   **sun**

A. _____ *revolves around* B. Earth *revolves around* C. _____

2. Write a sentence or two about the ideas shown in the concept map.

Gathering Evidence

1. In the Activity on page 8, how did you know where the force of gravity was the greatest and the slightest?
2. In the Activity on page 14, how did you know the shape of the path of light?

Doing Science!

1. *Create an activity* that would show how an object with less mass is more easily pulled by gravity than one with more mass.
2. *Design an activity* that would show the phases of the moon.

The Solar System

Our car is like this in the summer. You can't even sit in the seats.

Discover Activity

How can you trap heat?

Think about containers in your room that light can pass through. Which one traps the most heat from the sun? To find out, place a thermometer inside the empty container. Then, place the container in the sun. Put another thermometer outside the container. After 30 minutes, read each thermometer.

For Discussion

1. *What happens to the temperature inside your container?*
2. *How could you make it trap more heat?*

2.1 The Inner Planets

What is it like on other planets?

It's a good thing that Earth is part of the solar system. Without the pull of gravity between the sun and Earth, Earth would find itself traveling off into space. Without the sun's light and energy, Earth would be a very cold and dark world. However, Earth does orbit the sun and so it has a place in the solar system. But Earth is not the only planet that is affected by the sun's energy and gravity.

People have always wondered what it's like on other bodies in the solar system. The moon is the only place people have been able to visit in person to answer that question. On July 20, 1969, astronaut Neil Armstrong was the first human to set foot on the moon. Six other missions visited the moon after that to explore, collect samples, and conduct experiments. Space probes sent from Earth without crews have been able to travel vast distances through the solar system. The probes have found that the planets in the solar system are very different from one another.

Find Mercury, Venus, Earth, and Mars on the map. They are the inner planets because they orbit closest to the sun. The outer planets—Jupiter, Saturn, Uranus, Neptune, and Pluto—orbit much farther away. In this lesson, you will learn how being in the solar system affects the inner planets.

Pluto

Neptune

Mercury

Venus

Earth

Jupiter

Mars

Saturn

Uranus

▲ *The solar system*

◄ *The sun*

➤ *Mercury*

The Sun—The Shining Sphere

The sun is the largest, brightest, and hottest object in the solar system. It is also the center of the solar system. The sun has more mass than all the other objects in our solar system put together. As a result, gravitational force causes all the planets to orbit around the sun—even planets as distant as Neptune and Pluto.

The powerful sun is mostly made of a gas called hydrogen. In turn, the hydrogen is made of tiny particles called atoms. At the sun's center, hydrogen atoms may reach temperatures as high as 15 million degrees Celsius (°C). The higher the temperature, the faster the atoms move. Some of the atoms move so fast that they smash into each other and form a gas called helium. And when the hydrogen atoms change into helium, they also release energy. The energy heats up the sun and makes it shine. The sun has enough hydrogen to stay hot and shining for about 4 billion years.

Mercury—The Hot and Cold Planet

The closest planet to the sun is Mercury. Because it is so close to the sun, it is difficult to study Mercury from Earth. The brightness of the sun makes it hard to see. Spacecraft flying past Mercury have sent back to Earth pictures and information about this planet.

In some ways, Mercury is similar to our moon. This small planet is only a little larger than our moon and, like the moon, it is covered by dust, rocks, and bowl-shaped holes called craters. Thousands of **meteorites** (mē′tē ə rītz′)—chunks of rock from outer space—formed the craters by crashing into Mercury. You can see Mercury's rocky surface and some of its many craters in the picture shown below.

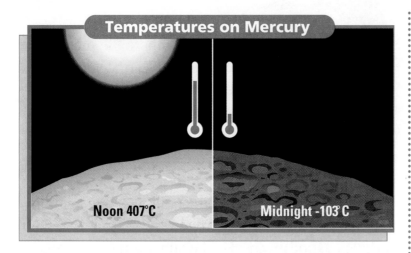

Temperatures on Mercury

Noon 407°C   Midnight -103°C

When Mercury has rotated once around its axis, 59 Earth days have gone by. Long days combined with closeness to the sun and a very thin atmosphere explain how Mercury can be so hot and so cold. During the day, Mercury's thin atmosphere can't protect the planet from the sun's heating rays. The diagram above shows that noontime temperatures on Mercury can reach 407°C. Afternoons can sizzle to 427°C. At night, the atmosphere can't keep the heat in, so the temperature can drop to about −183°C.

Venus—Cloudy Neighbor

Venus has a very thick atmosphere. The picture shows the thick, swirling clouds of carbon dioxide and acid that surround Venus. Powerful winds that move at speeds of over 300 kilometers per hour keep the clouds moving at all times. The atmosphere presses down on Venus like a very heavy blanket. In 1975, two large space probes from Earth landed on Venus. The probes lasted less than two hours before they were flattened by Venus's crushing atmosphere and damaged by the heat.

It takes Venus a little longer to rotate once around its axis than to revolve once around the sun. So, on Venus, a day is slightly longer than a year.

▼ *Venus*

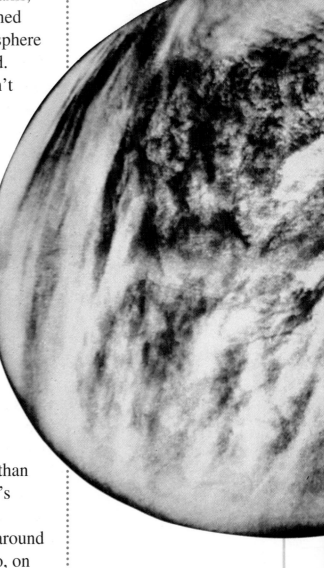

▲ Earth

Compare the pictures of Venus and Earth. Venus is about the same size as Earth. Like Earth, Venus has mountains, valleys, and plains. It even has a volcano bigger than any mountain on Earth. But Venus has no water. In the Discover Activity, you saw how heat can be trapped inside a container. The heat on Venus is unbearable—about 450°C, enough to melt some kinds of metal! The thick atmosphere on Venus traps the sun's energy and holds it close to the surface, day and night. Venus is hotter than Mercury, even though Mercury is closer to the sun. Life as we know it could not survive on Venus. Only rocks can exist in Venus's high temperatures and the crushing pressure of its atmosphere.

Mars—the Red Planet

Mars is a little bit like Mercury, a little bit like Venus, and a lot like Earth. As you can see in the picture on page 29, Mars looks reddish. Mars is about half as wide as the Earth.

As on Mercury, craters dot the surface of Mars. The nights are much colder than the days. As on Venus, the atmosphere of Mars is mostly carbon dioxide. But Mars's atmosphere is not thick enough to trap the sun's heat.

Like Earth, Mars has changing seasons, and days that are about 25 hours long. The average winter temperature on Mars is a chilly –125°C. Summer temperatures can sometimes get as high as 0°C. Mars also has north and south poles. The poles are covered with caps of frozen carbon dioxide, called dry ice. When the poles heat up, the ice caps melt and get smaller. When the poles cool down, the ice caps get larger.

Into The Field

How is Mars different from Earth?

Make a list of data about Mars. Make a list about what you observe about Earth. Compare the information.

Some of the ice at the poles may also be frozen water. Mars might have had a lot of water millions of years ago. The many valleys and canyons on the surface of Mars could have been formed by rushing rivers. The flat areas could be the bottoms of lakes that dried up long ago. However, the surface is now dry and the air contains only traces of water vapor. Notice in the picture below that the surface of Mars is dry, reddish, and dusty. The redness comes from rusted iron in the rocks.

Mars appears to be lifeless now. But does that mean there never was any life on Mars? In the summer of 1976, two space probes from Earth landed on the surface of Mars. The probes studied the air and the soil. They took pictures and sent the information back to Earth. Scientists found no signs of life after studying the information. Even so, some scientists think Mars could support life. Perhaps someday astronauts will go to Mars to try to answer this mysterious question.

▼ *Mars*

▲ *The surface of Mars is dry, dusty, and reddish.*

Checkpoint

1. In what ways does the sun affect the rest of the solar system?
2. How did Mercury get so many craters on its surface?
3. What causes Venus to be hotter than Mercury?
4. What causes Mars to be so cold?
5. Take Action! Use marbles, tennis balls, and golf balls to show how the inner planets compare in size.

Activity

What Affects the Temperature of a Planet?

Many planets in our solar system are very hot or cold. Try this activity to learn more about how the sun heats the planets.

Picture A

Picture B

Picture C

Gather These Materials

2 shoe boxes
marker
2 thermometers
tape

metric ruler
lamp
plastic wrap

Follow This Procedure

Part A

1. Make a chart like the one on the next page. Record your observations in your chart.

2. Use a marker to label two shoe boxes, A and B. Each shoe box will represent a different planet.

3. Tape a thermometer to the inside bottom of each box. (Picture A) Read and record the starting temperature in each box.

4. Using the metric ruler, place Box A 30 cm away from the light bulb in the lamp. The light bulb will represent the sun. Place Box B 60 cm from the light bulb. (Picture B)

Predict: **In which shoe box will the air heat up faster?**

5. Measure the temperature inside each box after 10 minutes. Continue taking temperatures and recording every 10 minutes for half an hour.

Part B

1 Make a copy of the chart you made in Part A.

2 Shut off the lamp and begin this part after both thermometers return to room temperature. Place Boxes A and B 30 cm from the lamp.

3 Cover the opening of one box with plastic wrap. (Picture C)

4 Measure and record the temperature inside each box every 10 minutes for half an hour.

Record Your Results

Temperature	Box	
	A	B
At start		
10 minutes		
20 minutes		
30 minutes		

State Your Conclusions

1. In part A, which box was warmer after half an hour? Explain what happened.

2. Use what you learned in Part A to explain how distance from the sun affects the temperature of each planet.

3. In Part B, which box was warmer after half an hour? Explain what happened.

4. Using what you learned in Part B, explain how the plastic wrap acted like an atmosphere.

Let's Experiment

Now that you have learned how planets heat up, design an experiment to explain why the temperatures on Venus can be hotter than on Mercury. Use what you know about scientific methods to find out.

2.2 *The Outer Planets*

What are the outer planets?

Gaze at a clear night sky for just a few minutes. You'll probably see a meteor—sometimes called a falling star. Meteors aren't really stars. But they're as bright as stars and they really are falling. **Meteors** (mē′tē ərz) are chunks of rock that burn up brightly as they fall through Earth's atmosphere. Luckily for us, most meteors burn up before they reach Earth's surface. Those that do reach the surface are called meteorites.

Some meteors come from the asteroid belt—a large group of rocks that orbits the sun just beyond the inner planets. Asteroids come in all shapes and sizes. The largest one is about as wide as the state of Texas. The smallest might be smaller than a basketball.

Asteroids often smash into each other. When that happens they crumble into pieces of rock that fly in all directions. Many head toward the sun. A few of these become Earth's meteors. Others speed toward the outer planets of the solar system: Jupiter, Saturn, Uranus, Neptune, and Pluto.

➤ *Jupiter*

Planets of Gas

The pictures on these pages show Jupiter and Saturn, the largest planets in the solar system. Each one is about ten times wider than Earth. Unlike the inner planets, Jupiter and Saturn are mostly made of layers of liquid hydrogen and helium, but they probably have solid cores. Thick, swirling, colorful clouds of gas surround both planets. The Great Red Spot of Jupiter has long been visible among its clouds of gas.

Unlike the inner planets, Jupiter and Saturn create more heat than they receive from the sun. Their centers may be as hot as 24,000°C. That's hot! But it's not hot enough to heat the clouds that surround both planets. Near the tops of the clouds on both Jupiter and Saturn the temperature is about –150°C. That's cold! Rings of dust and ice spin around the equators of these two giant planets. Jupiter's rings are so dark and thin they're almost invisible. Saturn's rings were first seen in the 1600s. But telescopes weren't very powerful then, so people thought there was only one ring. Since then seven major rings have been found. Notice in the picture that Saturn's rings appear as many colorful, bright bands.

Dozens of moons orbit above, below, and beyond the rings of each planet. Jupiter has at least 16 moons, Saturn has at least 24 moons. The moons are as different from each other as fire and ice. Io, a moon of Jupiter, has active volcanoes. Europa, another of Jupiter's moons, has a vast frozen plain of water. Titan, one of Saturn's moons, is larger than Mercury. Its atmosphere is thought to be similar to Earth's atmosphere when Earth was very young.

▲ Saturn has hundreds of thin rings made up of ice particles. The color in these rings was added by a computer. To your eye the rings would appear white.

New Worlds

You're about to visit the planets. But what will you bring?

Mercury The closest to the sun, Mercury is very hot during the day. It has little atmosphere.

Venus Earth's nearest neighbor, Venus has an atmosphere that is mostly carbon dioxide, and its thick clouds are made of acid.

Earth You explore this planet every day.

Mars Its red surface is similar to Earth's, but much colder. Any water is frozen all year long.

Jupiter The largest of all the planets, Jupiter is made mostly of gases and liquids.

Saturn Almost as large as Jupiter, Saturn is famous for its rings.

Uranus and **Neptune** Both are blue-green, very cold, and very far from the sun.

Pluto The smallest and farthest from the sun, Pluto takes 248 years to circle the sun.

Something cool would be nice on Mercury. But in this heat, it would evaporate right away.

Use at night on any planet. The clouds on Venus are so thick, you might need a flashlight all the time.

The very, very bright sunlight on Mercury would make it impossible to see without eye protection.

Think about it: if you're 12 years old on Earth, you'd be 48 on Mercury, 6 on Mars, and 1 year old on Jupiter.

Mercury has craters. Mars has extinct volcanoes. But for now, climbing mountains on Earth will do.

Distant Planets

Uranus and Neptune are smaller versions of Jupiter and Saturn. Like their larger neighbors, Uranus and Neptune probably have solid inner cores surrounded by layers of liquid and gas. They also have incredibly varied moons. One of these moons appears to have volcanoes that could have erupted water and ice.

Notice in the picture that Uranus and Neptune are nearly the same size and color. Both planets are about four times wider than Earth. Both are bluish in color and both have thin, wispy rings. Even though Neptune is much farther from the sun than Uranus, both planets have about the same surface temperature: an icy −215° C.

Cloudy Edges

The small picture below shows Pluto, the farthest known planet from the sun. Pluto is the only planet that a space probe hasn't studied, or flown by, so we know very little about it. We do know that Pluto has one moon.

▼ *Uranus*

➤ *Neptune, and Pluto on the far right.*

We also know that Pluto is the smallest planet—even tinier than Earth's moon. Unlike the other outer planets, Pluto is made of rock and ice.

Pluto's orbit differs from the orbits of all the other planets. Between 1979 and 1999 Pluto's orbit brings it closer than Neptune to the sun. It takes Pluto 248 Earth years to complete its long journey around the sun. Temperatures on Pluto are just a few degrees colder than those found on Uranus and Neptune. If you could stand on Pluto, the sun would look just like any other star: a distant point of light.

Does Pluto mark the edge of the solar system? Probably not. Billions and billions of kilometers from Pluto there may be a vast cloud of comets. Comets are icy balls of frozen gas and dust. The cloud of comets is called the Oort Cloud. The Oort Cloud may surround the entire solar system. It could contain more than a trillion comets orbiting the sun. Some comets disappear, never to be seen again. Others continually orbit the sun. Halley's comet, last seen in 1986, will return 76 years later, in 2062.

The comets that we sometimes see streaking through the night sky may come from the Oort Cloud. They are far different from the warm, comfortable planet we call Earth.

Checkpoint

1. How are Jupiter and Saturn similar to the sun?
2. Which group of planets has more in common, the inner or the outer planets?
3. List several ways that Uranus and Neptune are alike.
4. Where do most comets come from?
5. Take Action! Make a chart that compares the five outer planets. Compare how they are the same or different.

Planet Names

Are the day names related to the names of objects in the solar system? Let's investigate.

What To Do
A. Copy the two charts below; make each one long enough to fit all seven days of the week.
B. Fill in the English chart; start with Sunday.
C. Fill in the Spanish chart using an English-Spanish dictionary.
D. In the Sky Body column, match these sky bodies with the English or Spanish name that sounds most similar: Mars, Saturn, Venus, Sun, Mercury, Moon, Jupiter.

Day of the Week		Sky Body Name
English	Sunday	
Spanish	domingo	

What Did You Find Out?
1. *Are the names of the days related to the names of objects in the solar system? Explain.*
2. *Write a myth about how Sunday got its name.*

Activity

How Can You Make a Model of the Solar System?

A scale model is a small version of the real thing. In this activity, you can make a scale model of the solar system.

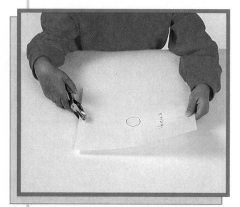

Picture A

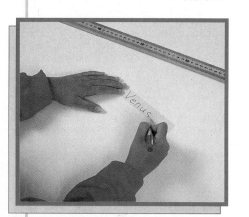

Picture B

Picture C

Gather These Materials

art paper
colored markers
metric ruler
hole punch

masking tape
meter sticks
ball of string

Follow This Procedure

Team 1

1. Members of Team 1 should draw and label each of the nine planets on a separate piece of paper. Draw in some features of each planet. Use the chart on the next page to find the diameter of each planet in this scale model. Use a metric ruler to draw each planet with its correct diameter.

2. Use a hole punch to make a hole at the top of each drawing. Put masking tape above and below the hole to reinforce it. (Picture A)

Team 2

1. Use the chart to find the distance from the sun to each planet. Your teacher will tell you where the sun will be in your scale model. Using that location as the starting point, measure the distance to each planet using a meter stick.

Predict: Which planets will be visible from the earth's position?

Planet	Diameter Scale: 1 cm = 2,000 km	Distance from the sun Scale: 1 m = 150 million km
Mercury	3.4 cm	0.38 m
Venus	6.2 cm	0.72 m
Earth	6.4 cm	1 m
Mars	3.4 cm	1.5 m
Jupiter	71 cm	5.2 m
Saturn	60 cm	9.5 m
Uranus	26 cm	19 m
Neptune	22.4 cm	30 m
Pluto	1.2 cm	39 m

2 Write out each planet name on a piece of masking tape. Place each label on the floor at its correct distance from the sun. (Picture B)

3 Thread the pictures of the nine planets in order on a piece of string. Nine students, each holding a drawing, should take a "space walk" along the string to its label on the floor. (Picture C)

State Your Conclusions

1. Are you surprised by the sizes or distances of the planets? Explain.

2. In your model of the solar system you have used one scale for the planets' size and another for their distance from the sun. Why do you think this was done?

3. Most of the solar system is space. Why do you agree or disagree with this statement?

Let's Experiment

Now that you have learned about scale models, why do you think some planets were not discovered for a long time? Use what you know about scientific methods to find out.

Mars

Ordering Planets

Suppose you found the index of this book on the first page and part of the first lesson on the last page. Imagine how hard it would be to read and understand.

Scientists organize facts into a certain order for the same reason a book is ordered in a certain way. Ordering facts makes them easier to understand.

Thinking It Through

How you order things depends on what you need to know about them. For example, suppose you wanted to know which planets take longer to orbit the sun. It would make sense to order the planets according to their distances from the sun.

Suppose instead you wanted to know whether Earth is a large planet, a small one, or somewhere in between. In that case, you would want to order the planets according to their size.

You can order things by finding the greatest number. For instance, look for the planet that is the greatest number of kilometers from the sun, or the planet that is the largest size. Then find the next greatest number, and so on until everything is in order.

Order may be shown by making a list, a table, or a drawing. In the drawing below the planets are shown according to their sizes. Note that you can easily tell which is the largest planet and which is the smallest. This way of ordering helps show how large Earth is compared to the other planets. Can you think of one other fact this order helps to show?

Your Turn

Choose a new way to order the planets. Order the planets according to your way. Explain why you chose this particular order.

Chapter Review

Thinking Back

1. What have **meteorites** done to the surface of Mercury?
2. How is Venus different from Mercury?
3. Why is Venus not a good place for humans to live?
4. How is Mars different from Earth?
5. What is a **meteor**?
6. What causes the rings around the equators of Jupiter and Saturn?
7. Which two planets are closer to the sun than Earth is?
8. In what ways are Uranus and Neptune similar to the two giant planets?
9. In what ways is Pluto different from the other outer planets?

Connecting Ideas

1. Copy the concept map. Use the terms at the right to complete the map about the planets.

Earth   Mars   Neptune
Pluto   Uranus   Saturn
Venus

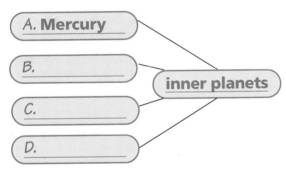

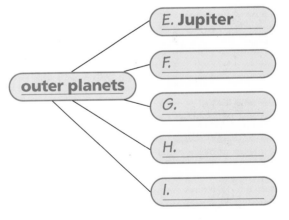

2. Write a sentence or two about the ideas shown in the concept map.

Gathering Evidence

1. In the Activity on page 30, how did you conclude how the sun heats the planets?
2. In the Activity on page 38, how did you conclude that the solar system is mostly space?

Doing Science!

1. *Choose one planet* and make up an animal that could survive there.
2. *Choose one planet* and write a skit about a journey to that planet.

The Blue Planet

It's sticking to my hand
so it must be wet!

Wear cover goggles
for this activity.

Discover Activity

Is there water in soil?

Take a clump of soil and feel it with your hands. Do
you think it contains water? Can you see the water?
Can you smell it? Find a way to collect any water
that the soil might contain.

For Discussion

1. How did you show that soil contains water?

2. How can you show that water is in the air?

3.1 System of the Spheres

▶ **Why do astronauts wear spacesuits?**

On July 20, 1969, astronauts Neil Armstrong and Edwin Aldrin became the first people ever to walk upon the dry and airless surface of the moon. In order to breathe, the astronauts had to wear bulky spacesuits that provided them with air. The spacesuits also protected them from extreme temperatures, harmful solar rays, and even tiny meteorites. Without their suits, the astronauts would have died instantly.

Looking up into space they could see the planet we call Earth. How inviting Earth must have looked to them! They could see enormous blue oceans shimmering beneath the fluffy white clouds in Earth's atmosphere. They could also see solid masses of land.

Unlike the moon and other planets, Earth has air that you can breathe and water that you can drink. It has soil in which plants can grow. Earth has all the ingredients necessary to support life as we know it. On Earth you don't need to wear a spacesuit.

▼ *Part of Earth as seen from space*

Our Planet's Spheres

Earth's three spheres provide all that living things need.

The **atmosphere** is Earth's outer covering of air. It provides the gases that plants and animals need to survive. It protects living things from being damaged by too much sunlight.

The **hydrosphere** (hī′ drə sfir) provides living things with water. Oceans, lakes, rivers, and streams are all part of the hydrosphere. Earth alone has water in its liquid state available in such great abundance. In fact, water covers almost three quarters of Earth's surface.

The **lithosphere** (lith′ ə sfir) is Earth's solid, rocky outer shell. It contains soil, rocks, and minerals that are needed for plants. And, plants provide the food that animals need.

The Interactive Spheres

The picture below shows the interactions of Earth's atmosphere, hydrosphere, and lithosphere. While each sphere is quite different from the others, parts of each sphere can be found in the other spheres. For example, the atmosphere contains drops of water from the hydrosphere and bits of dust from the lithosphere. Solids and gases mix in the oceans and lakes of the hydrosphere. You found out in the Discover Activity that even the ground beneath your feet—part of the lithosphere—can hold water.

The three spheres together form a system in which each sphere affects the others. How can they form a system? The answer begins with the sun! Because of the sun's energy, different parts of the spheres are able to move from one sphere to another. For example, the water of the hydrosphere travels constantly between ocean, air, and land. The journey begins when the sun's energy heats the ocean, causing water to evaporate.

▼ The hydrosphere, atmosphere, and lithosphere are in close contact.

Rising water vapor can cool and change back into tiny droplets of liquid. These droplets form clouds that move with the air across the ocean and over the ground of the lithosphere. Rain pours down on the land in mighty storms. The water carries dirt and rocks into rushing streams.

The streams flow together into large rivers, which empty into the oceans. Soon the water will evaporate again. It will continue its never-ending journey through the atmosphere, the lithosphere, and the hydrosphere.

The Sphere of Life

The interaction of the atmosphere, the lithosphere, and the hydrosphere creates another sphere—the sphere of life. No other planet that we know of in the solar system contains life. The system of the spheres makes life possible on Earth.

Life thrives in each of the three spheres. Living things need air, water, and nutrients, found in each sphere. Living things are found in the lower atmosphere and upper lithosphere. Life is found all through the hydrosphere—even to the darkest depths of the oceans. The sphere of life is called the **biosphere** (bī′ə sfir).Within it live fish of the ocean, birds of the air, trees of the forest, and you.

Checkpoint

1. What important things can be found in each of the three spheres that enables living things to survive?
2. What allows parts of one sphere to move into another?
3. Where is the biosphere found on Earth?
4. Take Action! Pour water into a container of soil. Notice the air bubbles on the soil's surface. Where does the air come from?

Activity

Is There Life in All Three Spheres?

Living things can be found in the strangest places. Try this activity to find out where the living things are near you.

Picture A

Gather These Materials

paper cup
spoon
soil
white paper towel
hand lens
reference books

pond water
petri dish
medicine dropper
depression slide
microscope

Follow This Procedure

Part A

1 Make a chart like the one on the next page. Record your observations in your chart.

2 Use a paper cup and spoon to collect some moist soil. Your teacher will tell you where to look.

Predict: What kinds of living things are you likely to see in the soil?

3 Empty the soil sample onto a white paper towel. (Picture A)

4 Use a hand lens to look at the living things that you see in the soil. (Picture B) You may need a book to help identify the living things. List their names on the chart. Draw pictures of the living things that you find.

5 Wash your hands when you have finished.

Picture B

Picture C

Part B

1 Get a sample of pond water. Place a small amount in a petri dish.

2 Look for movement of tiny living things. Use a medicine dropper to place 1-2 drops of pond water onto a depression slide. (Picture C)

Predict: *What kinds of living things are you likely to see in the pond water?*

3 Place the slide on the stage of a microscope, and examine it under low and high power. Draw a picture of any living things that you see. You may wish to use a reference book to help identify the living things. Record their names on your chart. (Picture C)

Record Your Results

Soil	Pond Water

State Your Conclusions

1. How do the animals from the soil compare with the animals from the pond water?

2. Did you find any one kind of living thing in both soil and pond water?

Let's Experiment

Now that you have explored soil and water, do you think the air contains any tiny living things? Place one slice of fresh bread in a sealable plastic bag. Place another slice on a counter for an hour, and then put it in a second bag. Moisten both pieces of bread with sterilized water. Observe for one week. Use what you know about scientific methods to find out what happens.

3.2 *A Living Planet*

Can plants grow in the ocean?

Imagine you're on a raft in the ocean. All around you stretches an unbroken view of water, water, water. There are no trees, no bushes, no flowers—not even a blade of grass. Could anything grow in this huge, wet world?

The answer is floating right next to your raft. If you look at just one drop of ocean water under a microscope, you'll see hundreds of individual, tiny, living things. All those tiny things live together in a floating carpet of life. This living carpet floats on or near the surface of most of the earth's oceans.

▼ *Below, left: Adult acorn barnacles*
Center: Gooseneck barnacles with feet extended
Below, right: Enlarged photo of a water flea

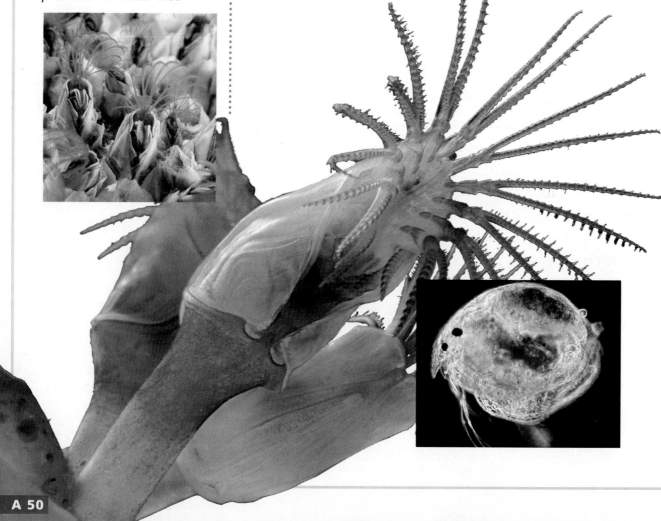

▲ *In the shallow, well-lit water of this tide pool many different kinds of living things thrive.*

These tiny living things are called plankton. They float near the surface of oceans where they get sunlight. They can also be found in tide pools like the one shown above.

The many types of plankton are not the only kinds of living things found in the biosphere. In this lesson you will learn about the incredible variety of life found in the different areas of the biosphere.

The Living Shores

All along the seashore the salty ocean waves meet the land. The waves carry more than water. Some tiny organisms roll in with the waves. Some attach to the rocks along the shore as the waves slide back into the ocean. Barnacles, for example, begin their lives as floating eggs. When the eggs hatch in the ocean water, the baby barnacles drift as they begin to grow. When the water brings a barnacle near a rock, it glues itself to the rock. Then it grows a shell. Find the feet of one of the gooseneck barnacles in the picture. Barnacles eat by extending their legs outside the shell. The legs catch bits of plankton that come in with each new wave. Then the food is passed into the barnacle's mouth inside its shell. When the wave has gone, barnacles are left high and dry on their rocks. But, their shells keep them from drying out in the sunny air.

INVESTIGATE

Water Habitats

Can certain animals live in fresh water? Let's investigate and find out.

What To Do
A. Cut the tops off of two empty plastic 2-liter bottles.
B. Label one bottle "fresh water" and fill it with tap water that has been sitting out for a day.
C. Label the second bottle "salt water" and fill it with the salt water prepared by your teacher.
D. Add 1/2 spoonful of brine shrimp eggs to each bottle.
E. Observe the bottles each day for the next five days. Record what you see taking place in each bottle. A magnifying lens may help.

	Daily Movement				
	1	2	3	4	5
Fresh water					
Salt water					

What Did You Find Out?
1. *In which liquid did the eggs hatch into small brine shrimp?*
2. *Can brine shrimp live in fresh water?*

How many types of living things can you observe?

Observe the outdoors for 10 minutes. Make a list of as many living things as you can find. Compare your list with someone else's.

The Diversity of Life

The gooseneck barnacle is just one kind of living thing. About one and one-half million different types of living things in the biosphere have been identified. Millions more might exist that have not yet been discovered. The picture below shows just some of the diversity found in the animal world. Some life forms, such as bacteria, are so small you can only see them under microscopes. Others, like giant redwood trees of California, can be as tall as 30-story buildings. Some, like polar bears, live in bitter cold polar regions. Others, such as colorful parrots, live in the sweltering heat of rainforests. From the tops of mountains to the dark bottoms of the ocean, life exists.

The Nepalese swift, for example, soars above some of the highest mountains in the world, more than 6 kilometers above sea level. It often flies with its mouth wide open catching any insects that cross its lofty path.

► *The students in the photo are holding a greenwing macaw, a red-tail boa, and Molly the cat.*

Far below the Nepalese swift, the blue lanternfish swims through the deep, deep water of the ocean. The days here are the same as the nights—pitch-black. But the darkness is no problem for the lanternfish. The fish has special organs that give off light.

Life abounds in the ocean. But much of it we can't see. It's easier for us to see the plants and animals of the land around us, such as oak trees. These lovely plants spread their green leaves far above our heads. They provide both shade and fresh air. Acorns from the oak trees fall to the ground. Other oak trees will grow from them and join the biosphere.

Sharing the Sphere

You, your friends, and all the people of Earth are members of just one kind of living thing. We are called *Homo sapiens*. Look at all the living things in the picture on page 52. We share a place in the biosphere with them and with all the other living things on Earth.

Like all other living things, we depend on the biosphere. Without the biosphere, we couldn't exist.

▼ *This bumblebee is searching for nectar on the flower of a thistle.*

▲ *This fish is one of many living things found in the biosphere.*

Checkpoint

1. In which sphere does the gooseneck barnacle live?
2. How do the Nepalese swift and the blue lanternfish survive where they live?
3. Living things are very different from one another, but how are they alike?
4. Take Action! Collect pictures of different living things. What helps each survive in its part of the biosphere?

How Many Living Things Can You Find in a Square Meter?

As you look around your schoolyard, you probably see many living things. But what might you find if you take an even closer look?

Picture A

Picture B

Picture C

Gather These Materials

meter stick
4 wooden stakes
string

large sheet of drawing
    paper
pencil

Follow This Procedure

1. Make a chart like the one on the next page. Record your observations in your chart.

2. Select an area of the schoolyard to investigate.

3. Use a meter stick to measure off 1 m on the ground. Push a wooden stake into the ground at each end of the length of the meter. Connect the stakes with string. (Picture A)

4. Measure off the rest of a square, and mark with two more stakes in the other corners. Tie the string around the remaining stakes to form a square. (Picture B)

5. The area inside the stakes and string is 1 square meter of space. Make a pencil drawing of your living square meter on a large sheet of drawing paper.

Predict: **What kinds of organisms will you find in your square meter?**

Record Your Results

Kinds of living things	Observations	Approximate number
Plant life		
Small animals (insects, worms, etc.)		
Larger animals (birds, frogs, etc.)		

6 Carefully examine every part of your square meter. Turn over rocks and look on the underside of leaves. Make a list of all the living things and nonliving things you find on your chart. Count or estimate the number of organisms in each category. (Picture C)

7 Look at your living square meter a week later. How has it changed? Which animals really make their home there? Which are just feeding or passing through?

State Your Conclusions

1. How do your lists compare to your predictions?
2. Which living things are the most common in your square meter?
3. Use your lists to show how the plants and animals are dependent on one another.

Let's Experiment

Now that you have observed the organisms that live in your square meter of space, do you think the same group of organisms live in your space as the seasons change? Use what you know about scientific methods to find out.

Observing

At a large library, you can find hundreds of books about all kinds of animals. Where does that information come from? How do we know so much about animals and other living things? Scientists learn about living things mostly by observing them. When scientists observe, they use their senses to gather as much information as they can. Observing is an important skill that you can sharpen every day.

Thinking It Through

Suppose you had an assignment to gather as much information as you could about a squirrel by observing it. One quick look might tell you that it's a small, brown animal with a bushy tail. But there's more to observing than that. Here's a list of questions you might ask yourself as you take time to observe the squirrel.

1. How would I describe this animal to someone who's never seen one?
2. What can I say about the looks of its paws, legs, head, nose, and so on?
3. How does it move? Does it walk slowly, hop, run, or jump?
4. Does it make any sounds I can hear? How would I describe those sounds?
5. Where does this animal spend its time? How much of its time is spent in trees? in bushes? in open areas?
6. How does it spend its time?
7. How much of its time is spent gathering food?

Your Turn

Now, use questions like these to observe a squirrel, bird, insect, or other animal in your area. You might think of other questions. Write your observations in a journal.

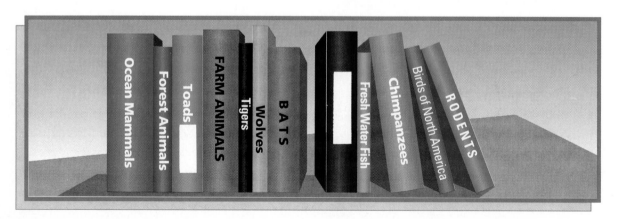

Chapter Review

Thinking Back

1. What would be missing for life on Earth if one of the three spheres was missing?
2. Explain how the sun's energy moves water from one sphere to another.
3. Which spheres are part of the **biosphere?**

4. Why are the **atmosphere**, **hydrosphere**, and **lithosphere** called a system?
5. What are some of the ways living things on Earth are different?
6. In what way does the system of spheres make life on Earth possible?

Connecting Ideas

1. Copy the concept map. Use the terms at the right to complete the map about the biosphere.

atmosphere   **hydrosphere**
lithosphere

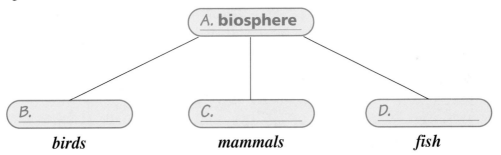

A. **biosphere**

B. _____   C. _____   D. _____

birds   *mammals*   *fish*

2. Write a sentence or two about the ideas shown in the concept map.

Gathering Evidence

1. In the Activity on page 48, what led you to conclude that life exists in each sphere of the biosphere?
2. In the Activity on page 54, what made you decide how many different kinds of living things existed in your schoolyard?

Doing Science!

1. *Design an activity* that would show the special qualities of the hydrosphere, lithosphere, and the atmosphere.
2. *Create a display* that shows the type of life you might find in each part of the biosphere.

Kids in the Ground Crew

NASA is working with new scientists down here on the earth: kids! Students in kindergarten through twelfth grade have been helping the space agency. This partnership helps both sides. NASA gets a lot of new scientific data, while the kids learn earth and space science.

Some of these space seeds grew as much as four times bigger or faster than the ordinary seeds.

In one NASA activity, over 125,000 classes across the country planted tomato seeds that were given to them by NASA. This may not sound very exciting. But these were special seeds. They had spent almost six years in outer space! They had been kept aboard a U.S. spacecraft.

NASA asked the kids to help figure out if these space seeds would grow differently from seeds that had never left the earth. So the young scientists planted the space seeds next to ordinary seeds. They compared how the seeds grew. Kids from Stuart Elementary School in Patrick County, Virginia, had something interesting to report. They said that the space seeds grew much faster, bigger, and greener than the ordinary seeds. Some of these space seeds grew as much as four times bigger or faster than the ordinary seeds.

In another NASA activity, a group of Global Change programs were set up by the Aspen Global Change Institute of Colorado. This institute's goal is to teach kids how to gather information on the environment. For instance, kids may learn how to measure and track conditions of their town's streams and lakes. Or they may learn how to record air pollution near their community. This information can be compared with data collected about the earth by NASA satellites. By doing this work, kids gain an understanding of their local environment. They see how it is affected by changes around the world.

At the Jenison Junior High School in Michigan, the program has already begun. Students have used their own measurements, along with NASA's aerial photos, to examine how their town's natural landscape has changed.

So far, the Global Change program has been set up in only 12 schools. But it will soon expand to 60 schools. These schools will be all across the United States and in other parts of the world.

On Your Own

1. Write to NASA if you would like your school to participate in the space seed program.

2. You can find out how the water you drink is cleaned by visiting a water treatment plant. Find out where the water comes from and what kinds of pollution in your environment affect the water that you drink.

An Engineer in Space

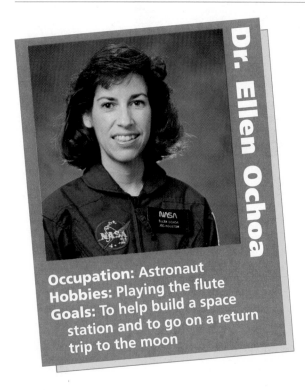

Dr. Ellen Ochoa

Occupation: Astronaut
Hobbies: Playing the flute
Goals: To help build a space station and to go on a return trip to the moon

Your safety belts are strapped. All systems are go. The engines roar. You try to remain calm. Four, three, two, one, blast-off!

Can you imagine what it would be like to fly to the moon? Lots of kids dream of becoming an astronaut. But Ellen Ochoa never did. "When I was growing up, there were no female astronauts. So it never occurred to me that I could be one." That's all changed now. Today, Ellen is one of seventeen female astronauts.

Who gets to be an astronaut?
About 2000 people apply for each class. And only about twenty are chosen. Ellen was one of the lucky ones. She thinks it's because she's always worked hard—at school and at her job. Her first job was being an engineer.

Does being an engineer help?
Ellen works with laser computers. They can solve problems that people usually handle. For example, imagine playing with a remote-control car. What would happen if you couldn't see where the car was going? It might crash into things. Now imagine a spacecraft, with no people on board, landing on Mars. A laser computer could guide the spacecraft to the perfect landing site.

Why did you want to be an astronaut?
"As a researcher I always enjoyed discovering things for myself. The space program is the only way to leave Earth and see for yourself what's out there."

What do you like best about being an astronaut?
"There's lots of variety. I work on the simulator and train for missions. When you train, you're given many unexpected problems. Then everyone in the crew works together to solve the problems."

Space Suit: Heavy Protection

One thing is certain—if you wanted to leave the earth's atmosphere, you would have to take along everything the air does for you just to stay alive. All the equipment you would need might weigh as much as 112 kilograms.

1 The primary life support system is worn like a backpack. It contains all the control systems and oxygen for breathing and for air pressure.

2 Astronauts talk to each other and to Control Central using microphones and headphones. They transmit their messages on a radio.

3 The helmet is covered by a solar shield that filters the sun and protects from excessive heat.

4 The gloves have silicone fingertips to give some sensitivity.

5 Since there is no gravity, an astronaut working outside the spacecraft must be attached to the craft to keep from floating away.

Find Out On Your Own

Write a letter to an astronaut asking him or her to describe the characteristics and functions of a space suit.

Module Review

Making Connections

Systems and Interactions

1. How does gravity affect the interaction between the sun and the planets?

2. Give an example of how the Earth and moon system and the Earth and sun system interact and explain why.

Diversity

3. In what ways do the inner planets differ?

4. What are some unique factors that enable Earth to support life?

Using What I Learned

Comparing

1. Compare Venus, Mercury, and Earth, and explain how their atmospheres affect the ability to sustain life.

Predicting

2. If you knew that a planet had a very thin atmosphere, what could you predict about life on that planet?

Categorizing

3. Name the physical characteristics you can use to classify the area of the biosphere in which an animal lives.

Communicating

4. Draw a diagram that shows how water moves through the biosphere.

Ordering

5. What would be the order of Earth, moon, and sun from the object with the most to least mass?

Applying

6. Why might humans wear masks and flippers when swimming?

Relating

7. What causes the three spheres of the biosphere to form a system? Explain why.

Observing

8. Tell in which sphere or spheres of the biosphere the animals in the pictures would live and how you would know.

Applying What I Learned

Action Project

Make a survey of the pets that people living in your community have. Find out in which sphere or spheres of the biosphere they live.

Drawing

Make a drawing to show the diversity of life in each sphere of the biosphere.

Science Theater

Prepare a skit for a news show describing the discovery of a new planet. Explain what type of atmosphere it has, its orbit, and whether life is possible.

Performance Task

Use a flashlight, a table tennis ball, and a larger ball to symbolize the sun, moon, and Earth to show how a solar and lunar eclipse occur and how they affect light.

Exhibition

Make a poster or bulletin board comparing two or more of the planets in the solar system.

What If

What if a nearby marsh, forest, or open land were to be made into a shopping center? What questions might you ask concerning the effect this might have on plants and animals in that area?

Water

Water

Water drifts through the sky and covers most of the earth. Water carves out the land and freezes in glaciers. Water flows through people and every other living thing. Without water, life on earth could not exist. In this module, you'll dive into the wide, wet world of water. Get ready for the plunge!

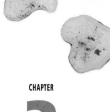

CHAPTER
2 Powerful Water

Tiny water drops crack huge rocks! When water freezes inside rocks, it splits them apart. That's just one way that water keeps changing the face of the earth.

CHAPTER
1 Water Molecules

Is a water drop the smallest form of water? Not by a long shot! Inside every drop of water, millions of water molecules are always on the move.

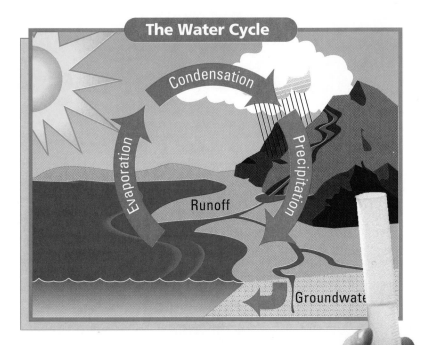

The Water Cycle

Condensation

Evaporation

Precipitation

Runoff

Groundwater

3 Water and Life

From head to toe, you're all wet.
Like all other living things on the earth,
you're mostly made of water. Your blood,
your bones, and even your teeth contain
this precious liquid.

Water Molecules

Alright, we're winning!

Discover Activity

What makes wet spots vanish?

Divide your class into teams. Each team will make a wet spot on the chalkboard and then make it disappear—fast. Before you begin, draw up the rules for this contest. For example, each group of students should have the same size and type of sponge. Make sure you decide on the size of the wet spot.
Then, ready, set, go!

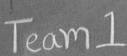

For Discussion

1. What makes the wet spot disappear quickly?
2. What helps water evaporate in nature?

1.1 *Water Changes*

How does water change?

It's a quiet, drizzly day. You're hiking a forest trail on the coast of southern Alaska. Big drops of water cling to ferns along the path, and mist drifts through the hemlock and spruce trees. Suddenly, a loud CRACK! stops you in your tracks. What was that noise? BOOM! Maybe it's thunder.

You run toward a clearing, and far ahead you see a wall of ice. It's a 60-meter-thick glacier stretching kilometers up the mountain! Just then, another chunk of ice, like the chunk in the picture, breaks off the face of the glacier. The chunk is as big as a house. With a thundering boom the ice slams into the salt water, splashing cold spray high in the air. Amazingly, however, this huge iceberg doesn't sink. It floats! How can a chunk of ice as big as a house float? That's one of the many wonders of water you'll read about in this chapter.

◄ *Ice breaks off the face of an Alaskan glacier. Dozens of glaciers dot the region of Alaska shown on the map above.*

Amazing Molecules

You hike close to the glacier and run your hand over its side. Brrr. It feels rough and cold. After all, a glacier is made of ice. Now you chip off a piece of the glacier and hold it for a few minutes. The ice in your hand starts to change to water. In time, that water will disappear, just like the water in the Discover Activity. How can ice change into water, and then disappear?

To understand these changes you need to know something about water molecules. A water **molecule** (mol′ ə kyül) is the smallest particle of water. In fact, a water molecule is so small it's invisible. Water molecules are so tiny that millions of them would barely cover the head of a pin.

Water molecules are always moving. Sometimes, water molecules move very fast. Other times, they move very slow. The temperature of the water determines how fast water molecules move.

▼ Alaska's Mendenhall Glacier moves 19 kilometers down the mountains to a lake. There, it melts into water.

As the temperature of water rises, water changes into a gas called water vapor. In nature, the sun provides most of the heat that changes water into water vapor. You can't see water vapor, but it's part of the air you breathe. As the temperature of the water falls, the water freezes, or changes to ice. Ice forms at 0 degrees Celsius (0°C).

Liquid, solid, gas—water is always changing forms, or states. From 0°C to 100°C, few other substances on the earth exist as a solid, liquid, and gas. You can find water in all three states at once. That's one thing that makes water special.

At any time, water vapor is in the air you breathe. Water and ice cover a large part of the earth. The picture below shows how much water and ice exist in a tiny corner of Alaska. Around the earth, water fills lakes, rivers, streams, and oceans. Snow and icecaps cover some mountains and the North and South Poles all year.

How Fast Is A Glacier?

You might think a snail travels at a slow rate. Glaciers move even more slowly!

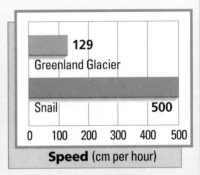

Greenland Glacier	129
Snail	500

Speed (cm per hour)

The speed of a glacier depends on its thickness, the surface under the glacier, and the season of the year. The graph shows that glaciers move at different average speeds in different parts of the world.

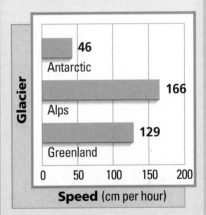

Glacier

Antarctic	46
Alps	166
Greenland	129

Speed (cm per hour)

What Did You Find Out?
1. *How much faster than the Greenland glacier does a snail move?*
2. *How far can the Greenland glacier move in one day?*

The Water Cycle

You learned that water can be found on the earth in all three states at once—water, ice, and water vapor. The movement of water through the earth's hydrosphere, atmosphere, and lithosphere is called the water cycle. This cycle provides all living things with a constant supply of fresh water to use.

Study the diagram of the water cycle on page 9. Notice that water moves from the earth's surface into the air and back to the earth's surface again.

How does the water cycle work? Every day, the sun heats millions of kilograms of water. The heating causes water to evaporate, or change into water vapor. More than three-fourths of the water evaporated each day evaporates from the oceans. Evaporation also takes place from lakes, rivers, puddles—even from your pet's water bowl. Plants, animals, and people give off water vapor, too. Water vapor can be carried thousands of miles by the winds. Some water vapor in the air you breathe may have come from the Pacific Ocean or the Gulf of Mexico.

◢ Water constantly cycles, like vapor that has changed into mist above. As the field notes below show, the water cycle brings heavy rain to coastal Alaska.

Alaska, near Juneau
Wednesday, June 11
Rain 16°C
It is raining very hard.
Thursday, June 12
Rain 14°C
It is still raining.
Friday, June 13
Partly Cloudy 15°C
The sun is starting
to come out.

When the air cools, water molecules in the air begin to move more slowly. They collect on invisible particles of dust and salt in the air. This collection of water molecules forms tiny droplets of water. Look at the dot over the *i* in the word "tiny." Each droplet is smaller than that dot!

Clouds form from many millions of these tiny water droplets. Often the temperature of the air where clouds form is below freezing. Then the droplets begin to freeze into tiny bits of ice. The tiny bits of ice grow larger and heavier. When the ice bits become too heavy to float in the air, they fall through the clouds. More water freezes to the ice, forming snowflakes. If the air is cold enough, the falling snowflakes reach the ground. Or they might melt on the way down and fall as rain.

The rain or snow adds water to lakes, streams, ponds, and rivers. It seeps into the ground. In time, streams and rivers carry water back to the oceans. And during all this time, the water cycle continues.

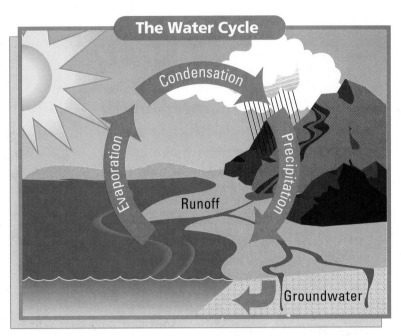

The Water Cycle

Condensation

Evaporation

Precipitation

Runoff

Groundwater

▲ *Water changes from one state to another as it moves through the water cycle.*

Checkpoint

1. Describe how temperature affects water molecules.
2. Describe the water cycle.
3. **Take Action!** See how fast you can change an ice cube into water vapor. What did you do to cause the change?

Now You See It...

Have you ever tried mixing lemonade or washing up an oily spill? Which substances will mix evenly in water? Try this activity and find out.

Picture A

Gather These Materials

cover goggles	tea
clear plastic jar	pepper
measuring cup	sand
room temperature water	milk
spoon	ink
salt	vinegar
sugar	oil
instant coffee	

Follow This Procedure

1. Make a chart like the one on the next page. Record your observations in your chart.

2. Put on your cover goggles.

3. Pour 250 mL of water into the plastic jar. (Picture A) Predict which of the substances will mix evenly throughout the water.

4. Measure 1 spoonful of salt, and add it to the water. (Picture B)

5. Stir it slowly for 30 seconds, and observe what happens. (Picture C) Record your observations.

6. Empty out the water and rinse the jar.

7. Repeat steps 3 through 6, but instead of salt, use a spoonful of each of the following solids: sugar, instant coffee, tea, pepper, and sand.

Picture B

Picture C

Record Your Results

Substance	Prediction	Mixed evenly	Didn't mix	Observations
Salt				
Sugar				
Instant coffee				
Tea				
Pepper				
Sand				
Milk				
Ink				
Vinegar				
Oil				

Predict: *What might happen when you try to mix other liquids in water?*

8 Repeat steps 3 through 6, but instead of salt, use a spoonful of each of the following liquids: milk, ink, vinegar, and oil.

State Your Conclusions

1. Which solid substances mixed evenly in the water?
2. Which liquids disappeared in the water?
3. Classify the substances you tested by what they did when mixed with water.

Let's Experiment

Now you've found out which substances mix evenly in water. How do you think the temperature of the water will affect the rate at which sugar cubes will mix evenly? Use what you know about scientific methods to find out.

1.2 Wonders of Water

What makes something wet?

Nothing else on the earth can do what water does. Traveling through the water cycle from the oceans to the air to the land and back again is just the beginning. Think about what happens when you spill water on your slacks or your shirt. Think about what happens when you take a shower or bath. Each time the same thing happens. The water sticks to your clothes or skin!

Water Clings

Water clings to surfaces because of something that water molecules do. Water molecules cling to, or strongly attract, other water molecules. But water molecules are also attracted to molecules that make up glass, wood, fur, cloth, leaves, and many other substances. The picture at the left shows how water molecules cling to a person's skin. When millions and millions of molecules stick to your shirt, your bike, or your dog, those things are wet.

▼ Water molecules cling to many surfaces, including your hand.

➤ Water molecules cling tightly to each other and form a "skin" that lets water bulge over the top of this glass.

Because water molecules cling together, water does something else. If you fill a glass with water to the rim, what happens? The picture below shows that the water bulges above the rim of the glass! You might be able to add a little more water and make the water bulge a little more. How can the water bulge above the rim of the glass without spilling?

Pretend your classmates are water molecules. They are standing close together in a straight line with their arms linked. You push gently on one of your classmates, but she or he doesn't break away. The link will not break unless you push harder and are stronger than the link.

Water molecules at the surface of the glass act in a similar way. The molecules are attracted to each other so strongly that they have "links" between them. They cling tightly together and form a sort of surface "skin." The "skin" has what is called surface tension. Surface tension keeps the water in the glass from overflowing. The picture on the right shows how strong surface tension can be. A water strider can tiptoe across a pond on a watery "skin." Even so, the "skin" is not strong enough to hold heavier things.

Water's surface "skin" can support insects like the water strider.

Mixing with Water

By now you may be getting the idea that water is very unusual. It is. Water can be found on the earth as a liquid, solid, and gas. Water molecules cling to one another tightly enough to form a "skin." Yet there is something else unusual about water.

Water mixes with other substances. The picture of the water below shows water mixed with rocks and dirt, forming a mixture.

A **mixture** is two or more substances mixed together. However, the substances in a mixture keep their own properties, and they can be separated. Many things on the earth form mixtures. Cereal, fruit, and nuts form a mixture. Smog is a mixture of gases and particles.

Sometimes you can't see the substances that form a mixture. Have you ever jumped into the ocean and swallowed a gulp of water? If you have, you know that ocean water is salty. Ocean water is a mixture of water and salt, as well as other substances. But you can't see the salt in ocean water. The salt is **dissolved.** When salt dissolves in water, it is broken into invisible particles that spread evenly throughout the water.

▼ *Pebbles, soil, and water form a mixture.*

Not all mixtures have particles that are spread out evenly. For example, the sand and water in a stream form a mixture. Unless the water is moving fast enough, the sand particles will settle to the bottom of the stream. When particles of salt or other substances dissolve in water, they form a mixture called a solution. In a **solution**, all the atoms or molecules of the dissolved substance spread out evenly. Water can dissolve many different solids, liquids, and gases. In fact, more substances can be dissolved in water than in any other substance on the earth.

The picture on the right shows a colored tablet dissolving in water. Notice how the color of the tablet is beginning to spread out into the water. When the tablet completely dissolves, its particles will have spread evenly throughout the water. The water will take on a lighter shade of the tablet's color, forming a solution.

Imagine you're standing on the grassy banks of a river or lake. Look into the water. What do you see? Do you see oxygen or other gases? Although you can't see gases in the water, they are there. The gases are dissolved in the water, forming a solution. Fish take dissolved oxygen from the water with their gills. Plants that live under the water take in carbon dioxide dissolved in the water.

The blood inside your body also contains water. Oxygen and nutrients dissolve in your blood. The blood can then carry them to all parts of your body. The fact that water can dissolve so many things helps make life possible on the earth.

▲ As particles of the green tablet dissolve in water, they form a solution.

Sink or Float

Water does something unusual when it freezes. Remember the huge iceberg that broke off the glacier? The picture below shows that an iceberg floats in water. However, if you toss most rocks into water, what do they do? They sink!

Unlike the rock above, chunks of glacial ice float because they're less dense than water.

Ice floats because water does something that is very unusual as it becomes a solid. When most substances change to solids, their molecules move more slowly. The molecules also move closer together, causing the solid to become more dense. When water freezes, the water molecules also move more slowly. But the molecules do not keep moving closer together. In fact, below 4°C, the water molecules move farther apart. When they move farther apart, they take up more space. At 0°C the water molecules form ice.

The picture below shows what happens when water freezes. Each graduated cylinder contains the same amount of water. When the water in the second cylinder was frozen, space between the water molecules in the ice increased about ten percent. As a result, the ice takes up more space in the graduated cylinder than the water does. Also, the greater space between the molecules causes the ice to be less dense than water. In other words, you have the same number of water molecules spread out over more space. A substance with a lower density than water will float. Therefore, ice floats in water.

On a hot day, floating ice clinks in a glass of water. But floating ice does something much more important than just cooling drinks. In the winter, ice forms on the surface of lakes and parts of rivers. If the ice couldn't float, it would sink to the bottom. The summer sun would melt some of the ice, but not all of it. The next winter more ice would form and sink, and the same thing would happen year after year. In time, ice would fill the lakes and rivers and freeze them solid. Living things in the water would die. Since the ice floats, life within these waters can survive beneath the ice. They are protected from extreme cold because the water is warmer than 0°C.

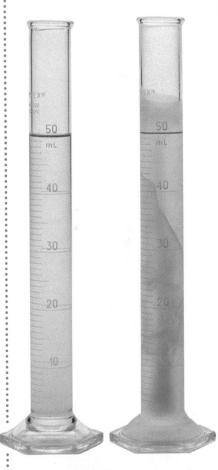

▲ *Water fills the cylinder to the 50 mL line. When water freezes, the ice expands and takes up more space.*

Checkpoint

1. Explain why water can make your skin feel wet.
2. What happens to salt when it is added to water?
3. Describe why ice floats.
4. **Take Action!** Take a lump of clay. Clay is more dense than water. Try to make the clay float.

How Can You Clean Up Dirty Water?

Water used in city supplies is taken from rivers and lakes. This water has to be cleaned. In this activity, you'll learn how to clean dirty water.

Picture A

Picture B

Picture C

Gather These Materials

cover goggles
1 L dirty water
3 plastic jars
strainer
tap water
20 g alum
1 2-L plastic bottle
big spoon

piece of window screen
 (5 cm by 5 cm)
rubber band
cotton balls
small pieces of charcoal
small pebbles
coarse, clean sand
scissors

Follow This Procedure

1 Make a chart like the one on the next page. Record your results in your chart.

2 Put on your cover goggles.

3 Pour 0.5 L of the dirty water into a clear plastic jar. Examine it, and record your observations in your chart. Let the dirty water stand for five minutes. Examine it again; record your observation.

4 Use a strainer to skim off material floating on the water. Then pour the water into another jar, being careful to leave the sediment behind. Examine the water, and record your observation.

5 In another jar, mix 20 grams of alum with 0.25 L of tap water. Add 3 spoonfuls of alum solution to the dirty water. (Picture A) Stir. Let the water stand for five minutes. Record your observations.

6 After five more minutes, check the water. Record your observations. Compare this water with the untreated dirty water.

7 Cut the 2-L plastic bottle in half. Use a rubber band to attach the window screen to the neck of the bottle. (Picture B)

8 Place the top half of the bottle upside down in the other half of the bottle. Make a filter by stuffing a 1 cm thick layer of cotton balls into the bottle neck. Add a layer of charcoal, a 5 cm layer of pebbles, and a 3 cm layer of coarse sand. (Picture C) Run tap water through the filter until it comes out clear.

> **Predict: *What do you think will happen when dirty water flows through the filter?***

9 Slowly pour the dirty water that has been treated with alum through the filter. Do not pour the sediment at the bottom of the jar. Compare the filtered water with the untreated dirty water and with tap water. Record your observations. *CAUTION: Do not drink the filtered water.*

State Your Conclusions

1. What happened to the dirty water after you added the alum to it? After you poured it through the filter?
2. Using what you observed, suggest an explanation for how the alum solution and the filter helped clean the water.

Let's Experiment

What do you think charcoal removes from the dirty water? Use what you know about scientific methods to find out.

Record Your Results

	Appearance of water
Before treatment	
After step 3	
After step 4	
After step 5	
After step 6	
After step 9	

1.3 Usable Water

How much water does the earth have?

Have you ever spun a globe and looked at all the blue water? The pictures below show that oceans cover a large part of the earth. In fact, three-fourths of the earth is covered by water. But just how much water is there on the earth?

Supply of Water

Scientists estimate that the earth has about 1239 billion billion liters of water. That's about 234 billion liters for every man, woman, and child on the earth! But most of the water, about 97 percent, fills the oceans. You already know that ocean water is too salty to drink.

Look at the chart on page 21 to find out where the other three percent of the earth's water is found. This small amount of the earth's water is fresh water. So humans and many other animals can drink it. About two of the three percent of all fresh water is frozen in ice caps, glaciers, and snow.

Where is the other one percent of the fresh water? Some seeps underground into spaces between rocks. The rest fills lakes, rivers, and streams and exists as water vapor in the air.

▼ *Three-fourths of the earth is covered by liquid water and ice.*

The amount of water on the earth stays about the same. Sometimes it seems that areas on the earth gain or lose water during floods or droughts. But water just moves from one place to another. Throughout time, the earth's water has traveled through the water cycle many times. Your last sip of water might have contained molecules from water that once cooled a dinosaur!

Enough Water

Does it seem like there's very little water for living things? Well, around 407,000 cubic kilometers of rain fall on the earth every year! That seems like enough rain for everyone. The problem is that rain doesn't fall equally everywhere. Wet, green Mt. Wai'ale'ale on the Hawaiian island of Kauai, gets about 1168 centimeters a year. Northern Chile, one of the driest places on the earth, can go for years without any rain.

Most places where people live aren't dripping wet or bone dry all the time. But rainfall does bring more water to some areas than to others. States east of the Mississippi River get an average of 103 centimeters of rain a year. Most of the western third of the United States gets less than 25 centimeters a year. Obviously, the western states are drier, but millions of people live there. How do western states get the water they need? You'll find out on the next page.

Into The Field

How is water used in your home?

Discover how many ways your family uses water at home. Keep a record of your observations.

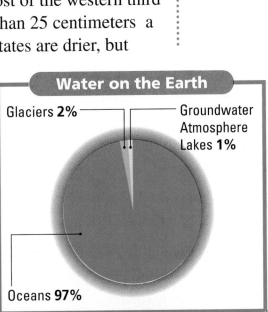

Water on the Earth

Glaciers 2%
Groundwater
Atmosphere
Lakes 1%
Oceans 97%

Stretching a Big River

Water from the Colorado River nurtures dry areas from Nebraska to California.

Like all rivers, the Colorado flows from higher elevations to the sea. But people have changed the Colorado's flow by building dams along its 2334 kilometer length. These dams form lakes called reservoirs. The energy of water flowing through the dams is used to produce electricity.

After providing energy, the water flows into tunnels, pipes, and canals. They carry the water across hundreds of kilometers to areas where little rain falls. Colorado River water washes clothes and fills bathtubs for more than 20 million people. Farmers use the precious water to change the desert into blooming farmland.

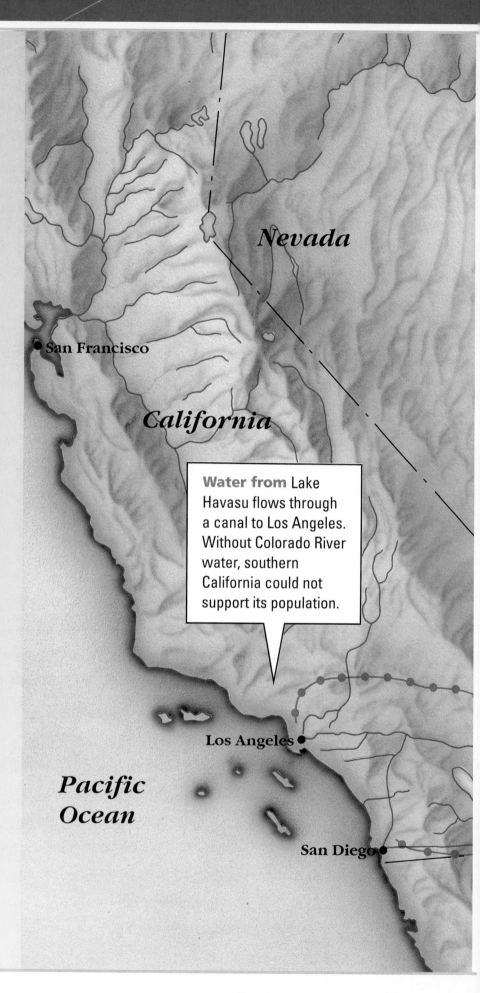

Water from Lake Havasu flows through a canal to Los Angeles. Without Colorado River water, southern California could not support its population.

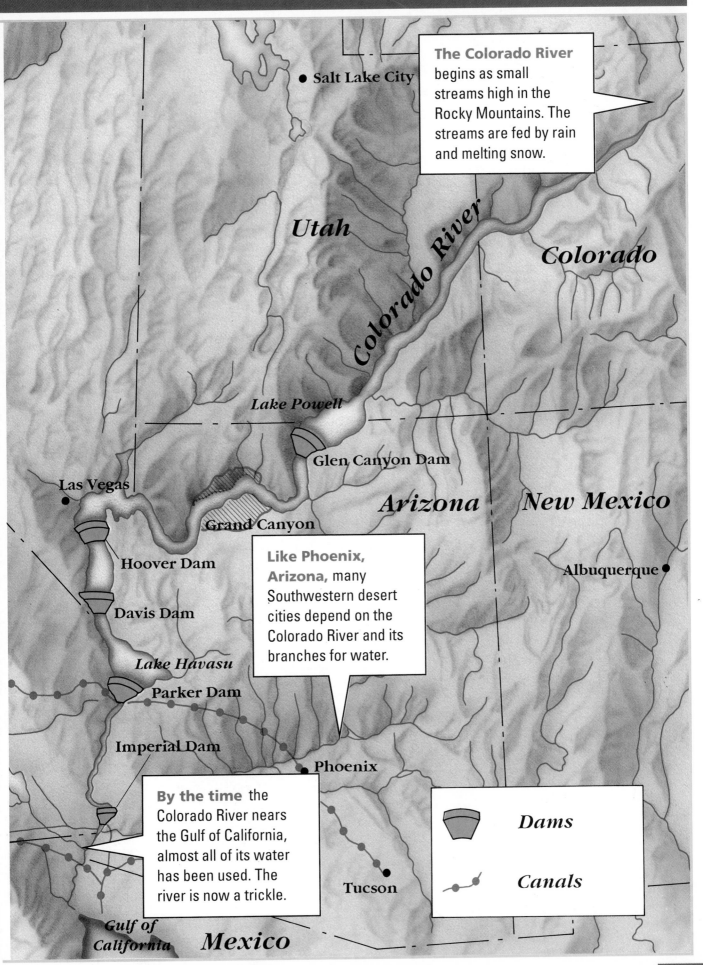

The Colorado River begins as small streams high in the Rocky Mountains. The streams are fed by rain and melting snow.

Salt Lake City

Utah

Colorado River

Colorado

Lake Powell

Glen Canyon Dam

Las Vegas

Arizona

New Mexico

Grand Canyon

Hoover Dam

Like Phoenix, Arizona, many Southwestern desert cities depend on the Colorado River and its branches for water.

Albuquerque

Davis Dam

Lake Havasu

Parker Dam

Imperial Dam

Phoenix

By the time the Colorado River nears the Gulf of California, almost all of its water has been used. The river is now a trickle.

Dams

Canals

Tucson

Gulf of California

Mexico

Saving the Water

You live at a time when the earth is more heavily populated than ever before. The United States has more than three times the people it had in 1900. Every person needs water to survive and uses more water each year. Modern appliances such as dishwashers and washing machines use water. It takes about 380,000 liters of water to make a car.

In addition to this, water can become polluted, or dirty. Pollution refers to the harmful chemicals and wastes that enter the water. The pictures below show that pollution harms the environment. Water pollution once killed nearly all the living things in Lake Erie, one of the Great Lakes. Even now, wastes are dumped into rivers and streams.

All living things need water to survive. So it's important to keep water clean and to use less water. Between one-third and one-half of all usable water is wasted. You can help save water by using only as much water as you need. Turn off the faucet when you brush your teeth. You might save nearly 20 liters of water a day. Take showers rather than baths, and shorten the time you spend in the shower.

▼ Pollution from communities and industries nearly destroyed Lake Erie.

OHIO'S LARGEST NEWSPAPER

THE

DEALER

CLEVELAND, OHIO

150

2A

25¢

25¢

DLIFE

INSIDE:

POLLUTED LAKE ERIE
TAKING TOLL ON WILDLIFE

"We can't drain the lake"

Manager Cleveland

— Margaret J

IS WEEK

What can you do to keep water clean? Easy. Learn what is polluting the earth's waters and where the pollution is coming from. Help your family choose household items, such as low-phosphate soaps, that don't pollute the water as much.

You can even help clean the water supply. The pictures show the results of many people working together to clean Lake Erie. You might join Beach Cleanup Day, which the Center for Marine Conservation holds every September. Last year workers hauled about 120 metric tons of trash from beaches in Canada, Mexico, Japan, and the United States. Or find out what organizations in your area volunteer to clean the local water supply. Volunteer to help with a project. Working to help save water, keep water clean, and volunteering to clean the water whenever possible is important. That way people help make sure they have a safe, clean supply of fresh water for years to come.

▼ *The cleanup of Lake Erie began in the 1960s. Today people can enjoy and use Lake Erie again.*

LAKE ERIE CLEAN AGAIN

It's true!
By Mary Beth Connelly
DEALER REPORTER

Checkpoint

1. What makes most of the earth's water undrinkable?
2. What affects how much water different parts of the earth have?
3. Explain why the Colorado River is so important to people in the West.
4. What can people do to help protect the water supply?
5. Take Action! Pour water from a 1-liter bottle into a plugged sink. Notice the level of the poured water. Use this information to estimate how much water you use when you fill the sink.

Gathering Data: Measuring Water

Scientists depend on correct data. They must know exactly how big, how cold, or how heavy something is. In order to gather such data, scientists measure. You depend on facts, too. Suppose you wanted to convince your family to conserve water. First you would need to measure the water your family uses every day.

Thinking It Through

You might begin by measuring how much water each member of your family uses to take a shower. To be a good scientist and to convince your family, your measurements have to be accurate. You also need to choose the right measuring tools for the job. You don't want to use a teaspoon to measure the water in your shower! You might use this method to gather information:

1. First, choose your measuring tools. Two possible measuring tools might be a timer and a 4-liter bucket.

2. Think about how you can use your tools. In this case, you can use the timer and the bucket to find out how much water comes from your shower in one minute. Then you can use the measurements to find out how much water each person uses per shower.

3. Make your measurements. Suppose you set the timer for one minute and hold a bucket under the shower. You find out that your shower puts out about 8 liters of water per minute. Time your next shower. If you take a 10-minute shower, you have used about 80 liters of water, since 10 x 8 = 80.

4. Now that you know how much water you use taking showers, persuade your family to cut its water use in half.

Your Turn

Figure out a way to get an accurate measurement of how much water you use to brush your teeth each day. What measuring tool or tools will you use? Why did you choose this tool? How can you use what you discovered?

Chapter Review

Thinking Back

1. Explain how temperature affects water **molecules.**
2. How does water vapor turn into rain?
3. What is surface tension?
4. What happens when a substance is **dissolved** in water?
5. How is a **mixture** different from a **solution**?

6. If a glass with five ice cubes is filled with water and the ice melts, will the glass overflow? Why or why not?
7. Explain why the Colorado River is so important to people in the West.
8. Since the earth has always contained the same amount of water, why is it important to keep water clean?

Connecting Ideas

1. Copy the concept map. Use the terms to complete the map of the water cycle.

cloud   droplet
rain

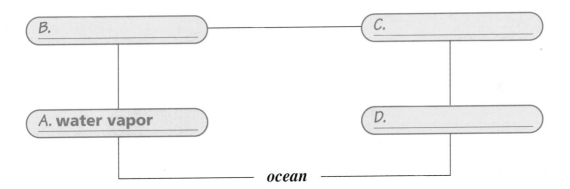

B. _____   C. _____

A. **water vapor**   D. _____

ocean

2. Write a sentence or two about the ideas shown in the concept map.

Gathering Evidence

1. In the Activity on page 10, how did you know if a substance had dissolved?
2. In the Activity on page 18, how did you know if the alum solution and the filter helped clean the water?

Doing Science

1. **Design an activity** that would show that water takes up more space as a solid.
2. **Design an activity** to show how a mixture of iron filings and salt could be separated.

Powerful Water

It's hard to see. Look how fast that one's going.

Discover Activity

What happens to sand in water?

Find a clear plastic bottle. Fill it to the top with water. Tape a strip of black paper on one side of the bottle. The paper will make a dark background as you look through the bottle. Now drop a pinch of sand into the water. Watch the sand particles very closely. What happens to them? What happens to the sand after you stir the water?

For Discussion

1. *What affects how fast the particles sink?*
2. *What affects the path of the particles?*

2.1 *Changing Rocks*

How can water drops break a rock?

Imagine you're back on the coast of Alaska near the booming glacier. The drizzle has stopped, and you're ready to go exploring again. Just a few meters from the edge of the forest you find a clear stream rushing over a bed of rocks. You look down at the rocks and study them. You notice that some of the rocks are brown. Some are gray. Some rocks are jagged, and some are smooth. Some of the rocks are much smaller than others. Where do you suppose all those rocks came from?

Ice Changes Rocks

Chips off a big rock—that's what you can call rocks like the ones in the picture. Slowly but surely a powerful force chipped these rocks from bigger rocks miles away.

◄ *Pebbles and rocks like these were once part of bigger rocks.*

People can't break a rock with their bare hands. But expanding ice can widen tiny cracks and eventually force a rock apart.

The force behind that handful of rocks is **weathering**—the breaking down of rocks. The sun's heat plays an important part in weathering. The freezing temperatures during winter play a part, too. But one of the strongest forces of weathering is—you guessed it—water.

As the picture shows, water is stronger than two people. Uuuuuuuhhhhh! The students can't break a rock that weighs less than one-half kilogram. But water can break apart rocks that weigh tons. How does water do it?

Rain falls onto boulders and cliffs and seeps into cracks that can be as thin as a hair. When temperatures fall, the water in the cracks in the rocks freezes. Remember what happens to water as it freezes? Its molecules move apart; the ice expands, or takes up more space. The expanding ice in each tiny crack pushes out against the insides of the crack. The tiny crack grows a little bigger.

With the next rain, more water seeps into the crack. When this water freezes, it wedges the rock even farther apart. The picture at the bottom of page 30 shows what happens to a huge rock after thousands of years of weathering. Gradually, the rock splits apart!

Water Dissolves Rock

Ice is strong stuff, but so is water. Over many, many years, water breaks big rocks into smaller and smaller rocks. How does this happen? It's a property of water to dissolve many substances. But how can water dissolve rocks? They seem so hard and solid. To understand, you first need to know a little more about rocks.

All rocks are made of one or more minerals. The minerals that make up rocks are nonliving solids from the earth. You may recognize granite from its gray, white, pink, and black flecks. The colorful flecks in granite are different minerals, including the minerals feldspar and quartz.

Water reacts with some minerals and changes them into other minerals. Over time, water reacts with feldspar in granite and changes it to clay, which is soft. Can you see what this means for a solid chunk of granite? Minerals that were once hard are now soft. Gradually the clay washes away. The granite rock breaks down into smaller chunks.

Checkpoint

1. How does ice change rocks?
2. How does water weather rocks?
3. Take Action! Press a pinch of sugar into the surface of a small, flat piece of clay. Put the sugar and clay mixture into water. Remove and examine it after 10 minutes. Compare your observations to what happens to granite.

Activity

Rolling Stones

Streams and rivers erode the land, forming valleys and canyons. How does water make such changes in the land? Make a model and find out.

Picture A

Picture B

Picture C

Gather These Materials

sand	marking pen
plastic bowl	masking tape
white glue	2 coffee cans with lids
spoon	water
waxed paper	2 large, clear plastic
3 paper towels	cups

Follow This Procedure

1 Make a chart like the one on the next page. Record your results in your chart.

2 Put two cups of sand into the plastic bowl. Stir in just enough white glue to make a stiff mixture. Shape the mixture into 30 small "stones" about the same size and shape. (Picture A) Place the stones on the waxed paper. Let them dry for one or two days until they have hardened.

3 Divide the stones you made into three equal piles. Place each pile on a paper towel. Label the piles A, B, and C.

4 Use the masking tape and marking pen to label the coffee cans A and B. Put the stones from pile A into can A and the stones from pile B into can B. (Picture B) Fill can A half full with water, and cover it tightly with a lid.

5 Hold can A with both hands, and shake it 100 times. (Picture C) Then ask your partner to shake the can 100 times.

> Predict: **What do you think will happen to the stones in can A?**

6 Open can A. Pour the water into a clear plastic cup. Put the stones on paper towel A. Record your observations about the stones and water.

7 Now fill can B half full with water, and cover it tightly. Have ten people each shake can B 100 times.

> Predict: **What do you think will happen to the stones in can B?**

8 Repeat step 6 with can B.

9 Compare all three piles of stones.

State Your Conclusions

1. How does water from can A compare with water from can B? Explain the differences you see.
2. How are the stones in piles A, B, and C different? Why are they different?
3. How are the stones like rocks in a stream bed?

Record Your Results

	Appearance	
	Stones	Water
Can A		
Can B		
Pile C		✕

Let's Experiment

Now that you've learned about erosion by moving water, investigate how freezing water weathers rocks. Use what you know about scientific methods to find out. You may want to experiment with the "stones" you made in this activity.

2.2 *Shaping the Land*

▶ *What can rivers and oceans do?*

Have you ever walked along a river or lake looking for smooth stones? You may find white stones shaped like eggs. Or maybe you'll find stones as small and flat as pennies. Do you know where those stones came from? Do you know how they became smooth? Make a guess and then read on to find out if you guessed correctly.

Hammers of Rain

If you guessed that water polished these stones, you guessed correctly. But did you also guess that water carried those stones for miles? That's just what it did. The people in the picture are demonstrating **erosion** (i rō′zhən), the moving of weathered rocks and soil by water. Erosion changes the shape of the land.

▼ *Erosion can begin as drops of water strike the soil and loosen tiny particles.*

Erosion can start with rain, which loosens dirt and particles of rock. During a heavy rain, drops of water strike the ground with an enormous force. Pow! Pow! In a way, each raindrop is like a tiny hammer pounding the rock and soil.

As rainwater flows over the ground, it carries away the loosened dirt and rock. The flowing water runs into streams. From there the water moves into rivers.

Grinding Rivers

If raindrops can erode the land like tiny hammers, imagine what rivers can do. Powerful running water can push big rocks out of its way. It can drive between cracks in rocks and break the rocks apart.

The picture at the right shows river water at work. But look at the diagram above to see beneath the river's surface. The water is carrying soil and rocks, which also cause erosion. Rocks carried by moving water crash into other rocks like wrecking balls. Sand and pebbles grind rock and the land like sandpaper scrapes wood. Rocks become smooth and round as they tumble and scrape against other rocks and boulders.

Over time, rivers carve valleys and canyons. Rivers also carry large amounts of soil and rock from place to place. Remember how the sand settled in the Discover Activity? As rivers reach flatter land and the water slows down, the soil and rocks settle to the bottom. Each day, the Mississippi River alone carries thousands of kilograms of mud, soil, and rock to the Gulf of Mexico. Turn the page to see an even bigger job of erosion done by moving water.

▲ Fast rivers carrying soil, stones, and logs erode the land. The yellow arrows in the drawing show how the river has scooped out its bed.

Carving a Canyon

Over millions of years, the Colorado River has carved through layers of rock.

The Grand Canyon is a giant sculpture carved by the Colorado River. The river began its work over eight million years ago when huge movements of the earth's surface lifted up the Rocky Mountains. As the mountains rose, the river flowed downhill faster and faster. Its fast-flowing waters eroded layers of limestone, sandstone and shale. The rocks had been laid down from 225 to 345 million years before by rivers and seas.

As the Colorado River cut deeper and deeper, beautiful layers of rock slowly came into view. Today you can see these colorful layers of rock because of eight million years of erosion and weathering.

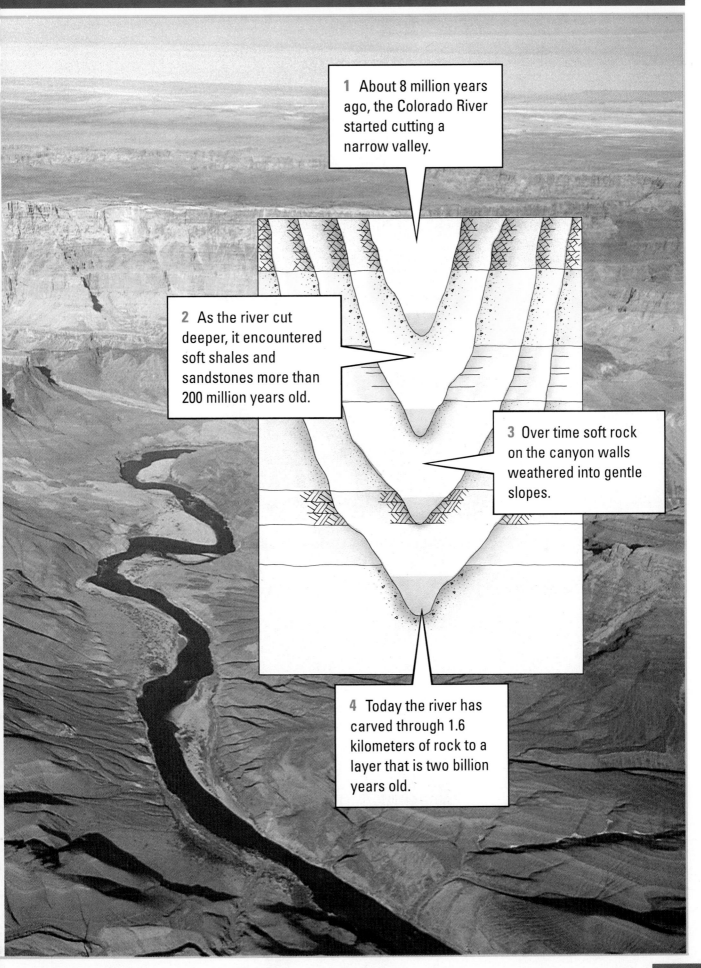

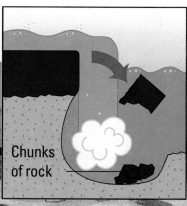

Crashing Waterfalls

Sometimes, rivers flow over a place where different kinds of rock meet. Some of the rock may be hard, and some may be soft. Can you figure out what happens then? The moving water erodes the soft rock, but leaves a lip of hard rock behind. The pictures show how the river flows over the hard rocky lip and forms a waterfall.

Imagine the force of all that water rushing over the rocky cliff. Minerals in the hard rock begin to dissolve. The rock weakens. Water from the river also seeps through cracks and dissolves minerals in the rock. As the diagram shows, the rocky lip eventually breaks off. Now the river has washed away the ledge, and the waterfall has moved farther upstream.

The fast-moving Niagara River washes away about a meter of the ledge at Niagara Falls every year. Over the past 12,000 years, the river has worn the falls 11 kilometers back up the river. At this rate it could take the river another 35,000 years to wear the cliff back 32 kilometers to Lake Erie. When that happens, the river will have lowered itself to about the same level as Lake Erie. The great roaring falls will be gone.

▼ *Waterfalls erode their own cliff faces through erosion and weathering.*

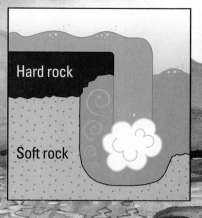

Hard rock

Soft rock

Chunks of rock

Pounding Waves

Imagine sitting on a beach and watching the roaring surf. Long rollers, or heavy waves, move toward shore, curl into frothy waves, and crash onto the sand. While rivers carve valleys and gorges, those ocean waves reshape the world's shores.

The picture below shows how water can erode rocky cliffs. Like rivers, ocean waves carry rocks and sand that grind away at cliffs and other land along the shore. In time, the steady pounding by waves, sand, and rock wears away the cliffs and changes the shape of the shore.

Waves driven landward by storms can change the shape of the shore even more quickly. One 6-meter storm wave can move a block of stone with a mass of 10,000 kilograms. That's a rock as big as a semi-truck with a flatbed! As the picture on the right shows, great storms can damage property. They can even reshape a coastline overnight.

As ocean waves tear down the land in one place, they build up the land in other places. Pieces of rock grind together in the surf and break into pebbles and sand. The waves carry them ashore along with sand from the sea bottom. There the pebbles and sand form strands of beach—just the place to play volleyball or watch the waves.

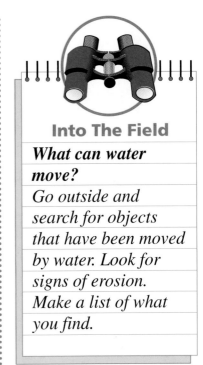

Into The Field

What can water move?

Go outside and search for objects that have been moved by water. Look for signs of erosion. Make a list of what you find.

▼ *Pounding ocean waves carrying rocks and sand can reshape coastlines and damage property.*

Earth-Moving Ice

Moving water is a strong eroding force, but it can't out-erode glaciers. The biggest glaciers are true giants. The one covering Antarctica is bigger than the United States, and its average thickness is about 2.5 kilometers! The most common glaciers are smaller valley glaciers that begin high in snowy mountains. But you wouldn't call these small glaciers weaklings by any means.

A valley glacier may be about 305 meters thick and several kilometers long—an enormous river of ice. Huge and heavy, the glacier creeps down the mountainside at a speed of about 30 centimeters a day. Because of its enormous weight, a glacier crushes the valley floor.

In addition, the glacier drags along rocks of every size—backpack-sized rocks, even house-sized rocks weighing many tons. Some rocks get stuck in the glacier's side; others get frozen on the bottom. As the glacier creeps forward, the rocks scrape soil off the valley floor. The rocks carve grooves into other rocks. In other places, the ice wedges into cracks in the rocky valley floor. As the glacier moves, it slowly breaks off rock from the valley floor.

▼ *Glaciers on each side of an Alaskan mountain carve a knife-edge ridge.*

Over thousands of years, glaciers carved features on land. The picture shows sharp mountain peaks chiseled by glaciers. How did they do it? Several glaciers formed on the high slopes of the mountain. As they moved forward, they shaved the sides into sharp ridges and the top into a point.

Farther down the mountain, glaciers changed V-shaped river valleys into U-shaped valleys. The U-shape comes from the glacier's powerful erosion of the slanted valley walls. Glaciers carved Yosemite Valley in California. The famous U-shaped valley is about 1.6 kilometers wide and about 1.6 kilometers deep.

As major eroders, glaciers carry loads of rocks and soil from place to place. Besides dragging rocks, they push loads of clay, sand, and rocks ahead of them. Other rocks are frozen into the edges of the glacier. When the glacier melts, it leaves behind piles of dirt and rocks. The piles form ridges called moraines. Today, moraines are clues that long ago, a huge glacier moved through.

Checkpoint

1. How does rainwater erode the land?
2. How do rivers erode the land?
3. Explain how the Grand Canyon was formed by weathering and erosion.
4. Explain how a waterfall moves upstream.
5. How do rivers and ocean waves erode in the same way?
6. How do glaciers carve U-shaped valleys?
7. Take Action! Fill a pan with soil. Sprinkle water onto the soil. What happens as water strikes the soil?

How Big Are Those Lakes?

Glaciers formed the Great Lakes, which make up the largest body of fresh water in the world.

The number on each lake shows how many square kilometers of land are now covered by each lake.

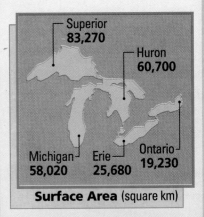

Superior
83,270

Huron
60,700

Michigan
58,020

Erie
25,680

Ontario
19,230

Surface Area (square km)

Glaciers can dig deep. The chart shows the deepest spot in each lake.

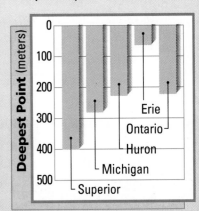

Deepest Point (meters)

Erie
Ontario
Huron
Michigan
Superior

What Did You Find Out?
1. *How much area do all the Great Lakes cover?*
2. *How much deeper is Lake Superior than Lake Erie?*

Activity

Grinding Away

Glaciers can carve through solid rock and shape mountains. How do they do it? Make a model to find out.

Picture A

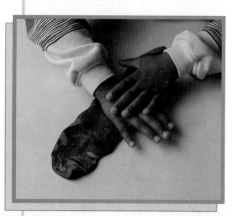

Picture B

Picture C

Gather These Materials

sand
pebbles
water

pie pan
clay

Follow This Procedure

1 Make a chart like the one on the next page. Record your observations in your chart.

2 Mix together some sand and pebbles in the pie pan. Add enough water to almost cover the mixture. (Picture A)

3 Put the mixture in the freezer and let it freeze solid. This will be your model glacier.

4 Roll out the clay to make a smooth, rectangular surface about 20 cm wide, 40 cm long, and at least 3 cm thick. (Picture B)

Predict: *What do you think will happen to the clay when you move the model glacier across it?*

5 Remove your glacier from the pie pan. Place it at one end of the slab of clay with the roughest side down. (Picture C)

6 Push your glacier across the clay. Record what happens to the clay and the glacier.

State Your Conclusions

1. What happened to the clay when you moved your model glacier across it?

2. What happened to the glacier when you moved it across the clay?

3. How is your model like a real glacier?

Let's Experiment

Now that you've learned how a glacier can erode the land, investigate how the size of the glacier affects the amount of erosion. Use what you know about scientific methods to find out.

Record Your Results

	Observations
Clay	
Glacier	

Analyzing Data: Time Relationships

Suppose you found some layers of rock that were exposed by erosion or construction. Could you figure out which was the oldest? You weren't there when the rocks were formed. You would have to use other clues to find the answers. Scientists often do this, too.

As you know, rivers carry loads of soil and rock. As rivers slow down, these sediments settle to the bottom. Over time, layers of sediment build up on top of one another and become a layer of rock. The kind of sediments that are deposited determine the kind of rock that is formed.

When streams and rivers erode soil, they expose those layers of rock. Scientists study the rock layers to learn about the history of a place. They begin by determining which layers are the oldest. The Grand Canyon is one place where scientists have studied rocks in this way.

Thinking It Through

Suppose you are a scientist trying to figure out which layer pictured on this page is the oldest layer. Here are questions you might ask:

Question: What do I know about how a layer of rock is formed?
Answer: A layer is formed when sediments are deposited over time.

Question: Which layer is usually on top?
Answer: The newest layer is deposited on top.

Question: As you dig through the layers, how would the age of each layer compare to the age of the layer above?
Answer: Each layer is older than the one above it. The oldest is on the bottom.

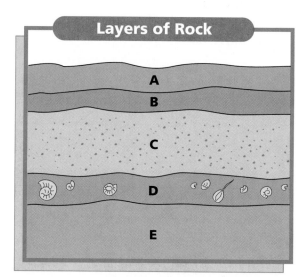

Layers of Rock

Your Turn

Study the layers of rock in the picture. Then answer the questions.

1. Which layer of rock is the newest?
2. Which layer formed earlier—layer E or layer C?
3. What can you tell about the area when layer D was formed?

Chapter Review

Thinking Back

1. Name two kinds of **weathering** by water.

2. Describe how **erosion** changes the shape of land.

3. Explain how erosion causes rocks to become smooth and round.

4. How does rain erode the land? How do rivers erode?

5. Explain how both weathering and erosion formed the Grand Canyon.

6. What happens to waterfalls as they erode their cliff faces?

7. In what ways do waves erode the shoreline?

8. What clues tell scientists that glaciers moved through an area long ago?

Connecting Ideas

1. Copy the concept map. Use the terms at the right to complete the map about erosion.

erosion   **rivers**

ocean waves   **rain**

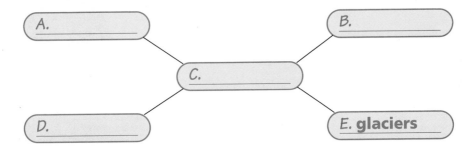

2. Write a sentence or two about the ideas shown in the concept map.

Gathering Evidence

1. In the Activity on page 32, how did you know that water eroded your stones?

2. In the Activity on page 42, how did you show that glaciers change the shape of the land?

Doing Science!

1. **Design an activity** that would show how ice breaks a rock apart.

2. **Design an activity** that would show how rivers can cause erosion.

Water and Life

How much water is in fruit?

Think about the fruits you like to eat. Which one do you think contains the most water? To find out, cut a fruit into thin slices. Then measure 20 grams of the fruit. Dry the fruit slices in the sun or in a warm oven. Next, find the mass of the dried fruit. Other students can try other fruits, and you can compare your results.

For Discussion

1. How much did the mass change by drying?
2. Which fruit contained the most water?

3.1 Water in Living Things

Why do you get thirsty?

Think about a steamy summer day. The sun is hot. The humidity is high. You feel your skin burning and warm beads of perspiration dribbling down your neck. Your forehead is sopping wet and your shirt is stuck to your back. Whew! You're probably thinking, "Where did all that water come from? Who would have thought one person could be so full of water?"

Full of Water

Believe it or not, the bodies of you and your friends contain a lot of water. The chart below shows that humans, like you, are actually more than two-thirds water. For an adult, that works out to about 47 liters of water. For fourth graders, it's about 23 liters.

▼ *Just like you, these students are made mostly of water. The chart shows how much of your body is water.*

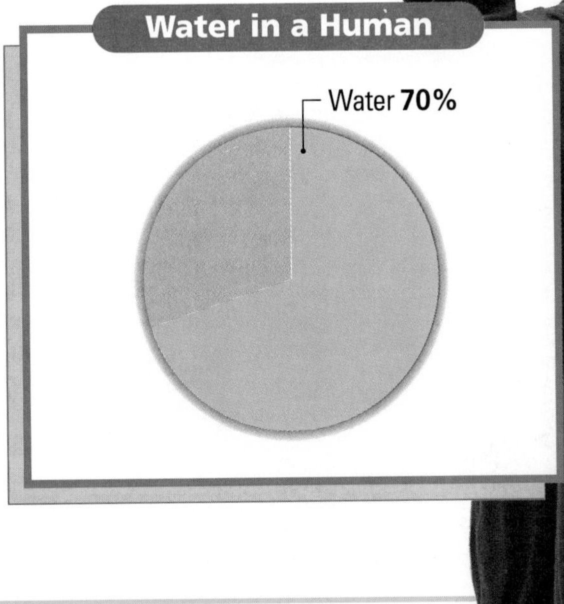

Water in a Human

Water **70%**

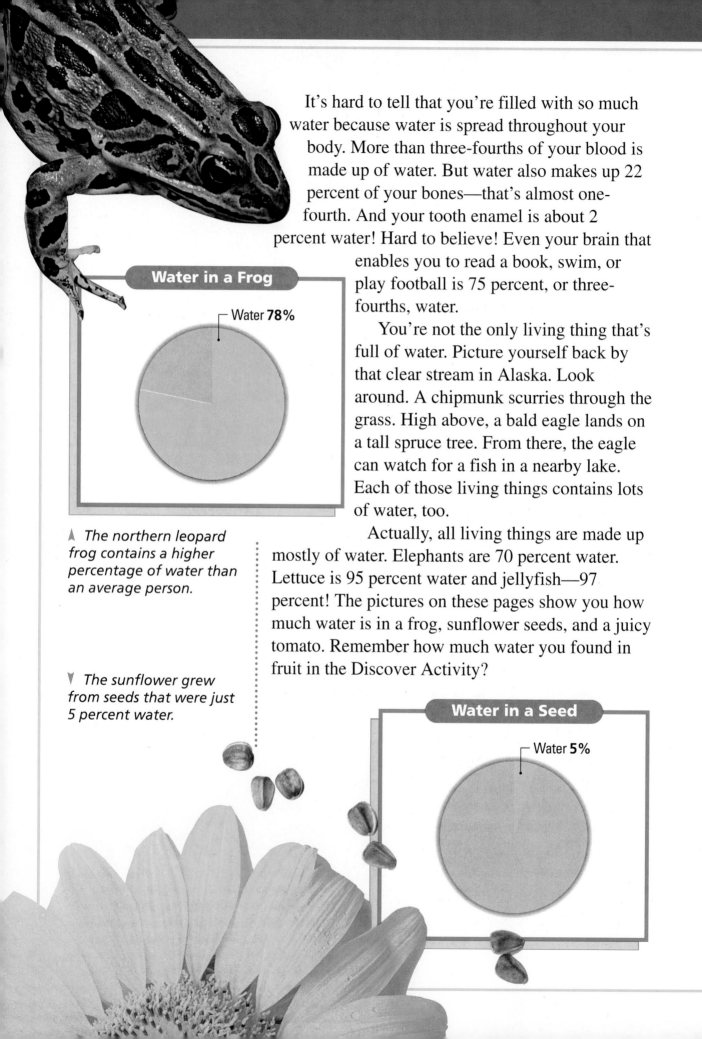

It's hard to tell that you're filled with so much water because water is spread throughout your body. More than three-fourths of your blood is made up of water. But water also makes up 22 percent of your bones—that's almost one-fourth. And your tooth enamel is about 2 percent water! Hard to believe! Even your brain that enables you to read a book, swim, or play football is 75 percent, or three-fourths, water.

You're not the only living thing that's full of water. Picture yourself back by that clear stream in Alaska. Look around. A chipmunk scurries through the grass. High above, a bald eagle lands on a tall spruce tree. From there, the eagle can watch for a fish in a nearby lake. Each of those living things contains lots of water, too.

Actually, all living things are made up mostly of water. Elephants are 70 percent water. Lettuce is 95 percent water and jellyfish—97 percent! The pictures on these pages show you how much water is in a frog, sunflower seeds, and a juicy tomato. Remember how much water you found in fruit in the Discover Activity?

Water in a Frog

Water **78%**

▲ The northern leopard frog contains a higher percentage of water than an average person.

▼ The sunflower grew from seeds that were just 5 percent water.

Water in a Seed

Water **5%**

Most living things lose water in many ways. People lose water through their skin; plants lose moisture through their leaves. For that reason, most living things must take in a lot of water each day to replace water that is lost.

But the amount of water living things need to take in each day isn't necessarily the same. Plants and animals that live in the hot, dry desert have ways of slowing down the water loss from their bodies. Some desert animals stay underground during the heat of the day. These animals do not need to take in as much water as other plants and animals do. Avoiding the heat of the day slows down the water loss from their bodies. The tiny kangaroo rat that lives in the desert doesn't drink water at all. It gets all the water it needs from the food it eats!

It's quite a different story with animals like the jellyfish. The umbrella-shaped jellyfish has no bones. Instead its body is filled with a moist, jellylike substance. To live, the jellyfish has to stay underwater where the water supports its boneless body and keeps it moist.

Plants also need varying amounts of water to live. Some need water almost every day; others can go several weeks without water. Trees and other plants that have thick stems with hard coverings can go longer without water than plants with thin stems. Desert plants, such as cactuses, have a waxy covering on their stems that cuts down on the water they lose each day. When it rains, cactuses can also take water and store it. That way, they can survive with less rain than many other kinds of plants.

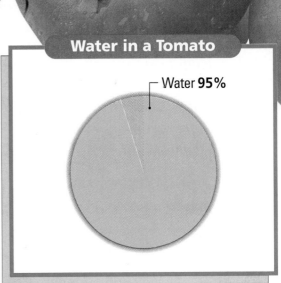

Water in a Tomato

Water **95%**

▲ Like other fruits and vegetables, the juicy tomato gained water as it ripened.

How much water do you take in each day? _Record the amount of each type of drink you have in one day. Also note the foods you eat that contain water. Compare your data with your classmates._

➤ Water keeps your eyes moist and provides moisture for tears.

Water for Life

Lick your lips. Blink your eyes. You couldn't do these things without water. Water does things for your body that no other liquid can.

Remember water's dissolving power? Nutrients in the food you eat are dissolved by water in your digestive system. These dissolved nutrients are then passed into the blood through the walls of tiny blood vessels, or capillaries. Oxygen enters the blood through capillaries in the lungs.

Your blood, which is mostly water, carries the nutrients and oxygen to all parts of your body. The diagram on the next page shows the maze of blood vessels in your body. Their total length is about 97,000 kilometers. That's more than 20 times the length of the United States from east to west!

Your muscles and other body parts use oxygen to get energy from nutrients. Your body uses the energy to help you exercise, study—even grow taller. As your body works, it produces wastes, such as carbon dioxide. The blood carries carbon dioxide to your lungs, and you breathe it out. Other wastes are carried to your kidneys, and then passed out of your body.

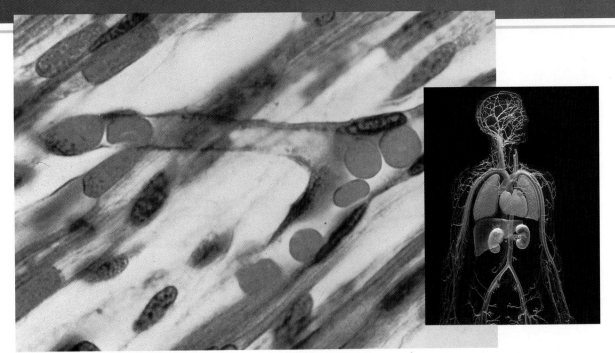

Saliva in your mouth and tears in your eyes are also made mostly of water. Saliva helps you begin to digest your food. Tears help keep the bright eyes of the student in the picture from drying out.

Yet each day, your body loses about 2 liters of water as waste. You breathe out another one-half of a liter. You also lose water as you perspire—an important way of staying cool.

Are you starting to see why you get thirsty? The amount of water in your blood needs to stay about the same all the time. That way all the parts of your body can do their jobs. When your water level drops, a part of your brain senses this change. The brain then signals you that you are thirsty, and you get a drink of water. Your water level returns to normal, keeping you waterlogged and healthy. You no longer feel thirsty.

▲ *Tiny, red blood cells, shown in the picture on the left, carry oxygen and carbon dioxide. The liquid part of blood, called plasma, carries nutrients from your food. Red blood cells and plasma reach all parts of your body by moving through a system of vessels, shown above.*

Checkpoint

1. Why might living things be thought of as waterlogged?
2. How does water help people stay alive?
3. **Take Action!** Exhale onto a cold mirror. Write an explanation of what you see.

Activity

Thirsty Flowers

All living things need water. You can even keep cut flowers by putting them in water. How much water do cut flowers need? Follow these steps to find out.

Picture A

Picture B

Picture C

Gather These Materials

water
graduated cylinder
test tube

fresh-cut flower
clay
scissors

Follow This Procedure

1. Make a chart like the one on the next page. Record your results in your chart.

2. Pour 25 mL of water into the test tube.

3. Cut 1 cm off the bottom of the flower's stem.

4. Place the flower in the test tube. Be sure that the stem extends at least 5 cm into the water. (Picture A)

5. Press clay around the flower stem to seal the top of the test tube. (Picture B)

6. Set the test tube in an upright position. Put it aside until the following day at the same time.

Predict: What do you think will happen to the water in the test tube?

7. On the following day, remove the clay seal from the test tube, and set the flower aside. Carefully pour the water from the test tube into the graduated cylinder. (Picture C) Record the amount of water that was in the test tube.

8 Pour the water back into the test tube. Be careful not to spill any.

9 Repeat steps 4 through 8 for three more days in a row. Record your measurements in your chart.

State Your Conclusions

1. How did the amount of water in the test tube change over the five days of the experiment?

2. What is the average amount of water missing from the test tube each day?

3. What happened to the water in the test tube?

	Amount of water in test tube
Day 1	25 mL
Day 2	
Day 3	
Day 4	
Day 5	

Let's Experiment

Now that you've found out how much water one kind of flower uses daily, what would happen if you used different kinds of flowers? Use what you know about scientific methods to find out.

3.2 *Living Underwater*

▶ Why can't I live underwater?

In some ways you're like a fish. For example, you and a fish are both made mostly of water. But imagine what would happen if you tried to live like a fish.

Suited for Land

Pretend that you're going to swim underwater, just like a fish. You dive down about 3 meters into clear ocean water. There's a lot to see here, but already you're having problems. The water is too cold. The salt water hurts your eyes. Before even a minute passes, you need air. You paddle back to the surface and break through. Gasp! Boy, that air feels good. Even though your body has a lot of water in it, you can't live underwater. Let's find out why.

▲ To stay underwater, people must protect their eyes with goggles and breathe through a snorkel (above).

You can't live like a fish because your body is suited to live on the land. It has all kinds of adaptations for living on land. An **adaptation** (ad′ap tā′shən) is a body part or behavior that helps living things survive in their surroundings. As a land dweller, your adaptations include lungs for taking in air. You also have long, strong legs for walking and running—great for land, but not so great for water.

If you wanted to spend some time under water, you'd have to use special equipment. The pictures on these pages show the gear you'd need to strap on for a short stay underwater. Find the mask to protect your eyes, the snorkel for breathing, and the flippers for speed. Look at the people in the picture below. They've outfitted themselves for a longer underwater stay with rubber suits and tanks of air. They've prepared as best they can. But they don't even come close to the perfectly adapted water dweller on the next page.

▲ People can swim faster underwater if they wear flippers, much like a frog's feet.

◄ To survive long dives, people need to carry tanks of air with them.

The Incredible Swimming Machine

The body of a rainbow trout is perfectly adapted to its watery environment.

The rainbow trout is a freshwater fish that lives in cool streams and lakes. The trout gets its name from the reddish band of color that runs along its sides.

Unlike humans, the rainbow trout doesn't need special equipment to live in water. It swims quickly with no trouble breathing. The water doesn't bother its skin, ears and eyes. In fact, water keeps the fish's eyes moist, so it doesn't need eyelids. Even when the water is dark or rough, the trout can find its way.

Ears Positioned inside the head, the trout's ears pick up changes in pressure.

Gills After water enters the mouth, it is forced through the gills. They absorb oxygen from the water.

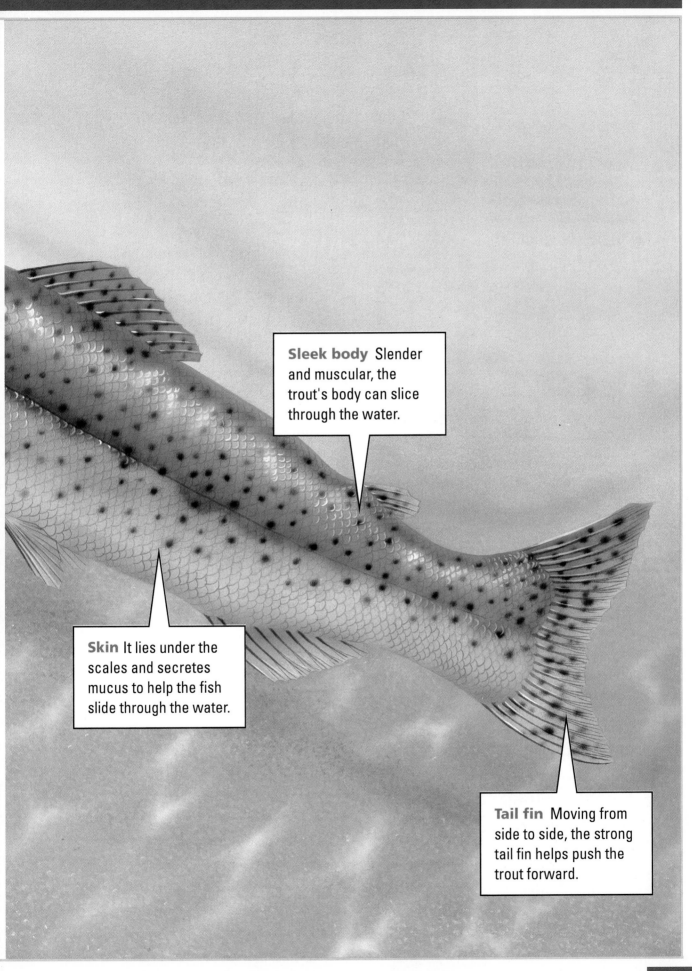

Sleek body Slender and muscular, the trout's body can slice through the water.

Skin It lies under the scales and secretes mucus to help the fish slide through the water.

Tail fin Moving from side to side, the strong tail fin helps push the trout forward.

Webbed Feet, Flat Leaves

The rainbow trout is built for water, but so are a lot of other living things. Almost 22,000 kinds of fish inhabit the waters of the world. Many other animals and plants are adapted to water living, too. To find out what some of these animals and plants are, let's explore a pond.

Take a look at the duck in the picture. It has webbed feet for walking along muddy pond bottoms and paddling along the surface. You can see its flipperlike footprints in the picture on page 59. Ducks also have oily feathers—like permanent raincoats—so they don't get soggy. Another water bird—the loon—is so adapted to water that it can't take off from land at all! A loon "runs" across the surface of a lake to pick up enough speed to lift its body into flight.

Frogs also live in freshwater ponds. In fact, frogs begin their lives in the water as fish-shaped tadpoles, like the ones in the picture on page 59. Tadpoles take in air through gills like a trout.

But tadpoles don't stay tadpoles for long. Their tails disappear and they grow legs. After a couple of months, the tadpoles lose their gills and breathe with lungs. They come out of the water as frogs!

▼ *Webbed feet and oily feathers enable ducks to spend hours in water. Long stems filled with air help keep the lily afloat.*

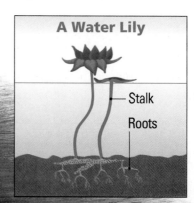

A Water Lily

Stalk

Roots

Many adult frogs are adapted for land or water living. On the shore of the pond, frogs like the one in the picture breathe air through their lungs. They leap away from danger using their strong hind legs. When frogs jump back into the pond, they swim powerfully, using their hind legs and webbed toes.

Many insects are also adapted for life in a pond. Some beetles have oar-shaped legs for paddling through the water. The water spider has a different adaptation—hairs on its body and legs that trap bubbles of air. When water spiders dive into the pond, they carry their own air supply—just as you'd have to if you took a dive.

Many pond and lake plants can't live out of water. The water lily in the picture gets much of its support from the water. The small picture of the lily shows its long, bendable stalks attached to stems and roots in the muddy bottom. The leaves have hollow spaces full of air to help keep the plant afloat.

Some plants, such as eelgrass, live entirely underwater. These plants have no stems. Their ribbonlike leaves, which float in the water, grow directly from the roots. Eelgrass grows in shallow water where it can get sunlight.

▼ *Without the legs or lungs of adult frogs, tadpoles must stay in the water. Adult frogs can live in water or on land.*

Checkpoint

1. What makes your feet a useful land adaptation?
2. How is a trout adapted to living in water?
3. What adaptations help animals live in water?
4. Take Action! Find "submarine" in a reference book. How are submarines designed to help people survive under water?

Activity

Gardening with Salt Water

Flowers, trees, crops, houseplants—all need water to survive. But what happens to plants when they're watered with salt water? Try this activity to find out.

Picture A

Picture B

Picture C

Gather These Materials

2 clear plastic jars   salt
water   2 slices of potato
spoon   2 identical potted plants

Follow This Procedure

1 Make two charts like the ones on the next page. Record your results in the charts.

2 Fill the two jars with equal amounts of water. Label one jar *Salt water.* Label the other jar *Fresh water.* Add three spoonfuls of salt to the *Salt water* jar. (Picture A)

3 Examine the two slices of potato. Try to bend them. What happens? Record your observations on your first chart.

4 Place one slice of potato in each jar. (Picture B) A potato is the underground stem of a potato plant, which depends on fresh water to live.

5 After one half hour, examine the slices again. What happens when you try to bend them?

6 Get two identical plants. These plants need fresh water to live. Describe their appearance in your chart. Water one plant with fresh water and the other plant with salt water. (Picture C) Label the plants *Fresh water* and *Salt water.*

Record Your Results

	Start	After one half hour
Fresh water potato slice		
Salt water potato slice		

	Start	Day 1	Day 2	Day 3	Day 4
Fresh water plant					
Salt water plant					

7 Except for the type of water you use, care for the plants the same way. Water them at the same time. Give them the same amount of water and sun.

Predict: *What do you think will happen to the plant that is watered with salt water?*

8 Check the plants daily for four days. Record your observations in your chart.

State Your Conclusions

1. Compare the potato kept in fresh water with the potato kept in salt water.
2. Compare the plant you watered with fresh water to the plant you watered with salt water.
3. Based on your observations, what effect does salt water have on these plants?

Let's Experiment

You have seen how table salt affects plants. Calcium chloride is a salt that is used to melt ice on sidewalks. Do table salt and calcium chloride have the same effect on plants? Use what you know about scientific methods to find out.

What can live in salt water?

Waterproof birds, floating plants, diving spiders—all of those interesting creatures live in just a tiny pond. Oceans are another matter. They're huge, deep, and salty. Let's take a look at the interesting things going on in the world's biggest bodies of water.

A Tough Life

Surf's up! Great for surfers, but not for other living things along the coast. When the tide is high, it means that everything along the shore is in for a pounding. The waves of high tide crash over the shore and wash back into the ocean. During high tide, much of the shore is under water.

During low tide, ocean water moves away from the shore. Within minutes, living things along the upper part of the shore are left high and dry. A few shallow pools remain in the sand after the tide goes out. But these pools get saltier and warmer as the sun causes some of the water to evaporate. How can ocean animals live without water or in water that gets saltier by the minute? Living things, such as the ones in the pictures, are well adapted to these shoreline changes.

▼ *Adaptations enable living things along the shore to survive high and low tides.*

Like many shore animals, the mussels, pictured on the right, have soft bodies protected by a hard shell. Thousands of mussels live in groups on shoreline rocks. How do the mussels hold on as waves pound the rocks, then roll away? Each mussel attaches itself to a rock with silky threads made by a gland near its foot. In time, the threads harden and anchor the mussel to the rock. Once the mussel is firmly in place, it won't be washed away by the waves. During high tide, the mussel opens its shell, and water and food flow into the shell. During low tide, the mussel pulls its shell closed. The closed shell keeps water in so the mussel doesn't dry out.

Acorn barnacles (bär′nə kəlz) also live inside a hard shell and stick to rocks. Their shells are made up of six pieces that overlap. One top piece has a hinge, so it can open and close like a door. During high tide, the barnacle opens the top plate. Then it sticks out a featherlike arm that gathers food. When the tide goes out, the barnacle closes the plate and stays moist and safe inside.

Animals called anemones (ə nem′ə nēz) also cling to shoreline rocks. When the water is high, the anemone's arms, or tentacles, make it look like a colorful flower. Find the anemone in the small picture on page 62. At low tide, some anemones pull their tentacles in. Then they produce a mucus that keeps them moist. Other anemones leave their tentacles out, but they still cover them with mucus. Until the tide comes in, these anemones look like soggy, sticky flowers.

Seeds and Salt Water

Will seeds soaked in salt water grow as well as seeds soaked in fresh water? Let's investigate.

What To Do
A. Soak ten radish seeds overnight in a cup of water.
B. Soak ten radish seeds overnight in a cup of salt water.
C. The next day remove the seeds from the water and wrap them in a wet paper towel.
D. Do the same for the seeds in salt water. Put each towel in a plastic bag and seal it. Check each day for signs of growth. Roots appear as the seeds grow. Record how many seeds show signs of growth.

	Number of Seeds Growing		
	Day 1	Day 2	Day 3
Fresh water			
Salt water			

What Did You Find Out?
1. *How does salt water affect the growth of radish seeds?*
2. *How could you find out how much salt is needed to prevent radish seed growth?*

Diving in the Alvin

By now you might be thinking that living things are adapted to almost any kind of environment. What lives a few meters under the ocean surface? What can survive kilometers down?

Hatch closed! You're inside the *Alvin*, a small submarinelike craft, called a submersible (səb mer′ sə bəl). Scientists use the *Alvin* to study the depths of the oceans. On this trip, you're traveling with biologists who study ocean life.

The *Alvin,* pictured below, has a strong covering to protect you as it dives. Why does the covering need to be strong? The deeper the *Alvin* goes, the more water there is pressing down from above. At 10 meters below the surface of the ocean, the pressure is twice as great. At 670 meters, the water pressure is 68 times greater than the pressure at the surface. Imagine the pressure at 3000 meters down where the *Alvin* goes! Without a strong covering, the *Alvin* would be quickly crushed.

▼ *Humans carry their environment with them when they dive in the Alvin.*

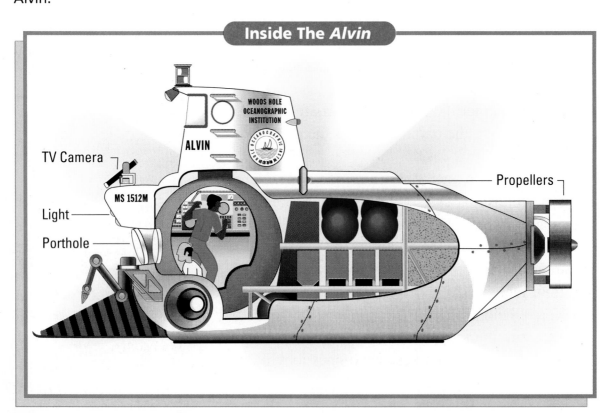

Inside The *Alvin*

WOODS HOLE OCEANOGRAPHIC INSTITUTION

ALVIN

MS 1512M

TV Camera

Light

Porthole

Propellers

Inside the *Alvin*, space is tight. You feel like you're squeezed inside a big metal beach ball with two other people. All around you are red, green, and orange glowing buttons. They're part of the panel that controls the *Alvin*. The controls keep air flowing from a supply brought along. They run the cameras, lights, and metal arms that help scientists gather information and samples. The controls also operate the motors that move the *Alvin* through the water. Diving in the *Alvin* is like riding a shuttle into space. You take your environment with you.

Into the Deep

Your trip in the *Alvin* will take you deep into the Pacific Ocean—the biggest and deepest ocean on the earth. The Pacific Ocean touches four continents besides North America. Near Hawaii, the ocean temperature is about 22°C —about room temperature. Along the coast of Antarctica, the surface water freezes during the winter. The Pacific Ocean is about 4000 meters deep on the average. But as the picture at the right shows, the ocean bottom isn't flat: plains, mountains, volcanoes, and valleys cover the ocean floor. The deepest known place in the world also lies under the Pacific. It's called the Mariana Trench, and it plunges to 11,033 meters below the surface. The distance from the bottom of the trench to the sunlit ocean surface is about one and a half kilometers —more than the height of Mt. Everest. And Mt. Everest is the tallest mountain on the earth!

Just think—all these places to live in one ocean! There's shallow water and deep water. There's a choice of sunny water or dark water, warm water or cold. The Pacific is alive with thousands of kinds of living things—each adapted to a certain habitat. Let's start exploring to see what forms of life live under the waves.

Like all oceans, the Pacific contains light and dark, warm and cold environments for life.

Life in the Light Zone

As you dip beneath the ocean's surface you enter the **light zone**, or the sunlit waters from the ocean surface down to 100 meters. Because of the sunlight, this ocean environment teems with a variety of life forms.

Remember the tiny living things called plankton that live in this part of the ocean? Most plankton are so small you need a microscope to see them. Some plankton are producers. They use energy from sunlight to make sugars from carbon dioxide and water. These plankton provide food for the animal life in the sea.

From the *Alvin* you see a few drifting jellyfish and swimming turtles. But mostly you see dolphins, whales, and fish—thousands of large fish. Why so many animals? The light zone has lots of plankton, so it's crowded with fish and other animals. But every shark, whale, shrimp, and squid is looking for food. The big fish that eats a little fish in the morning may become lunch for an even bigger fish.

One way animals can catch food and escape enemies in the light zone is to be able to swim fast. Notice the variety of streamlined fish in the picture. Like rockets, they're adapted for speed. Their heads come to a point and their bodies slope back. Tight-fitting scales make their bodies smooth, and a coating of mucus helps them slip through the water. A tuna can swim 48 kilometers an hour. That's almost as fast as a car travels on a city street. A sailfish can swim more than twice as fast as a tuna.

Smaller fish, like mackerel, swim in large schools for safety. To a hungry shark, the school looks like one big fish. Flying fish have another adaptation for escaping a hungry tuna. They can shoot from the water, stretch out their large fins, and glide through the air for 18 to 180 meters.

➤ *Like many light zone animals, whales and tuna are adapted to swim fast.*

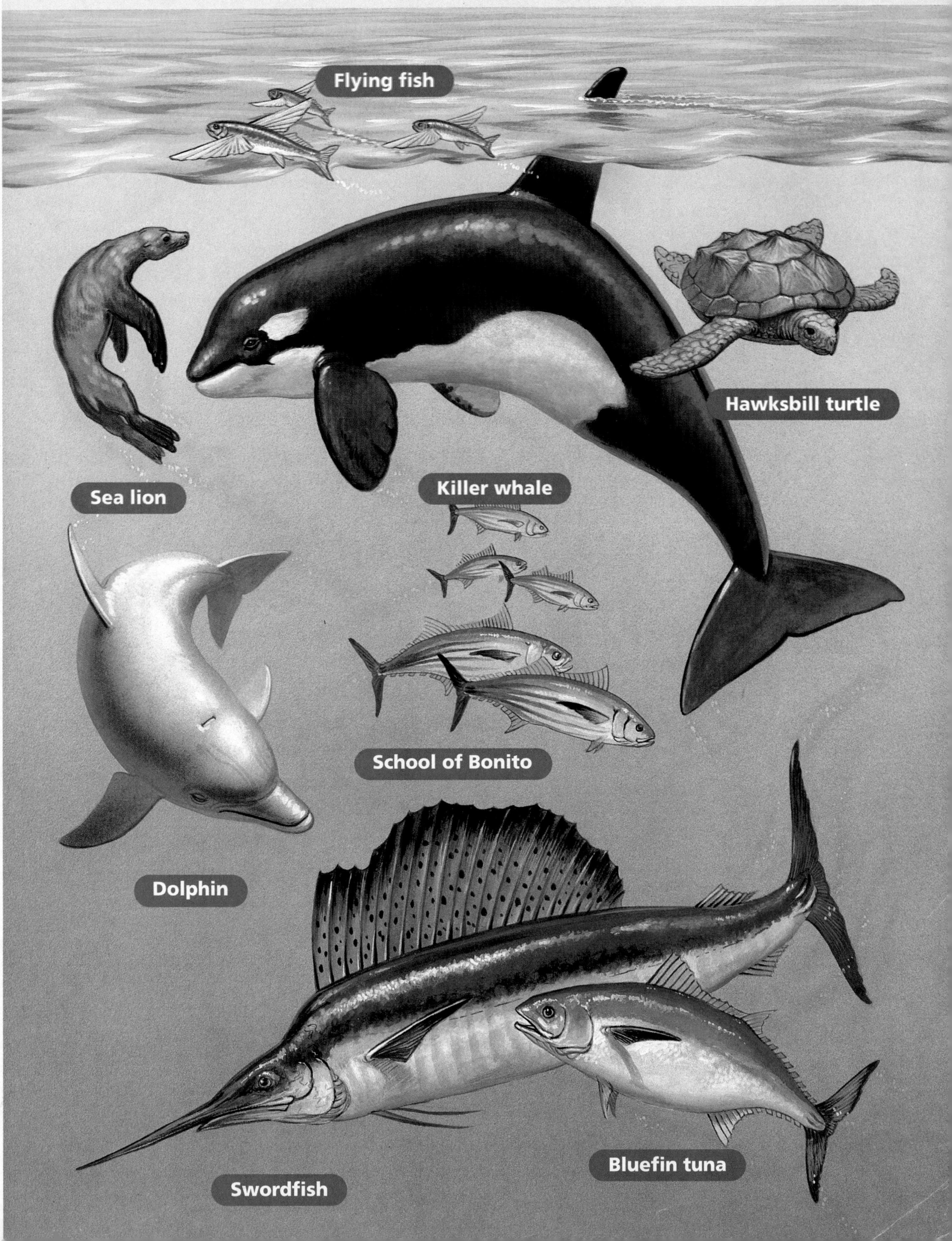

Flying fish

Hawksbill turtle

Sea lion

Killer whale

Dolphin

School of Bonito

Swordfish

Bluefin tuna

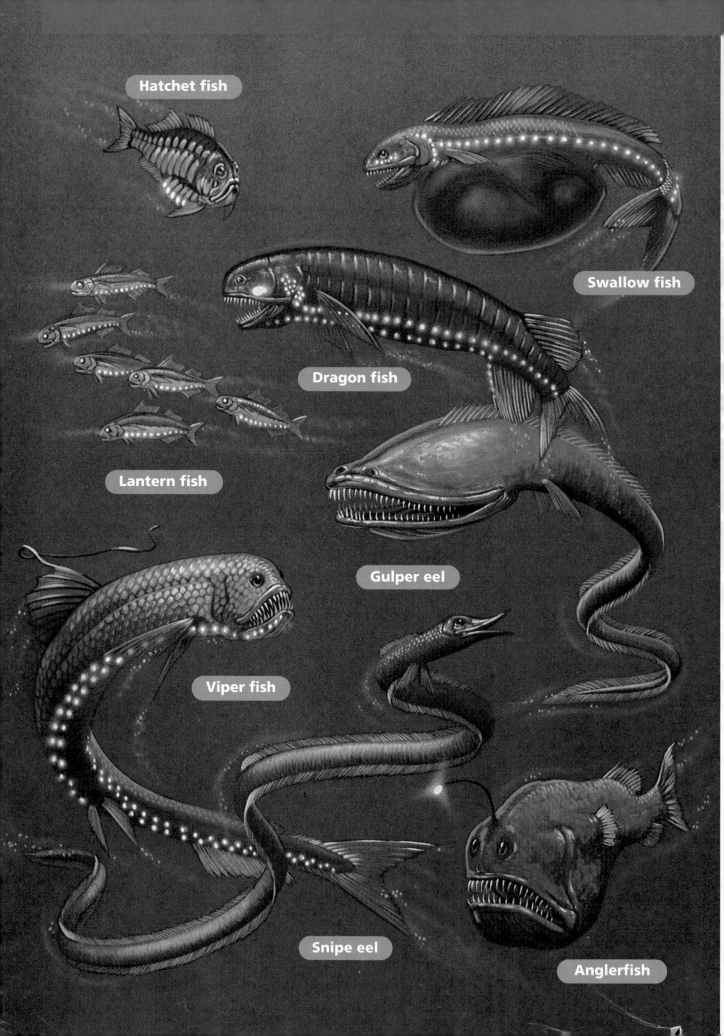

Hatchet fish

Swallow fish

Dragon fish

Lantern fish

Gulper eel

Viper fish

Snipe eel

Anglerfish

Life in the Dark Zone

You're moving deeper and deeper into the ocean. The blue water is getting black, as if night were falling. You're entering the **dark zone**—ocean waters between 1000 and 4000 meters deep where sunlight can't reach. You need to switch on the *Alvin's* floodlights.

Without the sun's light energy, there's not as much life in the dark zone. The water is cold, too, between 2°C and 4°C. With more than 1000 meters of water above you, the pressure is enormous. There's little food down here—no plankton to support the amount of life you saw higher up.

Suddenly, however, you spot the most unusual looking fish. It's shaped like a snake, and it has needle-sharp teeth. Viper fish, like the one in the picture, are well adapted to the dark zone. With little food, dark-zone fish eat other bottom-dwellers or whatever drifts down from above. When these fish get a meal, they need to hold fast so it can't wiggle away. The viper fish's sharp teeth make sure of that.

In the inky blackness, the only light comes from fish! Almost two-thirds of the fish in the dark zone make their own light with chemicals. Blink . . . blink . . . they're like fireflies on a dark night. These flashing lights attract a mate or a meal.

The anglerfish attracts food with a lure on its head that lights. To hungry fish, the lure looks like a glowing yellow-green worm. The angler waits for a fish to come close, then snatches the fish with its huge mouth and hinged teeth. The anglerfish's way of hunting is another dark-zone adaptation. In the cold water and extreme pressure, moving around burns a lot of energy. By waiting quietly, the angler uses little energy to trap meals that don't come around very often. Find the anglerfish with its glowing lure in the picture at the left.

◄ By producing their own light, many dark-zone fish can attract food.

▲ A big mouth and sharp teeth enable the fang-tooth fish to capture scarce food in the dark zone.

Life on a Reef

After a visit to the dark zone, sunny, blue waters look pretty inviting. But instead of going back to the light zone of the open sea, let's stop at a coral reef.

Look at the picture of a coral reef. It looks like an undersea garden. The reef is an undersea ridge built by billions of coral polyps (pol′ ipz)—tiny animals about 2 to 30 centimeters long.

Reef-building polyps are adapted to grow only in certain places. They live only in clear salt water not far from land. The water needs to be warm, more than 18°C. Polyps also need a lot of sunlight, so they can't grow deeper than about 40 meters. In these conditions, coral polyps grow like weeds.

Polyps use salt from sea water to build a hard skeleton around their bodies. When the polyps die, they leave their skeletons behind. Then new polyps grow on the surface and build up the reef. The Great Barrier Reef, the biggest coral reef in the world, stretches 2000 kilometers along the northeast coast of Australia. That's about the distance from New York City to Miami, Florida.

➤ Like many corals, the soft red coral below needs lots of sunlight.

The coral reef is filled with hiding places and food for thousands of ocean animals. Clams, starfish, snails, sea worms, and hundreds of colorful fish live on the reef. But the coral reef is one of the toughest places to live in the light zone: every animal can be another animal's meal. The adaptations of coral reef animals help them survive.

The lion fish has poisonous spines that protect it from being eaten. The scorpionfish looks like sandy rock. It can lie on the bottom and hardly be seen. Some creatures have protective armor—like the sea horse and the bone-covered box fish.

The bright yellow, blue, and orange fish on a reef are adapted for crowded living, too. Each kind has special colors and designs. That way, each fish can stake out a feeding area and find a mate of its own kind. Look, there goes an angelfish—a blur of neon yellow stripes on green and blue! Like viper fish and frogs, a rainbow trout, and you, the angelfish depends on water to live.

▼ *Colorful sweetlips and other fish find hiding places and food in the coral reef.*

Checkpoint

1. Why is a shell a good adaptation for shore living?
2. In what way is *Alvin* a kind of adaptation?
3. How can there be different places to live in one ocean?
4. How does life in the light zone depend on plankton?
5. Why is food scarce in the dark zone?
6. In what way are light zone and coral reef environments alike?
7. Take Action! Design an animal that could live in both the light and dark zones. Explain your creature to the class.

Problem Solving: Generating Data

Ellie and Zac are animal "detectives." They have discovered the facts below about a blue whale. But how can they "detect" the meaning of the facts?

Scientists often act as detectives to produce new data. They draw conclusions from the information or infer something new. Their conclusions may not always be right, but that's why conclusions need to be tested!

Thinking It Through

The blue whale is the largest animal that ever lived. It can weigh up to 200 metric tons. The blue whale has no teeth. Instead, it has hundreds of thin plates called baleen in its mouth. The baleen acts like a screen through which food can be filtered.

Ellie and Zac wonder what kind of food a huge animal with no teeth can eat to reach a weight of 200 metric tons.

Zac knows that other large animals such as bears and elephants often feed on very small animals or plants. Zac uses this fact to infer that the blue whale might eat something very small.

Ellie uses Zac's new idea. She concludes that if the blue whale does eat very small animals, or sea plants, it must eat huge amounts of these organisms.

Zac uses the fact about baleen to predict what might happen when the whale finds food. It probably takes huge amounts of water and food in, then filters the water out through the baleen.

Your Turn

Work with a friend. Discuss these facts about a blind cave fish: It's blind. Its skin has no color. Nerves help it sense movement in water.

What inferences can you make about why cave fish have these adaptations? What can you conclude about the fish's environment? What predictions can you make about finding animals with similar adaptations in this environment?

Chapter Review

Thinking Back

1. Why is water essential for life?

2. How are some plants able to survive with little water while others need a lot?

3. How does your body use water?

4. Explain how strong legs are an **adaptation** for living on land.

5. Explain how a rainbow trout is adapted to live in the water.

6. Explain how ducks and frogs are adapted to water.

7. Why are plantlike plankton found only in the **light zone**?

8. In what ways are fish in the **dark zone** adapted to that environment?

9. Explain why colorful designs are useful adaptations for coral reef fish.

Connecting Ideas

1. Copy the concept map. Use the terms at the right to complete the map of land and water adaptations.

adaptations   lungs
fins   legs
land   water

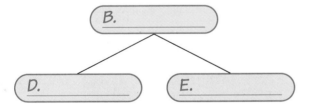
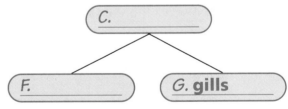

A. _____

B. _____

C. _____

D. _____

E. _____

F. _____

G. **gills**

2. Write a sentence or two about the ideas in the concept map.

Gathering Evidence

1. In the Activity on page 52, how did you know how much water the flower used?

2. In the Activity on page 60, how did you know the effect of salt water?

Doing Science!

1. ***Create a display*** that shows how water is used in the human body.

2. ***Develop a skit*** that shows how an animal is adapted for the place it lives.

Finding Ways to Save Water

We use an amazing amount of water every day. A running faucet pours out 12 to 20 liters of water a minute. A washing machine uses about 120 liters of water per load. Washing a car by hose uses almost 600 liters of water. In some parts of the country, there is no longer enough water to go around. How can we prevent permanent water shortages?

"Everyone can save water in some way."

Needs and Goals

There are two ways to avoid running out of an item or resource: use less, and recycle what you use. You can do both of these things with water.

Gathering Information

Using less: Think about all the ways you use water each day. As you review these uses, think of ways to conserve water, or use less. For instance, as you brush your teeth, turn off the running water. Here's a list of other ideas to spark your thinking:

- Install a "low-flow" shower head to cut down your water use while you take a shower.
- Never use the washing machine until you have a full load of laundry.
- Wash the car with a sponge, a bucket, and a hose with a shut-off nozzle.
- Plant flowers and grasses that need less water.
- Fix all leaky faucets.

How to Save Water		
Method of saving water	Good method for our family?	Reason
Planting desert plants in our yard		
Re-using water after defrosting freezer		
Taking showers, not baths		

▲ *Years with little rain caused this California reservoir to dry up. Conserving water is one way to help make sure people don't run short of water—even in dry weather.*

Recycling: You don't always need perfectly clean water for the lawn, house plants, or rinsing dirty dishes. One way to re-use water is to save water used for cooking boil-in bags of frozen food. Can you think of others?

Possible Alternatives

Not every family can cut its water use in exactly the same way. Some families don't have lawns. Others may rely on public transportation rather than owning a car that needs cleaning.

Evaluating Alternatives

Copy the table on page 74. You can add other water-saving methods that you know of. Fill in the second and third columns as they apply to you.

Making the Best Choice

Use the table to help you decide on water-saving methods you and your family can use. Remember, everyone can save water in some way. This is one matter where acting on your own really makes a difference.

Now You Do It

1. Which methods of saving water would be good ones for your family?
2. Which methods could you use every day?
3. *On Your Own* Run the water from your faucet for the time it would take to do several tasks, such as brushing your teeth or filling a saucepan to cook vegetables. Trap this water in a container and measure it. (Save it for later use, of course). How much water would you save or recycle doing this task if you used one of the methods described on these pages?
4. *Critical Thinking* Factories and farms use a lot of extra water. For instance, it takes about 11,400 liters of water to produce only one-half kilogram of beef. What might you do about this situation?

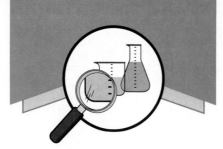

Tadpoles Lead to Big Fish

John Camper

Occupation: Assistant Curator of Fishes
Goal: To teach people to take care of the ocean, shores, and marshes
Hobbies: bicycling, cooking

Have you ever been to an aquarium where you see sand sharks, silver perch, tiny seahorses, and eels? John Camper's job is to help collect and care for the fish in a new aquarium in New Jersey. His first job there was to oversee collecting the animals.

How do you find sharks?

"It's easy—you go fishing. The hard part is keeping the shark calm for the trip home. If an animal gets too excited, it can hurt itself. But if it's kept in a cool, dark, and quiet tank, it will relax."

When did you start learning about fish and other "water life"?

"As long as I can remember, I would gather worms, insects, and other tiny things living in the stream near my home. I'd take them home and see if I could keep them alive in a jar with holes punched in the lid. Then when I was about 10 years old, I got my first aquarium—the kind you keep guppies in, not sharks."

What do you like about your job?

"I like being part of the team that keeps the animals alive and teaches the public about what these animals do in the wild. Some people can afford to take trips and see these animals in the ocean, but others can't. The aquarium gives these people a chance to identify with the ocean ecosystem and to have respect for these animals. You can't just read about the animals; you need to see them to appreciate them and to understand that we need to preserve their habitats."

How can kids help?

"Think about that plastic bottle before you throw it away. Where will it end up? When landfills get full, more trash is illegally dumped in the ocean. That hurts all ocean life. Kids can do a lot just by recycling."

Deep Sea Exploring: ROVs

Submersibles like the Alvin *can dive as deep as 4000 meters. The* Alvin *can support three people for three full days underwater. To extend their time underwater, scientists also use robots called Remotely Operated Vehicles (ROVs). One such ROV,* Jason Jr., *photographed the sunken luxury ship* Titanic. *The* Titanic *had been buried at sea for more than 70 years.*

1 A 61-meter cable connected *Jason Jr.* to the *Alvin.*

2 A strobe light and two smaller lights illuminated the inside of the *Titantic.*

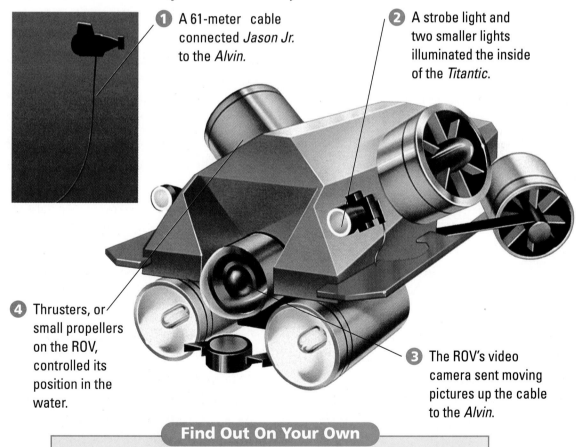

4 Thrusters, or small propellers on the ROV, controlled its position in the water.

3 The ROV's video camera sent moving pictures up the cable to the *Alvin.*

Find Out On Your Own

Find out what the bottom of the ocean might look like. Make a travel poster advertising a trip there.

Module Review

Making Connections

Patterns of Change

1. Explain the changes water goes through in the water cycle.
2. How do water and ice change the land over long periods of time?
3. Explain how your body gets water, uses water, and loses water every day.

Evolution

4. How have plants and animals adapted to a water environment? Give an example of each.
5. Show how human beings are adapted to a land environment.
6. Explain how water is necessary for life on the earth.

Using What I Learned

Comparing

1. Explain how trees and cactuses have adapted to different water supplies.
2. How are life forms in the light zone different from those in the dark zone?

Categorizing

3. Name two traits of an animal that lives on land and one that lives in water.

Predicting

4. If you have a graduated cylinder with 90 mL of water in it, which picture below represents what happens to the volume when the water freezes?

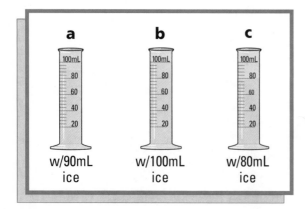

Communicating

5. Draw a picture that shows how a glacier erodes the land.
6. Draw a picture that shows the difference between a mixture and a solution of water and another substance.

Relating

7. Explain why it is important for you to drink water every day.

Ordering

8. Beginning with ocean water, put in order the following forms water takes as it moves through the water cycle: cloud, droplets, rain, water vapor, streams.
9. Record all the ways you take in water during a day. Include drinks and foods such as fruit juices, milk, water, soup, and fruits and vegetables that have a high water content. Then place all the drinks and foods on your list in order, from the source of the most water in your diet to the source of the least water in your diet.

Applying What I Learned

Action Project

Make a list of the ways water is wasted in your home, school, and community. As a class, think of ways to help conserve the water supply. Make a list of ideas and post them in your classroom.

Drawing

Draw a picture of a plant or animal that lives in water. Label the parts of the plant or animal that are adaptations to water living.

Performance Task

Use the materials shown in the picture to build a model of a beach. Now show how erosion changes your beach. Repair your beach and show ways you can protect it from erosion.

Science Theater

Prepare a skit of underwater exploration in the *Alvin*. Describe your crew, the submersible, and life under the ocean surface.

Exhibition

Make a poster or bulletin board showing a human being. Label the percent of water found in different parts of the human body.

What If

What if you learned a factory was polluting a nearby river? What arguments would you present to local officials to try to stop the pollution?

Volcanoes and Earthquakes

Volcanoes and Earthquakes

Do you judge the earth by its cover? If you do, you might not be aware of the powerful forces deep beneath the surface of the earth. In this module, you'll find out how these forces create volcanoes, start earthquakes, form mountains, and move continents.

CHAPTER 1 Beneath the Earth

Is the earth solid to the core? The layers of rock beneath the earth's crust are solid, liquid, and everywhere in between.

2 Explosive Volcanoes

Kaboom! From time to time, one of the earth's many volcanoes erupts explosively, forming a cloud of gas, rocks, and ash.

CHAPTER

3 Faults and Quakes

Are you ready for the big one? Major earthquakes can cause incredible damage, but you can protect yourself by playing it safe.

In this module

At the end of the book

Beneath the Earth

Sounds weird. What do you think it is?

Discover Activity

What is indirect evidence?

Get a shoe box from your teacher. The shoe box contains a mystery object. Find out as much as you can about the mystery object. There is just one rule: you can't look inside the box. Record what you did. What did you learn about the mystery object?

For Discussion

1. How can you find the weight of the object?
2. Why is the information you found called indirect evidence?

1.1 Liquid Rocks

▶ Do rocks melt?

The ground trembles. The earth cracks. The clock strikes twelve midnight. Just past midnight, on January 3, 1983, fountains of red-hot liquid begin spurting out of cracks along the eastern slope of Kilauea (kē′ lou ā′ə), a volcano on the island of Hawaii.

The thick liquid—called **lava**— glows like the coals of a fire. The lava rises dozens of meters into the air, then falls back to the earth. Wherever the lava falls, it sears the ground with heat great enough to melt rocks. Meanwhile, foul-smelling gas spreads throughout the air and joins the smoke of burning trees and other plants.

The sun rises, and still the lava keeps spurting from the ground. But now it begins flowing away from the lava fountains and spreading outward across the sloping land. As the lava spreads, it starts to cool. Over time, large masses of lava harden into thick carpets of black rock. In between these black carpets, rivers of red-hot lava, like the ones in the picture, continue to flow.

Over the next three weeks, 14 million cubic meters of lava will spurt out of the ground, covering almost 5 square kilometers of land. And this will be just the beginning. Time and time again, the lava will rise out of the ground, covering more and more land. Where did all the lava come from, and where will it go? You'll find out in this chapter.

▼ Lava erupts from Kilauea in Hawaii, and flows across the land.

The earth has three
main layers: the core, the
mantle, and the crust. The
continents and islands are
part of the crust. The core
has two parts: the inner
core and the outer core.

The Layers of the Earth

The earth is a slightly flattened sphere made of three major layers. The outer layer is called the crust. The middle layer is called the mantle. Some of the mantle is solid, some liquid. The inner layer is called the core.

The picture shows the three layers of the earth. The rocky crust covers the entire planet—from the top of the highest mountain to the floor of the deepest ocean. The rock that makes up the crust beneath the ocean is hard, black, and about 3 to 7 kilometers thick. The rock that makes up the crust of the continents is hard, coarse, and has many colors. This continental crust is usually thicker than the crust beneath the ocean.

The bottom of the earth's crust is much hotter than the surface. In its deepest parts, the crust is hot enough to melt some rocks. But, it's less than half as hot as the next layer, the mantle.

Like the crust, the mantle is mostly solid rock. But the mantle is far thicker and hotter than the crust. Silicon, oxygen, aluminum, and iron make up most of the rock in the mantle. The mantle is nearly 3000 kilometers thick.

The center of the earth, the core, is made of two parts. These parts are the inner core and the outer core. The outer core is made of melted iron and nickel. It is more than 2000 kilometers thick and hotter than the mantle. The inner core is a solid ball of white-hot iron and nickel. The distance from the edge to the middle of the inner core is about 1300 kilometers. The temperature of the inner core is even hotter than the temperature of the outer core.

The lava that spurted from Kilauea probably formed in the upper part of the earth's mantle. The temperature in the upper mantle is hot enough to melt some rock. Hot melted rock within the earth is called **magma.**

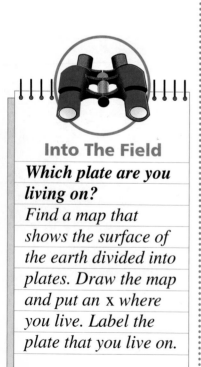

Into The Field

Which plate are you living on?

Find a map that shows the surface of the earth divided into plates. Draw the map and put an x where you live. Label the plate that you live on.

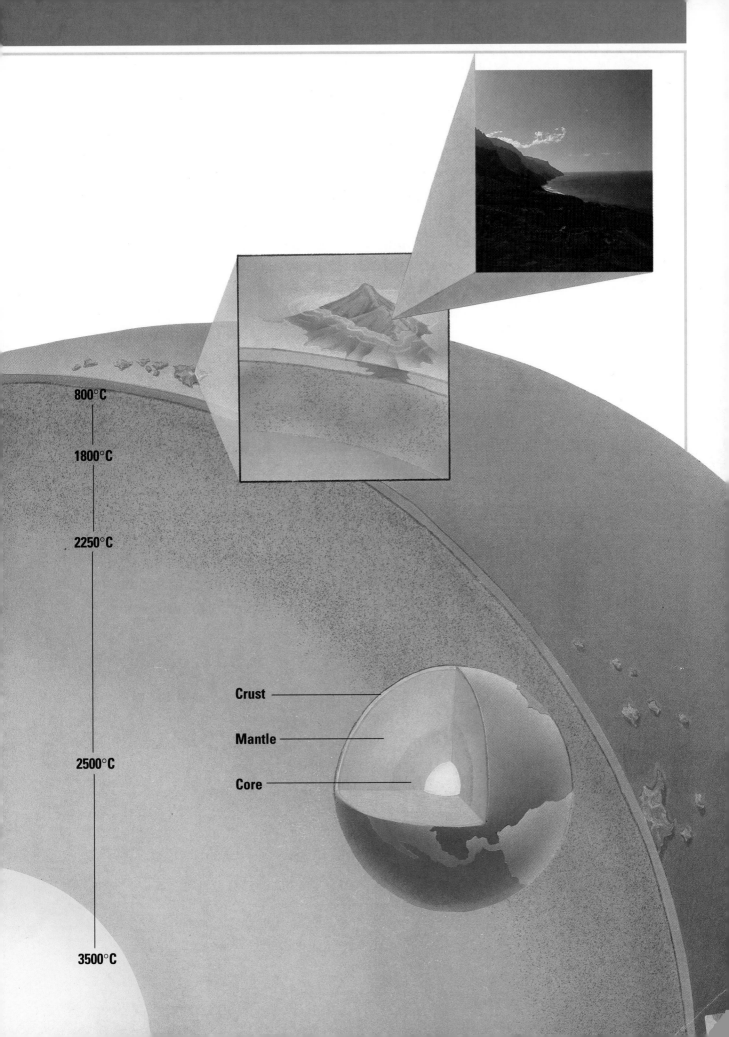

800°C

1800°C

2250°C

2500°C

3500°C

Crust

Mantle

Core

Rising Magma

Magma, which is hot melted rock, also contains gases. The gases within the magma push against the surrounding rock, producing a powerful force. This pushing force is called **pressure.** The pictures below show what happens next.

Magma rises because of its low density. Because of its heat and the high pressure, the magma slowly melts a pathway through the solid rock. When the magma reaches the crust, it forms a large underground lake called a magma chamber. These chambers can be just below the surface of the crust. Magma can gather in the chambers for hundreds of years.

When the magma breaks through the earth's crust, a **volcano** forms. Magma can break through the crust at weak spots. As the pressure in a magma chamber builds, the magma forces its way up through the weak spots, carving a wide channel in the solid rock. The magma then bursts through the crust of the earth, creating a large hole called a central vent.

When magma reaches a weak spot in the crust, it forms a magma chamber. Eventually, the magma bursts through the crust, forming a volcano.

Central vent

Hardened lava

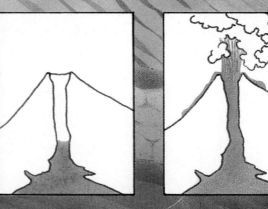

Magma chamber

When this type of volcano first erupts, the magma rushes up through the channel. The magma then bursts out of the central vent. The gases in the magma separate from the melted rock and rise high into the air. Now that the magma is on the earth's surface, it is called lava. The lava is still very hot, and it is liquid. The lava pours out onto all sides of the vent. The lava piles up in the shape of a mountain. When the lava stops flowing, it cools and hardens into rock. This volcano may erupt dozens of times in a single year. With each new eruption, the pile of cooled lava grows taller and taller, building up the volcano into a mountain.

Sometimes the central vent of a volcano becomes blocked. In the Kilauea eruptions that began in 1983, the magma burst through a weak spot in the side of the volcano. A new mountain of lava began building up around that vent. Within three years, a new mountain—called Puu Oo—was 250 meters high. Over a half billion cubic meters of lava spilled out of Puu Oo.

Some of the red-hot lava from Puu Oo flowed to the ocean, more than ten kilometers away. As the lava flowed into the cool water, the lava shattered into bits of black rock the size of sand grains. In turn, this sand drifted ashore on the coast of the island of Hawaii. This shattered lava forms Hawaii's famous black-sand beaches.

Checkpoint

1. Draw and label a diagram showing the three main layers of the earth.
2. What makes magma rise through the earth's mantle?
3. **Take Action!** Pour a small amount of cooking oil into a glass of water. Which liquid is like magma? Explain.

Blow Up

How high can a volcano get? The ash and lava shot out by volcanoes often build up into high mountains. The chart shows the heights of several volcanoes.

Volcano	Height Above Sea Level	
	m	ft
Aconcagua (Argentina)	6959	22,831
Mauna Loa (Hawaii, U.S.A.)	4169	13,677
Mount Fuji (Japan)	3776	12,388
Lassen Peak (California, U.S.A.)	3187	10,457
Paricutin (Mexico)	2808	9213
Mount St. Helens (Washington, U.S.A.)	2549	8364
Mount Katmai (Alaska, U.S.A.)	2047	6715
Vesuvius (Italy)	1277	4190
Surtsey (Iceland)	173	568

What Did You Find Out?
1. *In the chart given, which volcano is the tallest? Which volcano is the shortest?*
2. *When Mount St. Helens erupted in 1980, it lost 396 meters in height. How tall was Mount St. Helens before the eruption?*

C 9

Activity

An Erupting Volcano

What would it be like to stand near an erupting volcano? You probably would not want to be too near. Try this activity instead.

Picture A

Gather These Materials

cover goggles   250 mL beaker
plastic spoon   white vinegar
liquid detergent   trowel
plastic bottle   warm water
red food coloring   baking soda

Follow This Procedure

1. Make a chart like the one on the next page. Record your observations in your chart.

2. Put on your cover goggles.

3. Place 3 spoonfuls of liquid detergent into a plastic bottle.

4. Add 4 drops of red food coloring.

5. Add to the bottle 250 mL of white vinegar as shown in Picture A.

6. Bring the bottle outside. Scoop out a hole in loose dirt using a trowel. Pile up some dirt around the bottle so that the neck sticks out as shown in Picture B. If you cannot work outside, do the activity in a sink or in a large bucket.

7. Add warm water to the bottle until the bottle is three-quarters full. (Picture C)

8. Put 25 mL of warm water into the beaker. Mix 6 spoonfuls of baking soda into the water.

Picture B

Picture C

Predict: _What will happen when the baking soda is mixed with vinegar?_

9 Very quickly add the water with the baking soda to the bottle. What happens? Record your observations in your chart.

Observations

State Your Conclusions

1. What makes the detergent bubble?

2. How does this model of a volcano compare with a real volcano?

Let's Experiment

Now that you have made a model of a volcano, think of a way to make a model of how lava forms islands.

1.2 *Solid Plates*

▶ *Are you living on a moving plate?*

Your home is the place where you live. It's also the **plate** on which you live. You may not know it, but you've been living on a plate all your life, and so has everybody else who's ever lived on the earth. That's because the earth's crust and the upper part of the mantle is divided into about twenty sections. Each section is called a plate.

These plates fit together like the pieces of a jigsaw puzzle. But unlike jigsaw puzzles you've seen, the picture on this puzzle keeps changing. The picture changes because the plates are always slowly moving. The map on the left shows how the plates move. In some places, the plates are pulling apart. In some places, they are slowly sliding past one another. In other places, the plates are colliding, creating ocean trenches or mountain ranges.

▼ *Plates are sections of the crust and upper mantle. The arrows show the directions that the plates are moving.*

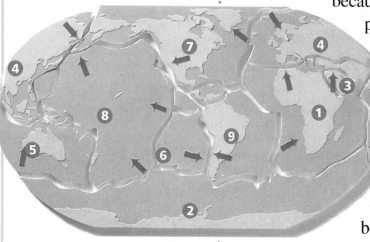

1 African Plate
2 Antarctic Plate
3 Arabian Plate
4 Eurasian Plate
5 Indian Plate
6 Nazca Plate
7 North American Plate
8 Pacific Plate
9 South American Plate

Plates, Pieces of a Puzzle

The plates that cover the earth are between 70 and 150 kilometers thick. Each plate contains a section of the earth's crust and a small part of the upper mantle. The plates float on the upper mantle. Some plates follow the edges of continents. Other plates cut across both land and sea. Together, the plates form the earth's lithosphere, or the layer of rock that lies under the oceans and the air.

Each plate drifts between 1 and 10 centimeters every year across the upper layer of the mantle, which is made of partly melted rock. Most scientists think that the plates move because of convection currents, as shown in the picture below.

In a convection current, differences in temperature force material to move in a circular pattern. Hot material rises, while cold material sinks. In the earth's mantle, hot magma rises up to the plates and spreads out sideways. The spreading magma acts like a conveyor belt and carries the plates along. As the magma spreads, it cools. The cool magma then sinks back into the mantle, where it heats and rises again.

Convection currents in the mantle sometimes bring magma up to where two plates meet. The magma pushes the plates apart as it melts through the weak area between them, forming a volcano.

Although many volcanoes form along plate boundaries, some form over what are called hot spots. Hot spots are areas, within the mantle, of extreme heat and melting action. The Hawaiian Islands formed as the Pacific Plate moved over a hot spot in the mantle.

▼ Circular convection currents in the mantle may cause the plates to move.

All in a Row

What happens when a hot spot stays put, but the crust above it keeps moving? A chain of islands forms!

Millions of years ago, a hot spot formed under the Pacific Plate. The hot spot melted the mantle and formed magma. The magma rose and formed a volcano. The volcano erupted many times and grew into an island.

Over many years, the Pacific Plate slowly moved away, but the hot spot stayed in the same place. A new volcano formed and grew into an island. As the plate continued moving, new volcanoes formed new islands. Over millions of years, the Hawaiian Islands formed. Today, a new volcano, Loihi, is growing over the hot spot. If it continues to grow, it will become a new Hawaiian Island.

Niihau Kauai Oahu Molokai Lanai Kahoolawe

Pacific Ocean

Pacific Plate

Mantle

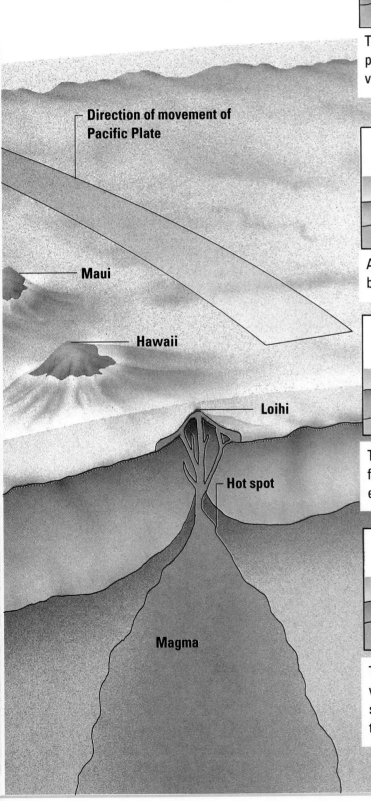

Direction of movement of Pacific Plate

Maui

Hawaii

Loihi

Hot spot

Magma

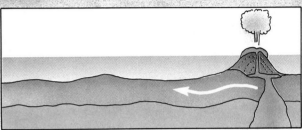

Pacific Ocean

Pacific Plate

Mantle

The hot spot causes magma to rise through the plate. The first volcano forms at the hot spot. The volcano erupts many times and makes an island.

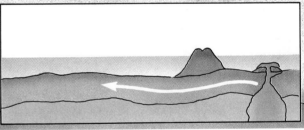

As the plate moves, the volcano moves with it because it is part of the plate. The hot spot stays put.

The first volcano stops erupting. A second volcano forms at the hot spot. It erupts many times and eventually another island forms.

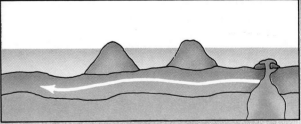

The plate continues to move, carrying the second volcano and island away from the hot spot. The steps repeat as another new volcano forms over the hot spot.

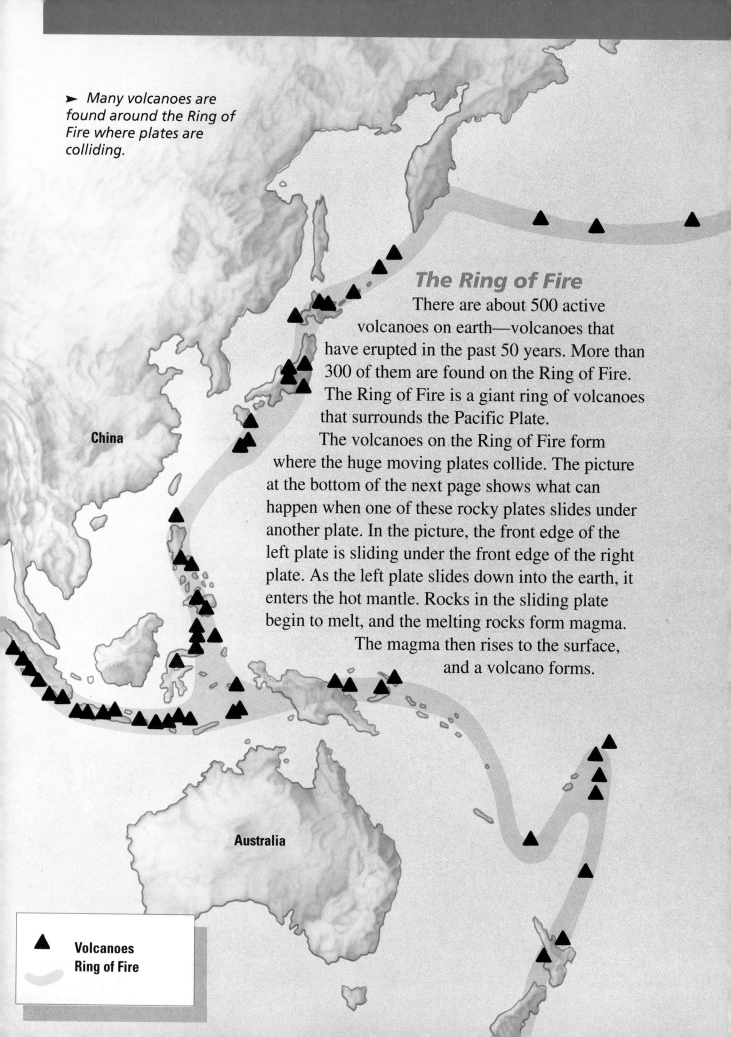

► Many volcanoes are found around the Ring of Fire where plates are colliding.

China

The Ring of Fire

There are about 500 active volcanoes on earth—volcanoes that have erupted in the past 50 years. More than 300 of them are found on the Ring of Fire. The Ring of Fire is a giant ring of volcanoes that surrounds the Pacific Plate.

The volcanoes on the Ring of Fire form where the huge moving plates collide. The picture at the bottom of the next page shows what can happen when one of these rocky plates slides under another plate. In the picture, the front edge of the left plate is sliding under the front edge of the right plate. As the left plate slides down into the earth, it enters the hot mantle. Rocks in the sliding plate begin to melt, and the melting rocks form magma. The magma then rises to the surface, and a volcano forms.

Australia

▲ Volcanoes
Ring of Fire

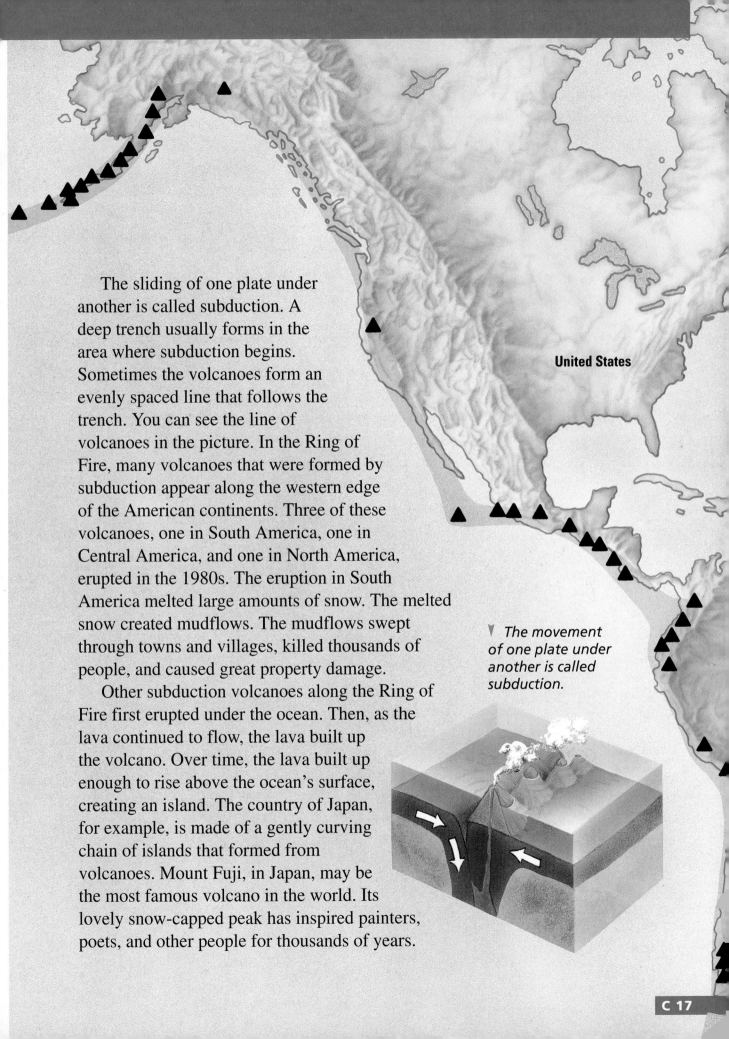

The sliding of one plate under another is called subduction. A deep trench usually forms in the area where subduction begins. Sometimes the volcanoes form an evenly spaced line that follows the trench. You can see the line of volcanoes in the picture. In the Ring of Fire, many volcanoes that were formed by subduction appear along the western edge of the American continents. Three of these volcanoes, one in South America, one in Central America, and one in North America, erupted in the 1980s. The eruption in South America melted large amounts of snow. The melted snow created mudflows. The mudflows swept through towns and villages, killed thousands of people, and caused great property damage.

Other subduction volcanoes along the Ring of Fire first erupted under the ocean. Then, as the lava continued to flow, the lava built up the volcano. Over time, the lava built up enough to rise above the ocean's surface, creating an island. The country of Japan, for example, is made of a gently curving chain of islands that formed from volcanoes. Mount Fuji, in Japan, may be the most famous volcano in the world. Its lovely snow-capped peak has inspired painters, poets, and other people for thousands of years.

United States

▼ The movement of one plate under another is called subduction.

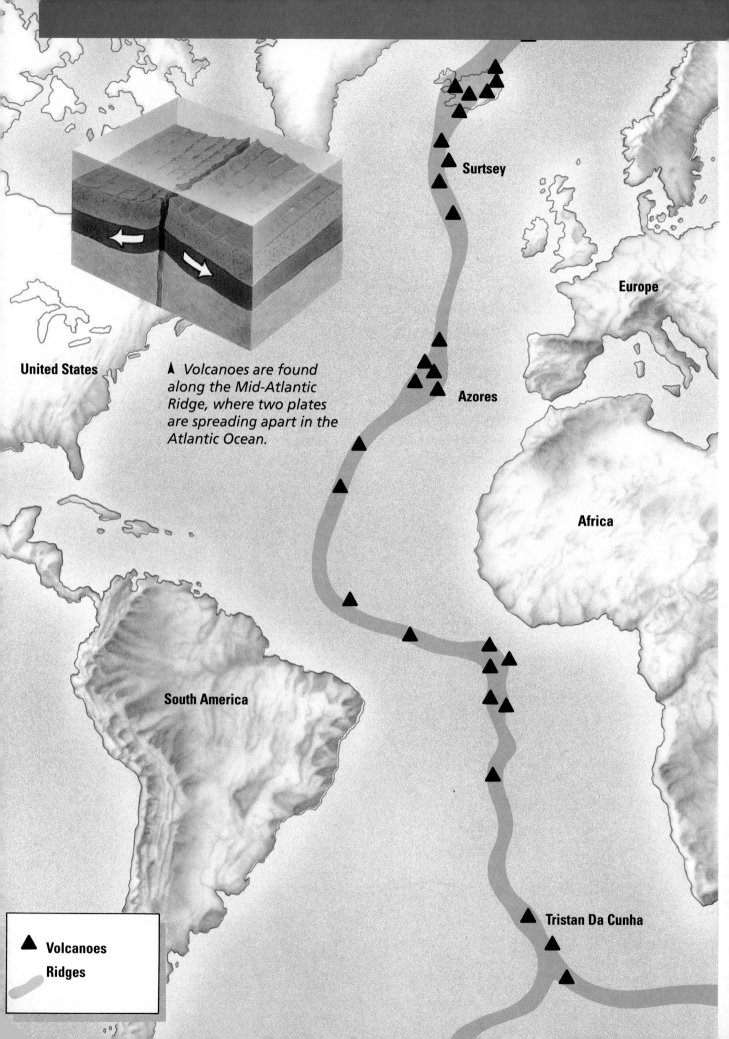

Volcanoes are found along the Mid-Atlantic Ridge, where two plates are spreading apart in the Atlantic Ocean.

United States

Europe

Surtsey

Azores

Africa

South America

Tristan Da Cunha

▲ Volcanoes

Ridges

Volcanoes Under the Atlantic

Halfway around the world from the Ring of Fire, another line of volcanoes stretches for thousands of kilometers along the Mid-Atlantic Ridge. But people rarely see the eruptions of these very active volcanoes. Why? Because nearly all of them lie deep beneath the Atlantic Ocean.

The pictures on the left show that the Atlantic Ocean floor is slowly splitting due to movement of the plates under the ocean. One set of plates moves east. The other set moves west. As the plates move apart, magma rises up and erupts under the ocean. The erupting magma forms volcanoes and ridges.

The eruptions of these volcanoes are usually calm and quiet. The great pressure of the ocean water changes the rising magma into harmless chunks of rock called pillow lava. Instead of blasting up into the water, the pillow lava spreads out across the ocean floor. Sometimes, Atlantic volcanoes rise above the ocean's surface and form islands. Surtsey, shown on the right, is an example.

▲ In 1963, Surtsey, an island near Iceland, rose above the ocean. It formed from an underwater Atlantic volcano that had been building up for many years.

Checkpoint

1. Explain what may make plates move.
2. What happens to a volcano when it moves away from a hot spot?
3. What happens to the sliding plate when it slides under another plate?
4. Why are eruptions deep in the ocean calmer than eruptions on land?
5. **Take Action!** Float several pieces of an old puzzle on water in a bowl. Gently stir the water. How do the pieces move? How is this movement like the movement of plates on the earth's surface?

Activity

Egg-citing Earth

When is an egg not an egg? When it is a model of the earth. Use a hard-boiled egg to show the layers of the earth.

Picture A

Picture B

Picture C

Gather These Materials

cover goggles
2 hard-boiled eggs that have been soaked in vinegar to soften

plastic knife
cutting surface
clear, plastic straw

Follow This Procedure

1 Make a chart like the one on the next page. Record your observations in your chart.

2 Put on your cover goggles.

3 Place a hard-boiled egg that has been soaking in vinegar on a cutting surface. (Picture A)

Predict: *What do you think the inside of the egg will look like?*

4 Firmly hold the egg with one hand. In the other hand hold a knife. Carefully cut the egg in two, shell and all. The egg will be soft after soaking in vinegar. (Picture B) *CAUTION: Handle the knife with care.*

5 In your chart, draw a cross section of the egg. Label it with the 3 parts of the earth that you have learned about.

6 Take the second hard-boiled egg. Push a clear, plastic straw into one end of the shell. (Picture C) Twist the straw to get it into the egg.

Record Your Results

Cross section of egg	Section in the straw

7 Push the straw from one end of the egg all the way out through the other end.

8 What do you see inside the straw? In your chart, draw a picture of the layers of the egg. Label your drawing with the names of the layers of the earth.

State Your Conclusions

1. How many layers can you observe in the first egg? How does the thickness of each layer compare to the other layers?

2. In what ways do the layers of an egg make a good model of the earth?

3. To study the earth's crust, scientists drill into the crust and mantle. Then, they remove long, thin strips of earth. How are the layers in the straw like the layers of the earth?

> **Let's Experiment**
>
> Now that you have used an egg for a model of the earth, how could you make a scale model of the earth using clay?

Drawing a Diagram

Did you ever help someone put together a toy from a kit? A diagram probably came with the kit. The diagram showed you how the parts fit together.

Some information is easier to understand if shown in a diagram. A diagram is a good way to show how something works or is put together. Diagrams are often used in everyday life. They are also good study tools. Diagrams can help you remember what you have read.

Thinking It Through

Suppose you were asked to make a diagram of one way that rock is formed from magma. You might draw something like the diagram on this page. Before making a diagram, ask yourself these questions.

1. What do you think the diagram is supposed to show?

2. What parts do I need to label?

3. How can I show how the parts work together? Do I need to draw arrows to show movement from one part to the next? Must I write Step 1, Step 2, Step 3, and so on?

When the diagram is finished, you should ask these questions.

• Is the picture clearly drawn?

• Are all labels clear and easy to understand?

You might show the diagram to someone else to see if he or she understands it.

Your Turn

Use the information you learned in this chapter to make a diagram of how magma moves in the mantle and can form a volcano.

Chapter Review

Thinking Back

1. How is the crust under the ocean different from the continental crust?
2. Describe the earth's core.
3. Where does the **pressure** come from that forces **magma** to rise?
4. How does a **volcano** form?
5. What is the difference between magma and **lava?**
6. Name three ways that **plates** can move in relation to each other.

7. How could convection currents in the mantle cause the plates to move?
8. How does a volcano move away from a hot spot?
9. Describe how the volcanoes along the Ring of Fire formed.
10. How does the movement of the plates in the Atlantic Ocean create volcanoes in the ocean?

Connecting Ideas

1. Copy the concept map. Use the terms to the right to complete the map about how islands and ridges form.

volcanoes   ridges
pressure   islands

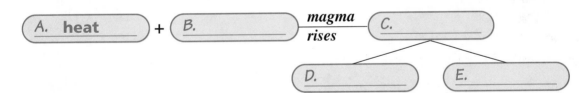

2. Write a sentence or two about the ideas shown in the concept map.

Gathering Evidence

1. In the Activity on page 10, how did the model of the volcano help you understand what a real volcano is like?
2. In the Activity on page 20, how were you able to use the egg as a model of the earth?

Doing Science!

1. ***Develop a skit*** that would describe how you would have reported the eruption of the Kilauea volcano in 1983 for a news broadcast.
2. ***Design an activity*** showing the different ways the plates of the earth move.

Explosive Volcanoes

Wear cover goggles
for this activity.

What can pressure do?

Punch a small hole in the lower edge of one side of a shoe box. Insert the neck of a balloon into the hole. The body of the balloon should be inside the box. Cover the balloon with sand or dirt. Predict what will happen when you blow up the balloon. Now blow up the balloon, and see what happens.

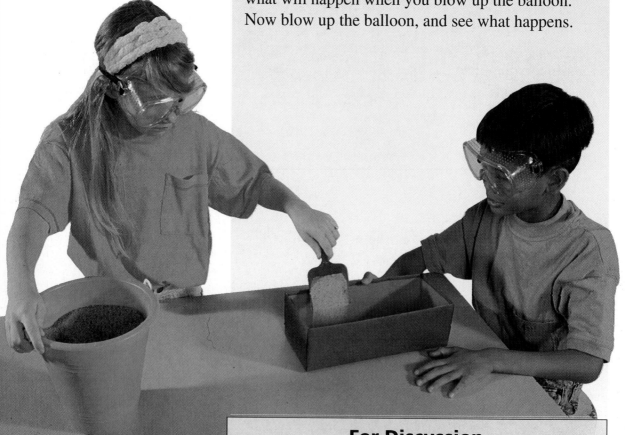

For Discussion

1. What happened when you blew up the balloon?
2. How does the amount of air in the balloon affect the result?

2.1 *Predicting an Eruption*

▶ *Can clouds carry rocks?*

At 8:32 on the morning of May 18, 1980, a huge sheet of rocks begins sliding down the north slope of Mount St. Helens in Washington state. As the rocks slide away, they uncover a gaping crack in the side of the mountain. Within seconds, a boiling hot cloud of rocks, ash, and steam blasts sideways out of the crack. Hugging the ground and moving faster than a race car, the cloud destroys almost everything in its path. It kills more than 60 people and millions of animals and trees. By the time it stops, the cloud has blasted a fan of death across more than 500 square kilometers of land. How can one cloud gather so much power? The answer lurks inside the mountain.

▼ *Before May 18, 1980, Mount St. Helens was covered with forest. The smaller photograph shows rocks, ash, and steam blasting out of the top of Mount St. Helens.*

Warning Signs

Scientists use seismographs to predict the eruption of a volcano. A **seismograph** detects movement, or vibrations, within the earth. The seismograph shows those vibrations by drawing lines on paper. The earth always has some vibration, so the lines are never straight. However, when the vibrations are strong, the seismograph lines begin to move up and down. When there are many strong vibrations, it is more likely that an earthquake will occur, or a volcano will erupt, or both.

Like other volcanoes in the Ring of Fire, Mount St. Helens sits over a magma chamber. When magma begins to rise, it causes earthquakes that can be measured by seismographs. In March of 1980, a seismograph near Mount St. Helens showed that earthquakes were shaking the area. Later that month, a loud explosion ripped open a small crater near the top of the mountain. Then the north side began to bulge outward.

Scientists measured the bulge and found that the bulge was growing, and growing fast. The magma under Mount St. Helens was on the move!

▼ Students study the record made by a seismograph.

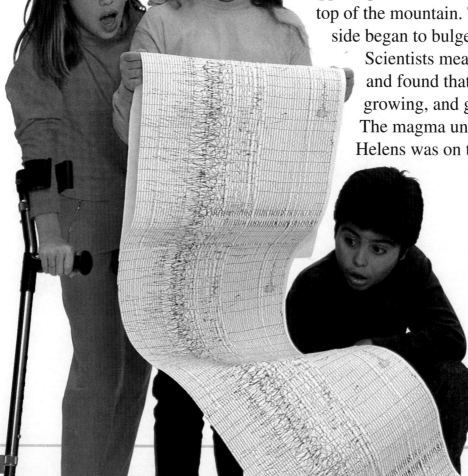

Bulging Rocks

When you boil water in a pan, the water slowly turns to steam and rises out of the pan. If you put a tight lid on the pan, the steam cannot get out. The pressure in the pan increases. If the pressure gets forceful enough, the pressure can blow the lid off.

Mount St. Helens was like a closed pan of very hot water. Over the years, magma and gases rose inside, and pressure on the crust increased. The magma and gases placed more and more pressure on the mountain's crust, creating the bulge. Then, an earthquake caused the rock atop the mountain to slide downhill. The pressure was suddenly released. The magma and gases rocketed out of the mountain, carrying along a deadly load of ash and rocks.

Because of warnings from many instruments, few people were near Mount St. Helens when it erupted. In 1991, similar instruments warned about the eruption of Mount Pinatubo in the Philippines. Tens of thousands of people left the area.

Into The Field

What warning signs can you find?

Volcanoes give warning signs before erupting. Use your senses to observe warning signs that happen before other events.

▲ *Children play with the ash dumped in their neighborhood by the Mount Pinatubo eruption.*

Checkpoint

1. How do scientists use seismographs to help predict an eruption of a volcano?
2. What made Mount St. Helens bulge outward?
3. **Take Action!** Pop off the cap of a bottle of warm soda. Explain how the soda is like the magma at Mount St. Helens.

Activity

Up from the Ashes

A volcano spreads black volcanic ash over the land. Can plants survive being covered by volcanic ash? Try this activity to find out.

Picture A

Picture B

Picture C

Gather These Materials

2 paper cups
soil
12 small fast-growing
  seeds such as beans
scissors

sheet of black
  construction paper
beaker
water

Follow This Procedure

1 Make a chart like the one on the next page. Record your observations in your chart.

2 Fill 2 paper cups with the same amount of soil.

3 Plant 6 identical seeds in each cup. (Picture A)

4 Use scissors to cut a sheet of black construction paper into tiny pieces. (Picture B) The black pieces will represent the black volcanic ash left after a volcano erupts.

5 Take one cup. Cover its soil with a layer of black paper pieces. The layer should be about 3 mm thick. (Picture C)

6 Water the 2 cups with the same amount of water. Put both cups in the same place.

Predict: *In which of the cups will the seeds grow first?*

Record Your Results

Observations		
Date	Cup without "ash"	Cup with "ash"

7 Record your observations. Record when you first see the sprouts, how many seeds grow in each cup, and how tall each plant grows.

State Your Conclusions

1. In which cup did you see sprouts first? Why?
2. How does this activity help explain what occurs to an area after a volcano erupts?
3. What did the seedlings under the black paper bits look like? Why?

Let's Experiment

You have now seen how a layer of ash affects the growth of seeds. Do an experiment to show whether the thickness of the ash makes a difference in how the seeds grow.

2.2 *Recovering from Eruptions*

Is there life after an eruption?

In the photograph below, firs, hemlocks, and other evergreen trees ring the calm waters of Spirit Lake, not far from Mount St. Helens. The photograph was taken before May 18, 1980. On that fateful May date, a deadly cloud of ash and rocks from the erupting volcano swept across Spirit Lake. The cloud knocked down trees and left behind a thick, heavy carpet of gray and gritty ash, as shown in the photograph at the bottom of the next page.

Would the land around Spirit Lake ever recover? The trees were dead, and the waters of the lake were thick with mud. Yet underneath that barren landscape, life stirred within hours of the eruption. Chipmunks scurried along their underground tunnels. Frogs underwater were still alive. They showed that Spirit Lake had a chance.

▼ *Spirit Lake, before the eruption of Mount St. Helens*

Underground Survivors

When plants or animals live through a disaster in a particular area, they are called survivors. Many plants and animals survived the eruption.

Chipmunks and pocket gophers live underground. When the ash and rocks fell around Mount St. Helens, many of them were safe beneath the soil. Over time, they dug their way up through the ash and poked their heads above ground. If they lived near water, they might have seen a few frogs, salamanders, crayfish, or snakes. Mud, water, and ice had protected these water animals.

But what about the plants? In between the fallen trees, a hardy plant called fireweed began growing within a month of the eruption. Fireweed gets its name because it grows soon after forest fires. It can grow after eruptions as well. All across Mount St. Helens, clumps of fireweed sprang out of the ground and bloomed with beautiful pink flowers. Other plants also grew, such as huckleberry. The plants attracted hungry animals from far away. These animals came from areas that the eruption had not damaged, so they cannot be called survivors.

▲ *Roots and bulbs buried under the soil survived the eruption of Mount St. Helens.*

▼ *Spirit Lake, after the eruption of Mount St. Helens*

Distant Colonizers

Colonizers are living things that come into an area to eat and live. After the eruption in May, deer and elk were among the first colonizers to enter the ash-covered land around Mount St. Helens. The deer and elk came to eat the fireweed and the other plants. As they picked their way across the land, they left deep hoof prints in the ash. They also left animal wastes filled with seeds. Over time, the seeds from the animal wastes sprouted and began to grow into plants. These seeds and plants were also colonizers because they came from outside the ash-covered land.

Rainfall and melting snow carved channels where plants could grow. Gophers broke through the ash from underground and shoved out small mounds of dirt. Seeds blown by the wind landed in these mounds and channels. Some of the seeds were from willow and cottonwood trees. Others came from blooming flowers. These seeds also sprouted and began to grow.

As the plants grew during the summer of 1980, they attracted more and more animals. Insects and spiders began to arrive. And wherever insects go, birds are sure to follow. Birds came to eat the insects and to build nests.

◄ *Lupine, a plant with lovely colorful flowers, grew through the ash of the Mount St. Helens eruption.*

The dead trees were home to many living things. Inside the trees, bacteria and fungi ate the wood, turning it into rotten matter that enriched the ground. Around the trees, a few saplings rose from the old roots and stretched their leaves toward the sun and the rain.

By autumn, many forms of life could be found in the area around Mount St. Helens. Some were survivors and others were colonizers, but all showed that life would go on. Someday soon, Spirit Lake and all the other places near the volcano would once again be green and growing.

The Healing of Mount St. Helens

Plants are key to the return of life.

On May 18, 1980, Mount St. Helens violently erupted. Only a few living things survived. The fireweed plant was the first to start growing. Deer, elk, and birds came through the area soon after the eruption. They did not stay because there was little food or shelter.

When the fireweed plants died, they fell into the ash and made the soil richer. The wind blew in new seeds. Many different plants started growing. The plants attracted insects, birds, and other animals. By 1990, the trees and shrubs were large enough to provide shelter, and there was enough food. Deer, elk, and birds once again were living on Mount St. Helens.

1980 Soon after the eruption, fireweed starts growing through the ash.

1983 Several years after the eruption, the soil has gotten richer. More kinds of plants are growing.

1980   1982

1986 Trees are the last plants to return. Here, Douglas fir trees have started growing, but they are still small.

1990 Many kinds of living things have returned. But the land is not yet the same as it was before the eruption.

| 1984 | 1986 | 1988 | 1990 |

➤ *Beautiful flowers also grow in volcanic soil.*

▼ *Ash from volcanoes makes the soil in Indonesia very fertile. Indonesia is a leading producer of rice.*

Benefits From Below

Volcanoes can kill people and reshape land, but they also provide many life-giving substances. Much of the air we breathe and the water we drink came from volcanoes. Without eruptions, many important gases would remain deep within the earth.

Volcanoes also help build the land on which we live by forming islands. Hawaii, Japan, and many other islands are volcanoes, although some of them are no longer active. But those are just the volcanoes that reach the surface of the ocean. Lava flows from volcanoes cover the deep ocean floor.

Another type of rock—granite—lies under the continents. Granite forms from magma that cools beneath the ground without erupting. Granite is very hard. People use granite to construct buildings that last for centuries.

The magma that erupts as lava contains many useful minerals. Obsidian is a shiny black volcanic glass that Native Americans used for making knives, arrowheads, and jewelry. Pumice, on the other hand, is a light, white, foamy-looking rock that when ground into a powder is used for polishing and scrubbing.

The ash that erupts from some volcanoes begins to break down soon after falling to the ground. Over time, it gives the soil nutrients important for plant growth. In the rich volcanic soil of Indonesia, for example, farmers grow rice, corn, peanuts, coffee, and many other crops. Volcanoes loom above the farmers' fertile fields, ready to erupt at any moment.

Italy's Mount Vesuvius has erupted several times in the past few hundred years, but farmers have always returned to its fertile slopes. There they grow apricots, grapes, tomatoes, beans, peas, and millions of beautiful carnations that are shipped all over Europe. Volcanoes may be dangerous, but for these farmers, volcanoes are well worth the risk.

Somewhat less risky are the underground steam fields that are found near volcanoes. People have begun using this underground steam to make electricity. At the Geysers power plant, located near volcanoes in northern California, the steam rises up to the plant through large pipes. The powerful steam drives huge turbines inside the plant. These turbines create enough electricity to serve one million people. That's a lot of electricity, but it's just a tiny fraction of the incredible power that is within volcanoes.

Checkpoint

1. What's the difference between survivors and colonizers?
2. How did deer and elk help life return to Mount St. Helens?
3. In 1981, the elk did not stay in the area around Mount St. Helens. Why?
4. In what ways do volcanoes contribute to life on the earth?
5. **Take Action!** Make a list of uses of the underground steam fields found near volcanoes.

Traveling Seeds

 Wear cover goggles for this activity.

Does the shape of a seed help it travel?

What To Do
A. Cut three squares, 5 centimeters on each side, out of paper.
B. Roll one square into a ball. Fold one square in half. Pretend that each piece is a seed.
C. Turn a fan on low speed. Drop each "seed" in front of the fan.
D. Measure how far away each "seed" landed from where you dropped it. Record your answers on a table like the one below.
E. Use the third square to invent a "seed" that will travel far. Test it with the fan.

Record Your Data

	Seed Number		
	1	2	3
Distance traveled			

What Did You Find Out?
1. *Which "seed" traveled farthest?*
2. *How did its shape help it travel far?*
3. *Which "seed" might travel on the wind to a volcano? Which might not? Why?*

Activity

Bulbs or Seeds?

Flowers such as tulips, crocuses, and daffodils grow from bulbs, not seeds. How are bulbs different from seeds? Do this activity to find out.

Picture A

Picture B

Picture C

Gather These Materials

cover goggles

bulbs such as tulip, crocus, or daffodil

seeds

paper towel

plastic knife

iodine solution

cups and flowerpots with soil

water

hand lens

Follow This Procedure

1 Make charts like the ones on the next page. Record your observations in your charts.

2 Put on your cover goggles.

3 Examine a bulb and a seed carefully. (Picture A) Write your observations on your chart.

4 Place a bulb on a paper towel. Carefully use the knife to cut off a small piece of the bulb. *CAUTION: Use the knife with care.*

5 Get the iodine. Iodine turns blue-black when it is put on something that has starch in it. Starch is a form of food found in plants. *CAUTION: Handle iodine with care. It is a chemical that can stain hands and clothes. Clean up spills and wash up immediately.*

Predict: *Will the iodine turn blue-black when you put it on a piece of bulb?*

Record Your Results

	Bulb	Seed
Name		
Description		
Iodine test		
Depth of planting		

Observations of growth

Date	Bulb	Seed

6 Place a few drops of iodine solution on the piece of bulb. (Picture B) What happens to the iodine? Record your results in your chart.

7 Try the iodine test on some seeds and record your results in the chart.

8 Plant several bulbs and seeds in the soil, following your teacher's directions or the package instructions. (Picture C) Record the depth of planting for each. Water the bulbs and seeds.

9 Observe your plants for several weeks. Record your observations.

State Your Conclusions

1. Do bulbs or seeds have more stored food for the young plant?

2. Which group is planted at a greater depth within the soil?

3. Which group would have a better chance of surviving after a volcano erupts? Why?

Let's Experiment

You have seen that bulbs and seeds store different amounts of starch and that they should be planted at different depths. Now find out if seeds and bulbs can grow at different temperatures.

Hypothesizing

One of the main volcanoes on the island of Hawaii is Kilauea (Kē′lou ā′ə). For more than seven years, streams of burning lava have flowed down its slopes. This lava has cooled into a hard, dark mass. You might think that nothing could grow here. But the Hawaiian Islands were formed by volcanoes that were built up from lava, and they are full of plant and animal life. Scientists used these and other facts to form the hypothesis that life would return to Kilauea.

A hypothesis is an explanation that scientists think is correct because it is based on known facts. A hypothesis is not a fact itself.

Thinking It Through

You are a scientist who is studying the return of living organisms to Kilauea. You observed the lava slopes, and learned the following facts:

Fact 1: Tiny plants called mosses are growing on the cooled lava.

Fact 2: The 'ohi'a trees on Kilauea were badly burned during the eruption. But some have an unburned side. The unburned sides of the 'ohi'a trees are growing new buds. These buds are growing little roots into the air. The roots get water from fog and rain.

Fact 3: Silversword plants are blooming on the volcano's crater. Bees, snails, wasps, beetles, and spiders have arrived.

Using what you observed, your hypothesis is that the cooled lava on Kilauea will be able to support further life. To test this hypothesis, you could see how many more living things arrive over time.

Your Turn

Use the facts in the chapter to form a hypothesis about why an island is forming at Spot A, a place where two oceanic plates are moving apart. List the facts that you used to form your hypothesis.

Chapter Review

Thinking Back

1. What tool do scientists use to predict the eruption of a volcano?
2. What does a **seismograph** detect?
3. How can seismographs save lives?
4. How do some small animals survive volcanic eruptions?
5. Why do animals come to areas where a volcano has erupted?
6. How do seeds get to an area where a volcano has erupted?
7. How did plants help animals return to Mount St. Helens after the eruption?
8. How do volcanic eruptions help produce air and water?
9. What useful rocks are formed by magma and lava?
10. Why do farmers return to the slopes of volcanoes?

Connecting Ideas

1. Copy the concept map. Use the terms to the right to complete the map about the benefits from volcanoes.

air and water ash
gases rich soil
useful rocks

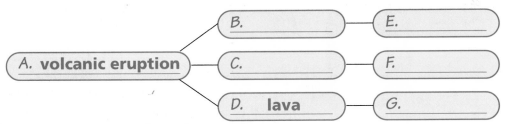

A. **volcanic eruption**
B. _____
C. _____
D. **lava**
E. _____
F. _____
G. _____

2. Write a sentence or two about the ideas shown in the concept map.

Gathering Evidence

1. In the Activity on page 28, what evidence did you use to decide whether ash is good or bad for plants?
2. In the Activity on page 38, which might better survive a volcanic eruption, a seed or a bulb? Why?

Doing Science!

1. ***Design a display*** that shows both the harmful and positive results of volcanic eruptions.
2. ***Write a news broadcast*** describing how an area recovered from the eruption of a volcano.

Faults and Quakes

Push and presto! It's an instant mountain.

Discover Activity

How do mountains form?

Flatten out three pieces of clay into rectangles. Place them on top of one another. Then put a block at each narrow end of the stack of clay. Press the two blocks toward each other. What happens?

For Discussion

1. Does it make a difference whether you press hard or soft against the blocks? What is the difference?

2. What do the blocks and the clay stand for?

3.1 *Raising the Ground*

▶ *Are all mountains volcanoes?*

Far to the south of Mount St. Helens, the rocky eastern side of Mount Whitney rises steeply out of the California desert. The jagged peak of the mountain soars more than 4000 meters above sea level. The peak is just one part of a long line of tall, jagged mountains that begins near Mount Whitney and stretches north for more than 600 kilometers along the eastern edge of California, as you can see in the picture. From a distance, the line of mountains looks like the blade of a giant saw covered with snow. For this reason, the Spanish settlers called them the Sierra Nevada—the snow-clad saw.

Did the Sierra Nevada erupt out of the ground like a volcano? Probably not. All along the eastern edge of the Sierras runs a fault. A **fault** is a crack in the earth's crust and upper mantle along which rock moves. The eastern side of the Sierras is slowly rising up along this fault in big blocks. Because the Sierra Nevada mountains are moving up in big blocks along a fault, they are called fault-block mountains. Their eastern side is steep, but their western side rolls gently down to California's central valley.

Fault-block mountains are just one of several types of mountains that cover the face of the earth. In this lesson, you will learn more about fault-block mountains and folded mountains. Both types can be found in the United States.

▼ *On this map of the western United States, you can see the Sierra Nevada near the eastern border of California.*

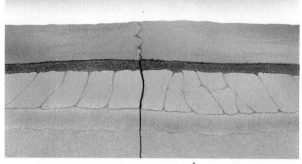

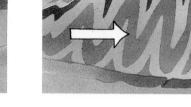

▲ *Folded mountains, like the Appalachians, form when two plates collide and crumple up.*

▼ *Appalachian Mountains*

Folded Mountains

To understand folded mountains, you have to remember that the earth is covered with slowly moving plates made of layers of rock. Folded mountains form when two plates collide. The force of the collision slowly crumples the edges of the plates, forming mountains. This mountain-building process can continue for millions of years, as the edges of the plates continue to crumple. The drawing above shows what the folded layers of rock under these mountains are like.

About 400 million years ago, the African Plate began smashing into the eastern edge of the North American Plate, forming the Appalachian Mountains. Over millions of years, the Appalachians slowly rose thousands of meters into the air. Then rainfall and wind wore down the Appalachians. The softer rocks washed away, leaving gently rounded mountains.

Today, the Appalachians are less than half as tall as the Sierras. Instead of being a single line of jagged peaks like the Sierras, the Appalachians are a series of ridges separated by valleys. These ridges and valleys follow the folds of the rock layers below the surface. If you stand on top of a ridge, you can see the other ridges stretching away from you like the crests of gentle waves. Judging from the view, you would never know that the Appalachians probably were once the tallest mountains on earth.

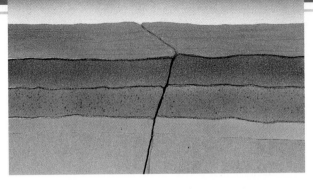

Fault-Block Mountains

The Sierras are much younger than the Appalachians. The Sierras began to form about 100–150 million years ago, when a plate separating from the Pacific Plate started sliding under the western edge of the North American Plate. As the Pacific Plate slid beneath the North American Plate and deep into the mantle, some of its rocks melted into magma. Instead of rising to the surface through volcanoes, some of the magma cooled underground and became granite. As more and more granite built up along the Sierra line, the granite began pushing upward in huge blocks.

As the granite blocks rose, they made cracks in the crust. One of these cracks is now the long fault that runs all along the eastern edge of the Sierras.

When the granite blocks move up along this fault, they create earthquakes. The east side of the Sierras has had many earthquakes in recent years. Based on these recent earthquakes and other available evidence, scientists think that the Sierras are still rising.

▲ *Fault-block mountains, like the Sierras, form when a block of rock moves up along a fault.*

Checkpoint

1. How do folded mountains form?
2. Why are the Sierras called fault-block mountains?
3. Take Action! Build your own mountain, then tell where your mountain is and how it formed.

Activity

Something Has to Give

What happens when two of the earth's plates collide with each other? Try this activity to find out.

Picture A

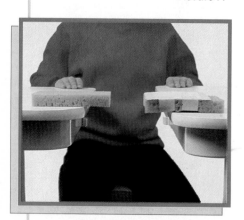

Picture B

Picture C

Gather These Materials

cover goggles
scissors
4 index cards
masking tape

4 dry sponges
2 desks
rubber bands

Follow This Procedure

1 Make a chart like the one on the next page. Record your observations in your chart.

2 Put on your cover goggles.

3 Use scissors to cut four index cards in half. Make a pile of the eight pieces, and tape the stack together.

4 Place the cards on one edge of a dry sponge. Attach them with masking tape. (Picture A)

5 Use two desks that are the same height. Move them close together so there is a distance of one "sponge length" between them.

6 Place the sponge with the index cards on one desk. Place a plain sponge of the same type on the other desk.

> **Predict: What do you think will happen when the two sponges collide?**

7 Slowly push the two sponges toward each other, as shown in Picture B. Record your observations.

8 Place a sponge on top of each of the original sponges. These second sponges will represent a continent on a moving plate.

9 Attach the top and bottom sponges together with rubber bands so that the top sponges are curved with the ends upward. (Picture C)

10 Move the sponges toward each other until the continents collide. Record your observations.

State Your Conclusions

1. What happens when 2 of the earth's plates collide? What do you think happens to the lower plate?

2. How does this activity help to explain how mountains are formed along the borders of the earth's plates?

Let's Experiment

The ocean floor is made of dense rock and is also riding on a plate. Make a model to show what happens when a plate carrying the ocean floor collides with a plate carrying land.

3.2 *Shaking the Land*

The top picture shows a fault before an earthquake. The bottom picture shows how the blocks of crust moved during the earthquake.

▼ *These houses in San Francisco collapsed during the earthquake of October 17, 1989.*

▶ *Can the earth stop the World Series?*

On October 17, 1989, baseball fans from all around San Francisco came to Candlestick Park for the third game of the World Series. At five in the afternoon, the crowd watched the players get ready for the first pitch. At that moment, about 40 kilometers south of Candlestick Park, part of the Pacific Plate near Loma Prieta suddenly moved northward and upward. A few seconds later, the baseball park and almost everything else in the Bay Area began to shake. Roads collapsed. Many houses collapsed, as shown in the picture. Fires broke out. Although the shaking lasted only 15 seconds, there was much damage. Back at Candlestick Park, the fans were terrified, but luckily no one was killed. The World Series was postponed. The Loma Prieta earthquake had just shaken the Bay Area, and normal life had come to a halt.

Sliding Along

Earthquakes begin at faults. Many faults occur where two plates meet. For example, the Loma Prieta earthquake began along the San Andreas Fault. This fault, which is 1200 kilometers long, is one of the places where the North American and Pacific Plates meet.

The Pacific Plate is slowly moving to the northwest. As this plate moves, it slides past the North American Plate. Both plates are made of layers of rocks. In some places, the rocks slide past each other easily. In other places, the rocks stick. These sticking places are usually several kilometers below the earth's surface. Pressure builds in the sticking places until the rocks break. Then the Pacific Plate suddenly lurches northward, starting an earthquake. The San Andreas Fault is one place where pressure often builds up and earthquakes occur.

Into The Field

Are you prepared for a natural emergency? *Think of all the things you would need in case of a natural emergency in your area. Make a list and prepare a box of those things.*

▼ *The San Francisco earthquake in 1906 was more powerful than the Loma Prieta earthquake. In 1906, most of the buildings, like the one in the small picture, were destroyed.*

Super-House

Special features in houses can help protect them during an earthquake.

Houses are damaged during earthquakes because the earth shakes back and forth. As a result, the house shakes back and forth. Imagine standing in your home. Imagine that an earthquake is shaking your house or apartment back and forth. What do you think might happen? The house might shake off its foundation (the part under the house that the house sits on). The roof might fall off, or the chimney might break. Pipes that carry water or gas might break. Furniture could fall over. Dishes, books, and other things could fall out of cabinets. Windows might break. The picture shows a house that has been built to be safe during an earthquake.

Safety film is put on the windows. The film sticks to glass and holds it together if the glass breaks.

Special bolts are used to connect the floor of the house to the foundation. Similar bolts are used to hold the roof to the walls of the house.

Pieces of metal are used to hold the water heater in place.

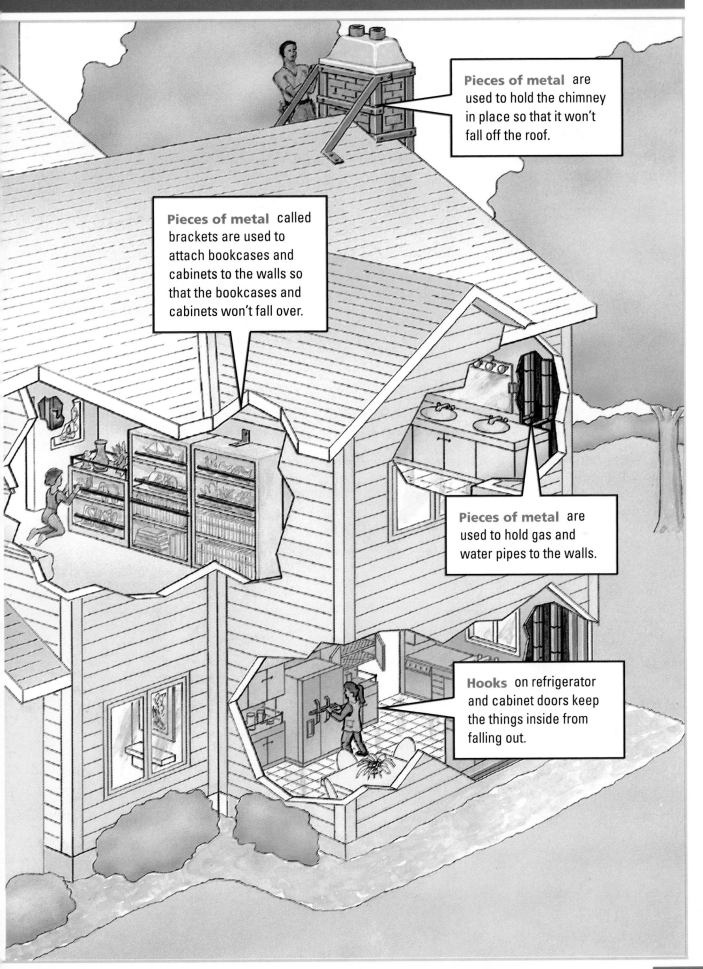

LANDSAT, a satellite, took this picture. It shows the San Andreas Fault in the Monterey Bay area just south of San Francisco.

These students are putting together an earthquake emergency kit.

Being Prepared

You can see where part of the San Andreas Fault is located in the photograph on the left. Scientists know that earthquakes are likely to occur along these faults, but they don't know exactly when. They can only make rough guesses based on past earthquakes and present warning signs.

In order to gather information about possible earthquakes, scientists use seismographs, tiltmeters, and laser reflectors—the same tools that can help them predict the eruptions of volcanoes.

When predicting earthquakes along a fault, scientists also consider how much time has passed since the last major earthquake. Along the San Andreas Fault, for example, earthquakes that measure 6 or more on the Richter scale occur about every 100 years. This information helps scientists predict when the next earthquake might occur.

But past history is not enough. Scientists also watch for warning signs. Sometimes small quakes occur just before a bigger quake. Sometimes animals behave in strange ways. But these warning signs don't always occur. Scientists have yet to find a warning that occurs before every earthquake.

Earthquakes can be very dangerous. If you live in an area that might have an earthquake, your best protection is to be prepared.

You should keep an earthquake kit in your home. The kit should include flashlights, batteries, a fire extinguisher, a portable radio, a first-aid kit, water, warm clothes, and canned food.

If you are inside during an earthquake, go under a table and cover your head. The table will protect you from falling objects. If you are in a car, tell the driver to pull over to the side of the road. Stay inside the car and keep away from bridges, power lines, and large buildings.

Checkpoint

1. What happens when sliding plates stick together?
2. What could you do to make your home safer during an earthquake?
3. What warning signs may show that an earthquake is about to occur?
4. Take Action! For a month, look in newspapers for reports of earthquakes. Record when and where the earthquakes occur.

Richter Scale

The Richter scale compares the strength of earthquakes. Each increase of one stands for an earthquake that is ten times as strong. For example, an earthquake of 6 is ten times as strong as an earthquake of 5.

Richter Number	Damage Caused
2.0–2.9	Not felt, but recorded
3.0–3.9	Felt by a few people
4.0–4.9	Felt by most people
5.0–5.9	Slight damage to buildings
6.0–6.9	Much damage to buildings
7.0–7.9	Great damage to buildings
8.0–8.9	Total destruction

What Did You Find Out?
1. *The Loma Prieta earthquake measured 7.1 on the Richter scale. The San Francisco earthquake of 1906 measured 8.3. Which was stronger?*
2. *Every day more than 1000 earthquakes occur, but no one feels them. What do these earthquakes measure on the Richter scale?*

Activity

Shake and Quake

Does the shape of a building help it remain standing during an earthquake? Try this activity to find out.

Picture A

Picture B

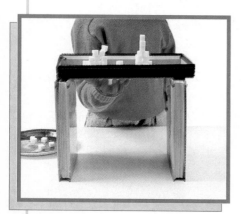

Picture C

Gather These Materials

shoe-box lid
metric ruler

2 books of the same size
30 sugar cubes

Follow This Procedure

1 Make a chart like the one on the next page. Record your observations in your chart.

2 In the center of a shoe-box lid, draw a square 12 cm long on each side. (Picture A)

3 Balance the shoe-box lid on 2 books.

4 Use sugar cubes to build a different "building" in each corner. Each building should have a different design and number. (Picture B)

Predict: **Which of your buildings will be the least likely to fall during an earthquake?**

5 Use your fingers in a flicking motion to strike under the center of the lid. (Picture C) Record your observations.

6 Strike the lid again, using slightly more force than before. Which buildings are still standing?

7 Repeat several more times, increasing the force each time until all the buildings have fallen. Record your results.

Record Your Results

Number of building	Strength of force needed (from 1 to 10 with 1 being the weakest) to make building fall
1	
2	
3	
4	
Your own design	

8 In one corner of the square, construct a building using at least 6 sugar cubes. Can you make it earthquake proof? Build it and shake it to see.

State Your Conclusions

1. Which building fell first? Why?
2. How did you use your shake and quake results to design your own building?
3. What would you recommend to someone who wanted to build a house in an area that has earthquakes?

Let's Experiment

Repeat your experiment. But this time, make a scale that shows how strong your earthquakes are.

Analyzing Information

When you need to solve a problem, you can analyze the information you have. When you analyze information, you study it carefully. Some ways to analyze information include finding time and space relationships and using diagrams.

Thinking It Through

Suppose you were asked to analyze the layers of sedimentary rock shown in the diagram at the right. You could begin by studying how the layers are related in time and space. You could then use this information to draw your conclusions about the history of the area. To draw your conclusions, you might ask questions like these.

What do I know about the way layers of rock are related?

I know that the oldest layers are usually on the bottom. Therefore, the location of the layers (space) is connected to when the layers were deposited (time).

How can I use this information to determine the age of any fossils that I might find?

Since the fossils are in the rock, they must have been deposited with the rock. Analyzing this information, I can conclude the older the layer of rock, the older the fossil.

Can I find out more about the history of this place from these layers?

Yes, I can. After looking at the diagram and analyzing the information it shows, I think the shell fossil layer might mean that at one time a sea was in this area.

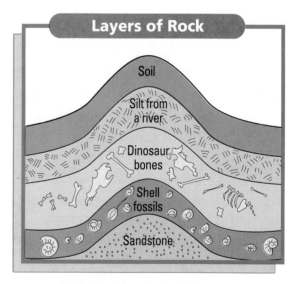

Layers of Rock

Soil

Silt from a river

Dinosaur bones

Shell fossils

Sandstone

Your Turn

Analyze the diagram to answer the following questions.
1. Do you think this area was ever covered by a river?
2. Did dinosaurs live in this area before or after it was a sea?
3. What do you think the fold in the layers might mean?

Chapter Review

Thinking Back

1. What is a **fault**?
2. What kind of mountains are the Appalachians and how did they form?
3. Why are the Appalachians no longer the tallest mountains in the world?
4. What kind of mountains are the Sierras and how did they form?
5. Why do earthquakes occur where two plates meet?
6. If you had a house in an area that has earthquakes, what would you do to your house to make it safer?
7. Can scientists predict exactly when an earthquake will occur? Why or why not?
8. Name some tools that scientists use to study earthquakes.
9. What goes into an earthquake kit?
10. What should you do if you are in a building or in a car during an earthquake?

Connecting Ideas

1. Copy the concept map. Use the terms to the right to complete the map about the formation of mountains.

fault-block   **folded**
          Appalachians

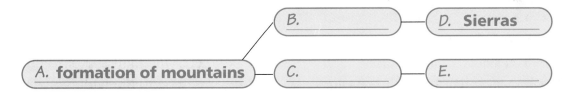

2. Write a sentence or two about the ideas shown in the concept map.

Gathering Evidence

1. In the Activity on page 46, how did the sponges show what happens to continental plates when they collide?
2. In the Activity on page 54, how could you predict which buildings were least likely to fall?

Doing Science!

1. *Design a model* to show the different ways mountains are formed.
2. *Develop a plan* for a person who lives in an area that has earthquakes. How could that person inform neighbors about ways to be prepared for an earthquake?

Earthquake-proof Buildings?

Earthquakes occur often in certain areas. Earthquakes can't be prevented, and so far they can't be predicted. However, if buildings are built in a special way, they are less likely to shake apart during an earthquake.

Needs and Goals

Suppose you are a building inspector. You are checking some tall buildings.You want to see if the buildings will hold together during an earthquake.

Buildings built in a special way are less likely to shake apart.

Gathering Information

Earthquakes usually happen along fault lines. Most of the earth's fault lines are known. Builders can choose to put the building as far as possible from the fault.

1. The shaking of an earthquake goes through solid rock as short, sharp jolts. Soft, sandy ground makes waves like ocean water, and shakes more than solid rock. A tall building is better off on ground of solid rock. A short building might be safe on sandy ground if it is built with special supports.

2. Some buildings have an open ground floor, for example, a building with a garage underneath. Such a building sways at two different rates. The solid upper floors sway less. The flexible first floor sways more. The building could collapse.

3. A building whose long side is parallel (running in the same direction) to the fault will be less likely to sway.

4. A building whose long side is crosswise to the fault will sway much more.

5. An L-shaped building, which has one wing parallel to the fault and one wing running crosswise to the fault, will sway at different rates. The two wings may break apart.

Possible Alternatives

There are many building types. Imagine you are comparing the buildings shown here.

Evaluating Alternatives

Copy the table. Then examine each of the pictures on this page. Fill in information about each building in the correct row.

Making the Best Choice

Decide which building is the safest and would be damaged the least during an earthquake. Use your table to help you.

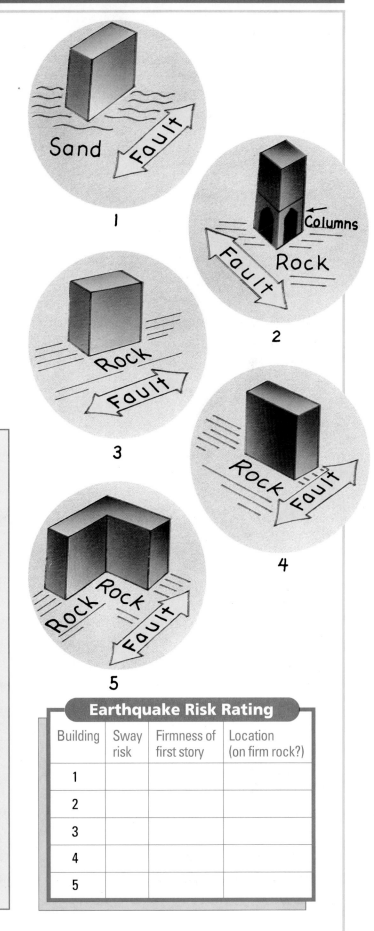

Now You Do It

1. Which building is the safest and would suffer the least damage in an earthquake? Why?

2. Which building seems almost as safe as the one you gave the top rating? Why?

3. *On Your Own* Look for pictures of buildings such as offices and schools. Of course, you can't tell whether they are built on sand or parallel to an earthquake fault. But examine things such as their height, whether they are L-shaped, and whether they have a solid first story. Tell whether they would be safe or unsafe in an earthquake zone.

4. *Critical Thinking* An earthquake is a natural disaster that can't be prevented. What preventable disasters do you know of? How can they be prevented?

Earthquake Risk Rating

Building	Sway risk	Firmness of first story	Location (on firm rock?)
1			
2			
3			
4			
5			

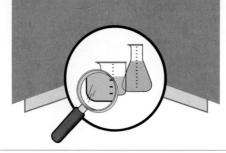

Reading the Quakes

Terri Hauk

Occupation: Seismologist
Current Project: *Expanding Your Horizons,* a program that encourages girls to become scientists

In 1964, a huge earthquake struck Anchorage and Valdez in Alaska. Terri Hauk was fascinated by the reports on television. "Roads were breaking apart, a tidal wave formed a huge wall of water, and everything started shaking like a bowl of gelatin. Then one whole area sank into the ocean, houses and all. I was in awe of the forces of nature, and I wished that I could have helped to save those people's lives." Now Terri Hauk is a seismologist—she studies earthquakes.

How do you study earthquakes?

"I live near the San Andreas Fault in California. Tiny earthquakes happen there every single day. You wouldn't be able to feel them, but special instruments called seismometers measure the waves from each tiny quake. The tiny quakes are called tremors. I look for a pattern in the tremors—where they occur and how strong they are. Over time, these patterns and other data may show if the small tremors are related to the occurrences of large earthquakes."

When is the big one coming?

"We could save a lot of lives if we were able to predict exactly when an earthquake will hit. That's still the hard part. But we can do a lot just by knowing where an earthquake might hit and how strong it might be. We can say where it's not safe to build, and we can advise how strong a building should be to make it safe during earthquakes."

What do you like best about your job?

"It's good to know that my job helps other people, but I also like what I do every day in the lab. It's exciting to be a part of important research and to work with the top people in my field. There are new methods and new information. I'm learning something new every day."

Mining: Extracting Iron From Ore

Iron is found in a rock called iron ore. Once the iron is made pure, it is used to make steel. Iron and steel are used in almost every kind of machine.

1 Large pieces of iron ore are crushed into lumps or powder and sent to a tall tower called a blast furnace.

2 Ore and special chemicals are loaded into the top of the blast furnace.

3 Hot air is sent from stoves into the blast furnace. Chemical reactions occur. The iron melts and trickles down.

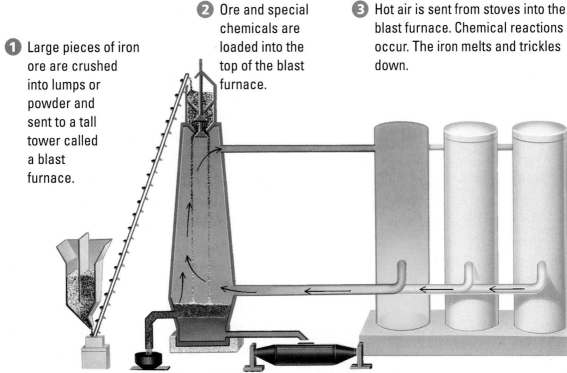

4 Liquid iron and the leftover material, called slag, are let out through different pipes at the bottom of the furnace.

Find Out On Your Own

Iron is one kind of ore. Use books to find out about other kinds of ores. List the ores, the metals found in them, and what the metals are used for.

Module Review

Making Connections

Energy

1. What causes magma to rise to the surface?
2. Explain what may make the plates of the earth move.
3. Explain why an earthquake occurs.

Patterns of Change

4. Explain two ways mountains form.
5. Name one instrument that scientists use to measure vibrations within Earth.
6. Explain why predicting earthquakes and volcanic eruptions is important.

Using What I Learned

Comparing

1. Explain how fault-block mountains and volcanoes are alike and different.
2. What is the difference between magma and lava?

Predicting

3. If you were a scientist and saw the lines on a seismograph move a great deal, what might you predict?

Categorizing

4. Name two differences between the Appalachian and Sierra Nevada Mountains.

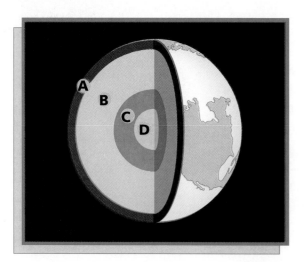

Communicating

5. Write a paragraph that describes how life returns to an area after a volcanic eruption.

Ordering

6. What is the correct order of the following layers of Earth from the outer part to the center: crust, inner core, mantle, outer core?

Relating

7. Why do scientists think that the Sierras are still rising?

Observing

8. Observe the diagram of the earth. In which layer, A, B, C, or D, are magma chambers found? Explain how magma chambers develop. Use the letters in the diagram in your explanation.

Applying What I Learned

Action Project

Find out about the results of earthquakes in other countries and the extent of damage caused by them. Contrast how the United States prepares its citizens for this type of disaster.

Drawing

Make a series of drawings to show what happens when a volcano erupts.

Science Theater

Write a TV news report describing either a volcanic eruption or an earthquake. Tell your viewers why this occurred, if there were any warning signs, and what they should do in the future to prepare for any similar occurrence.

Exhibition

Create a poster or bulletin board by drawing or tracing a large map of the United States. Find and label the major mountain ranges and the way in which they were formed.

What If

What if you read or heard that earthquakes were likely to occur in your area? What preparations might you make? How would you prepare others?

Performance Task

Use clay to show how folded mountains are formed and how fault-block mountains are formed.

Flying

MODULE D

Flying

Wave good-bye to solid ground. You're headed up into the clouds—up where the birds soar and the jets zoom by. How do they stay up here, so far above the ground? You'll find the answer in this module. It's an answer filled with flapping wings, invisible oceans, and the roar of modern engines.

CHAPTER

2 Born to Fly

Great fliers are born, not made. Birds use their muscles and wings to create thrust, lift, and the marvel of flight. But not all birds fly alike.

CHAPTER

1 Invisible Ocean

How can you hit what you can't see? Birds can fly thanks to the atmosphere—the invisible ocean of air that surrounds the earth.

CHAPTER

3 Learning to Fly

Fasten your seat belts! We're taking off! It took people thousands of years to learn how to fly. Now their jets and planes crowd the skies.

Invisible Ocean

I'd need a hurricane to get this thing to move.

Wear cover goggles for this activity.

How can you make a breeze detector?

Cut a piece of tissue paper into a thin strip. Blow on it. What happens? What happens when you blow on it even harder? Design an instrument for measuring the strength of the wind. Then make your instrument and find out how well it works.

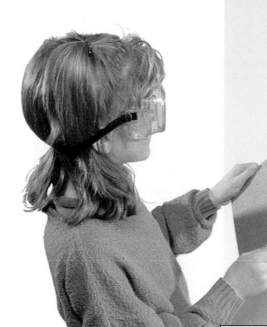

For Discussion

1. *How is where you measure the strength of the wind important?*
2. *How does your breeze detector work?*

1.1 Up, Down, and All Around

What is the air?

Far above the rocky ocean coast, a sea gull soars through the sky. It clutches a hard-shelled mussel in its beak. Suddenly, the bird lets go of the mussel, and it falls to the rocks. The hard shell cracks as it smashes into a rock, revealing the mussel's soft inner meat. Before anyone else can steal its prize, the gull swoops down, eats the meat, and flies off to find more mussels. A gull drops mussels from the sky all day long. Why can't mussels stay up in the sky like the gull in the picture?

Gas All Around

Part of the answer is the air, which lies between the gull and the ground. The air is part of the **atmosphere**—the layer of gases that surrounds the earth. Like solids and liquids, a gas is a form of matter that has mass and takes up space. Unlike solids but like liquids, a gas takes up the space available to it. Near the earth, gases are lighter and thinner than liquids or solids. The most common gases in the atmosphere are nitrogen and oxygen. You can't see them, but they're all around you. On the next two pages you'll see just how big the earth's atmosphere of gases is.

▼ Sea gulls and other birds can fly through the sky because air has mass and helps support them.

What Makes Up Earth's Atmosphere?

Layers of air are like an ocean above you!

You live at the bottom of layers of air held down by gravity. These layers weigh 5000 million, million tons! Just above Earth is the troposphere, the atmosphere's lowest and heaviest layer. Most weather is in this layer. The higher you go in it, the colder the air becomes, and the less oxygen there is to breathe.

Next comes the stratosphere. Airliners fly in the stratosphere to avoid the weather below. The ozone layer is in the stratosphere. It protects Earth from ultraviolet radiation.

Beyond, two more layers of atmosphere exist between Earth and outer space. The air in these layers gradually gets thinner and thinner.

Thermosphere

Mesosphere

Stratosphere

Troposphere

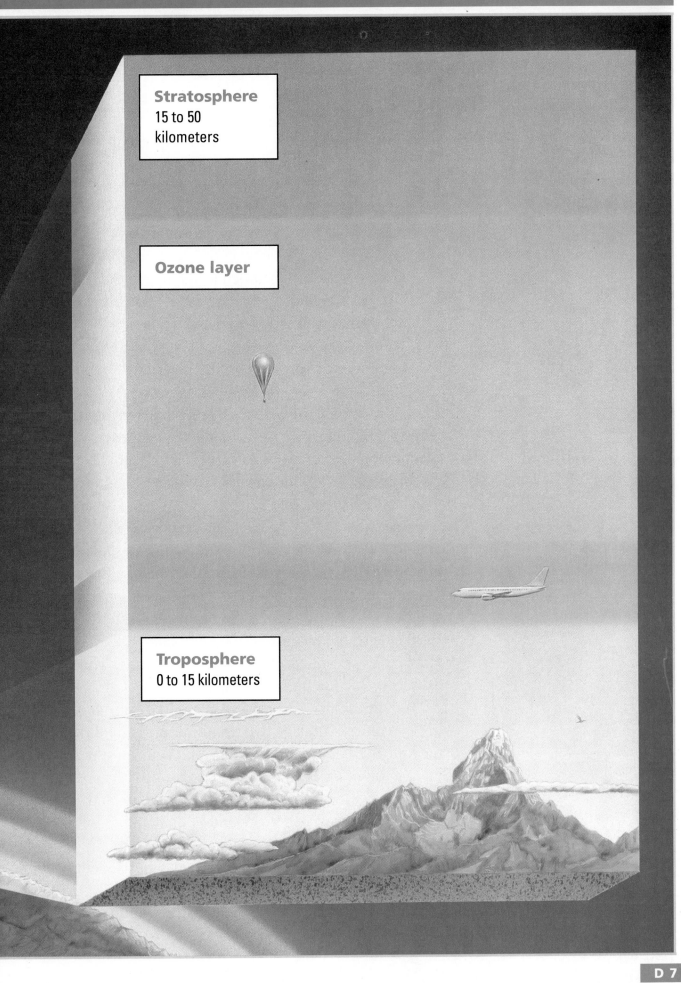

Stratosphere
15 to 50
kilometers

Ozone layer

Troposphere
0 to 15 kilometers

Air Pressing All Around

In the gravity of the earth, the atmosphere weighs a lot. When things have weight—like air—they press down on the earth. All over the earth, the atmosphere presses down—on oceans, beaches, hills, and mountains. Air pressure is the force of the atmosphere pressing down on a particular area.

Imagine that you have drawn a square on the back of your hand. The square is 1 centimeter long on each side, so it's called a square centimeter.

If you stand on an ocean beach, the weight of the air pressing down on that square centimeter on your hand will be about 1 kilogram. If you stand on the top of a mountain, the air pressure will be lower.

Why would the air pressure be different at the top of the mountain? Because the top of the mountain is higher up in the atmosphere than the ocean beach. Less air exists above the mountain top than above the beach.

Now imagine you're back on the ocean beach and you've drawn a square in the sand. The square is 30 centimeters long on each side. Imagine that your square is at the bottom of a column of air that stretches all the way to the top of the atmosphere. Each side of the column is 30 centimeters wide. How much do you think that column weighs? The answer is 907 kilograms—almost one ton of air!

Step inside that imaginary square like the student in the picture. Think of that ton of air pressing down on you. Why don't you feel this air? You can stand up to a ton of air because the air presses in all directions at once—up, down, in, and out. When you stand in that column of air, it presses on you equally from all sides. Air inside of you also pushes out with the same pressure. That's why you don't feel the weight of the air.

▼ *A column of air 30 centimeters square and as high as the atmosphere weighs as much as a small car.*

1 ton =

= 1 ton

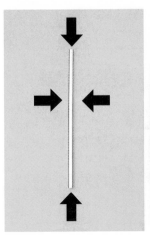

▲ *Air presses on a straw from the outside in and the inside out. This is why you can pull water up through a straw or hold it inside a straw by covering the top.*

The pictures above show how air pressure helps you drink a glass of water through a straw. Notice that the air is pressing on the first straw equally in all directions. When you suck on the straw, you pull air out of it, thereby lowering the air pressure inside the straw. The higher pressure of the air around the straw presses down on the water and forces the water up the straw and into your mouth.

If you put the straw in the glass and then cover the top with your finger, you can trap water in the straw. As you lift the straw out of the glass, the water stays inside. Why? Because air presses up on the straw from below. If you lift your finger off the straw, the water will fall back into the glass.

Checkpoint

1. How is a gas different from a solid?
2. In what layer of the atmosphere does weather take place?
3. Why don't you feel the weight of the air above you?
4. Take Action! What would happen if you could suck all the air out of a straw and cover both ends? Draw a picture of what the straw would look like.

Measuring Oxygen

How can you find the percent of oxygen in air? Let's investigate.

What to Do
A. Place a piece of wet steel wool in a test tube.
B. Turn the test tube upside down in a cup with 1 cm of water in it.

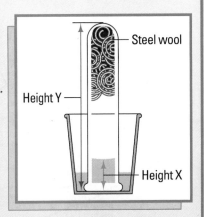

Steel wool

Height Y

Height X

C. Wait 4 days. A chemical change will use oxygen from the air in the tube.
D. Measure the height in mm that water rises in the tube. Record it as Height X.
E. Measure the total height in mm of the test tube. Record it as Height Y.

Record Your Results

Height X	
Height Y	

What Did You Find Out?
Find the percent of oxygen in the air. Divide Height X by Height Y and multiply by 100.

Activity

Soft Landing

You've probably seen a parachute float to the earth. In this activity you'll make your own mini-parachute.

Picture A

Gather These Materials

square piece of
  lightweight cloth
marker
scissors
gummed reinforcement
  rings

string
paper clip
ball of clay
metric ruler
timer

Follow This Procedure

1 Make a chart like the one on the next page. Record your observations in your chart.

2 Fold a square piece of lightweight cloth in half and then in half again. Then fold it so that your piece looks like the cloth in Picture A.

3 Draw a guideline to round off the edge of the piece of folded cloth using a marker. Then carefully cut off the edge using the scissors. Use the scissors carefully. (Picture A)

4 Open up the cloth and place a gummed reinforcement ring on every rounded edge of the cloth as shown in Picture B.

5 Cut several lengths of string that are about twice the diameter of the parachute. Cut a piece for each ring.

6 Tie each piece of string to a reinforcement ring. (Picture B)

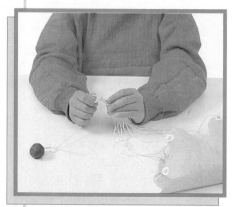

Picture B

Picture C

7 Gather the strings and tie their ends together with another piece of string.

8 Insert the paper clip into a ball of clay.

9 Then tie the string from your parachute to the paper clip. (Picture C)

Predict: *Does a parachute's height affect the time it takes to land?*

10 Drop the parachute from different heights. Use the timer to find out how long the parachute takes to land. Record the heights and times.

11 Try to land your parachute on a target. Can you control where it goes?

Record Your Results

Height	Time to soft landing

State Your Conclusions

1. Why does the parachute come down slowly?
2. What can you do to the parachute to keep it up in the air longer?
3. Suppose two parachutists release their rip cords at the same time, but one parachute is much larger than the other. Which do you predict would land faster and why?

Let's Experiment

Now that you have constructed a mini-parachute, what material makes the best canopy for a parachute? Set up an experiment using tissue paper, facial tissue, cotton, silk, nylon, plastic wrap, and aluminum foil. Use what you know about scientific methods to find out.

1.2 Rising and Falling

How strong is air?

Imagine you're a professional sky diver flying 4500 meters above the earth. Without a thought, you jump from the plane and dive toward the earth. When you're 600 meters above the ground, you pull a ring, and a parachute comes out of your backpack. In seconds, the parachute fills with air, and you float to earth like a gently falling leaf.

You may not be able to see air. But it's there all right. And it can exert a strong force.

Air Resists Motion

If you tried to ride your bike through a brick wall, you wouldn't get very far. You'd smash into the brick's atoms which are packed together making the brick dense. The atoms stop most objects that try to move through them.

Air is also made of atoms joined as simple molecules. When you ride your bicycle, you're smashing into molecules of air. Unlike the atoms of bricks, the molecules of air don't stop you. But the air molecules do slow you down, or resist your motion.

▼ A rider who sits upright on a bike offers many surfaces for the air to resist.

The force that tends to slow you down is called **air resistance.** But why don't the air's molecules stop you? They aren't as close together as the bricks' molecules. The air molecules also are not bound to each other. You can push the molecules of air apart as you move through them.

Air resistance affects the way you ride your bike. If you sit up straight like the girl in the picture, all the surfaces on the front of your body are pushing against the air. Your face and chest both push against the air, so air resistance slows you down. You can go much faster by bending forward over your handlebars. Why? Because your face and chest are no longer pushing against as much of the air. The less surface you present to the air in front of you, the less air resistance there is to slow you down. What is the boy below doing to reduce air resistance as he rides?

Speed also affects air resistance. The faster you go, the greater the air resistance. Bicycle racers go so fast that they do many things to cut down air resistance. Bicycle racers often wear tight clothes and a curved helmet. Some racers even shave the hair off their arms and legs. When you're going fast, even hairs can slow you down.

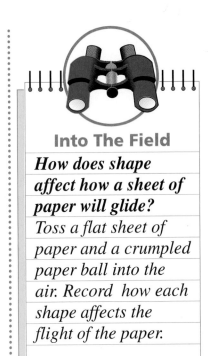

Into The Field

How does shape affect how a sheet of paper will glide?
Toss a flat sheet of paper and a crumpled paper ball into the air. Record how each shape affects the flight of the paper.

◄ Bikers who streamline their bodies with tight clothes and a crouched position cut down their air resistance.

Moving Air

You can feel air when you move by riding a bike. But sometimes air moves by itself as wind. How does that happen? Notice the balloon in the top picture on page 15. The balloon hangs loosely because it has very little air inside. In the bottom picture, the balloon is filled with air. What caused this change? The bottle with the balloon was placed in a pan of hot water. As the air became warmer, it moved from the bottle into the balloon.

Here's how. Before the bottle was heated, the air pressure inside and outside the bottle were the same. As the bottle sat in hot water, the molecules of air inside the bottle heated up and moved faster and faster. They tried to spread farther apart but couldn't because of the sides of the bottle, so their pressure increased. When the air pressure in the bottle became stronger than the elastic force in the balloon, the air molecules could move apart and begin to fill the balloon. When they expanded, the air became less dense.

As long as the bottle stays hot, the balloon will be filled with warm air. But if the bottle cools down, the air in the balloon will cool down, too. Then the molecules of the air will move closer together. The air contracts and takes up less space. The balloon's elastic force pushes the cold air back into the bottle.

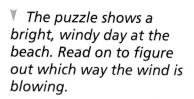

▼ *The puzzle shows a bright, windy day at the beach. Read on to figure out which way the wind is blowing.*

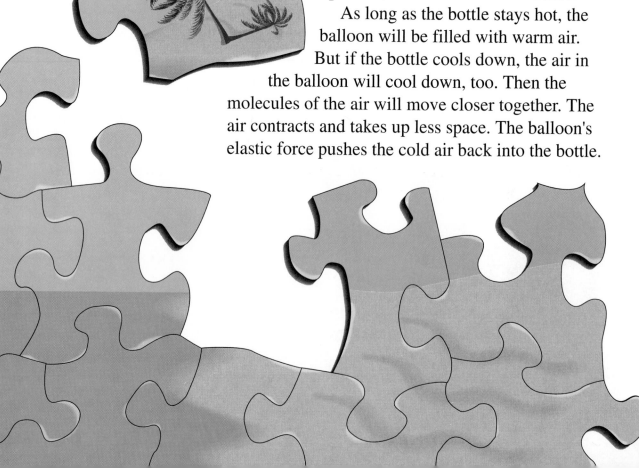

The balloon shows that hot air expands and cold air contracts. You can use these concepts to explain wind.

First of all, it's important to know that when air expands it becomes less dense and rises. Second, remember that air pressure is the force of the atmosphere pressing down on a certain area. Cold air in the atmosphere is more dense and presses down harder than rising hot air. So you can say that cold air creates higher pressure than hot air. Finally, you should know that air moves from areas of high pressure to areas of low pressure. For example, the air inside your bicycle tire is under higher pressure than the air outside. If you punch a hole in your tire, the high-pressure air will rush out.

Now, let's put all of these ideas together to explain the wind. On a warm day, the air over land heats up faster than the air over water. The warm air rises and it creates an area of low pressure. The high-pressure air above the water then moves into the low-pressure area above the land. This movement of air is called wind. Use this information to pick the right piece for the wind puzzle on page 14.

All over the earth, wind blows from areas of high pressure into areas of low pressure. The greater the difference in pressure, the stronger the wind, as you saw in the Discover Activity.

▼ *Before the bottle was placed in hot water, the balloon had little air inside. After the bottle sat in hot water, it filled with warmer expanding air.*

Checkpoint

1. Why does your bike go faster when you bend over the handlebars?
2. How does hot air produce wind?
3. Take Action! Find out how a hot-air balloon works and then draw one.

Activity

Full of Hot Air

You know that balloons are filled with air. But does it make any difference if the air is hot or cold? See what happens to a balloon in this activity.

Picture A

Picture B

Picture C

Gather These Materials

cover goggles
balloon
plastic bottle

masking tape
bucket of hot water
bucket of cold water

Follow This Procedure

1 Make a chart like the one on the next page. Record your observations in your chart.

2 Put on your cover goggles.

3 Carefully stretch the opening of a balloon over the mouth of a plastic bottle as shown in Picture A. Use masking tape to help keep the balloon in place.

4 Fill a bucket with cold water.

5 Fill a second bucket with hot water. *CAUTION: Be careful when using hot water.* Place the bottle in the bucket of hot water and hold it in the water as shown in Picture B.

Predict: *What do you think will happen to the air in the balloon?*

6 Observe any changes in the balloon. Record what you observe.

7 Remove the bottle from the bucket of hot water. Quickly place it into the bucket of cold water as shown in Picture C. Keep the bottle in the water until the bottle gets cold. Observe and record any changes in the balloon. Remove the bottle from the water.

State Your Conclusions

1. What happened to the air in the balloon as it was heated?

2. What happened to the air as it was cooled?

3. Suppose you go to a party on a very cold day and get some inflated balloons. As you bring them outside, what might happen to the balloons? Why?

Let's Experiment

Now that you have seen what happens when air is heated and cooled, use the same materials to show that hot air rises. Use what you know about scientific methods to find out.

Asking Questions

"Why is the sky blue?"
"When's dinner?"
"What is the atmosphere?"
We learn by asking questions of ourselves and others. Scientists learn the same way. They ask themselves questions and then try to find answers through experiments or observations.

Thinking It Through

When you think about something you notice, the questions you ask will lead to other questions. These may lead you to a way of finding answers.

Suppose you see a balloon drifting up to the ceiling. Why does that balloon rise? As you think about this, here are some questions you can ask yourself.
The balloon is pretty light. Do other light things rise too?
A feather is light. But I've never seen a feather drifting upward in a room.

Do all balloons rise the same way?
I've never seen a small balloon rise. I remember blowing up a large balloon and hitting it up into the air. It didn't keep rising either. But it *did* seem to come down more slowly than a small balloon. So you might wonder, "Is there something inside *some* balloons that makes them rise?" At last you have a more specific question. The next step is to find an answer through experiments and observation. If you can find out the answer, it may help you to understand why some balloons drift upward.

Your Turn

Suppose that you brought home a balloon from a fair. When you went to bed, you left it touching the ceiling. The next morning it was halfway between the ceiling and the floor, with part of the string on the floor. What questions can you think of that might help explain what happened overnight? List your questions and what you think the answers might be.

Chapter Review

Thinking Back

1. In what ways is a gas like other forms of matter?
2. In what layer of the atmosphere is the ozone layer?
3. What causes the **atmosphere** of Earth to have weight?
4. Explain how air pressure helps you drink through a straw.
5. How does the amount of surface area you present when riding a bike affect the amount of **air resistance?**
6. What effect does heat have on air molecules?
7. How does the pressure of air affect air movement?

Connecting Ideas

1. Copy the concept map. Use the terms at the right to complete the map about air movement.

cold air
rises

warm air
sinks

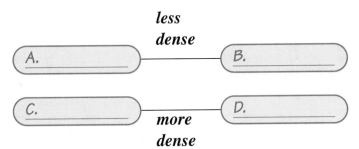

2. Write a sentence or two about the ideas shown in the concept map.

Gathering Evidence

1. In the Activity on page 10, how could you predict the length of time it would take for the parachute to land?
2. In the Activity on page 16, how did you know whether the balloon was in a bucket of hot or cold water?

Doing Science!

1. *Design an activity* that shows that air has mass.
2. *Design an activity* that shows that air takes up space.

Born to Fly

Why does it do that?

Discover Activity

How are things affected by moving air?

Tape a piece of string to an apple. Tie the other end of the string to a hanger. Blow on the apple. What happens? Now suspend another apple in the same way about 3 centimeters from the first apple. What do you think will happen when you blow in between the two apples? Try it.

For Discussion

1. How might you explain why this happened?

2. How can you show the same effect with paper?

2.1 How Birds Fly

Why walk if you can fly?

Early in the morning, the small bird called a chimney swift flies away from its brick-lined home. The swift is only 14 centimeters tall but nearly 30 centimeters wide, thanks to its outstretched wings. Those wings flap rapidly as the swift darts around the sky with its mouth wide open. Airborne insects flow into that wide-open mouth. The swift eats them, flying all the while.

Morning turns to afternoon, and still the swift keeps flying. It has already flown more than 100 kilometers, and it gives no signs of letting up. But now the swift is thirsty, so it swoops down and skims across the surface of a lake, scooping water into its open mouth. Along the way it gives itself a quick bath, flying all the while.

Afternoon turns to evening, and still the swift keeps flying. At last it turns homeward. The swift circles the top of its chimney home and dives inside. There the swift finally pauses for a well-deserved rest—by clinging to the steep sides of the chimney's brick walls. Even at rest, this amazing bird seems to defy gravity.

Chimney swifts fly through the air, day after day, year after year. They eat, drink, and bathe in the air, returning to their nests only to sleep. How do they do it? Just as you're adapted to walk, birds like the swift in the picture are adapted to fly through the air. You will learn more about birds' amazing adaptations as you read this chapter.

▲ Long wings are an adaptation that enables chimney swifts to fly almost constantly.

Moving Forward

When birds like the owl in the picture take off from the ground, they move in two directions: forward and upward. The force that moves the owl forward is called **thrust**. The force that moves the owl upward is called **lift**. The source of both thrust and lift can be found in the owl's wings.

Like your own arm, the owl's wing has three main parts: the hand, the lower arm, and the upper arm. And just like you, the owl can bend its wing at the wrist, at the elbow, and at the shoulder. Unlike you, however, the owl has a row of feathers attached to its hand and its lower arm.

The first step in flying is to create thrust—the force that moves the owl forward. When owls flap their wings, the feathers on the lower arms just flap up and down. Those feathers don't create thrust. The hand feathers, however, move backward while flapping up, then forward while flapping down, as if drawing a circle. This circular motion of the hand feathers does create thrust and move the owl forward. Notice the owl's wings below as they move the owl forward.

Lifting Upward

To understand how owls lift upward, take a closer look at their wings. The diagram on page 23 shows how the bottom of the wing is nearly flat while the top curves, like a gently rolling hill. As the owl flaps its wings to lift itself into the air, this shape lowers air resistance.

▼ *The owl produces thrust by moving its hand feathers in a circular pattern.*

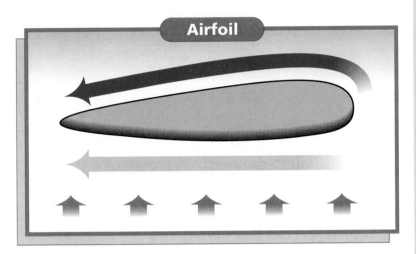

Airfoil

▲ *The curved shape of a wing helps cut air resistance.*

As the owl moves forward, air flows over and under its outstretched wings. But the air that flows over the wing travels faster than the air that flows under the wing. That's because the curved top is longer than the straight bottom, so air has to travel farther in the same length of time.

Fast-moving air can't press down as hard as slow-moving air. So the fast-moving air creates a low-pressure area over the wing. The high-pressure air under the wing tries to rise into this low-pressure area, but the wing blocks its path. The rising air pushes the wing up, helping create lift. Remember how the apples moved together in the Discover Activity for the same reason.

Birds also create lift by tilting their wings. When a wing is tilted, the front edge of the wing is higher than the back edge. As the tilted wing travels forward, air pushes against the bottom of the wing. The pushing air forces the wing upward.

Wings and Arms

How similar are chicken wings and human arms? Let's investigate.

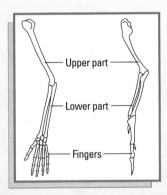

Upper part

Lower part

Fingers

What To Do
A. Observe the number and location of the bones in the human arm in the drawing.
B. Fill in the Arm row in your chart.
C. Observe the number and location of the bones in the chicken wing.
D. Fill in the Wing row in your chart.

Record Your Results

	Number Present		
	Upper part	Lower part	Fingers
Arm			
Wing			

What Did You Find Out?
1. *Compare human arms and bird wings.*
2. *How do jobs of arms and wings differ?*

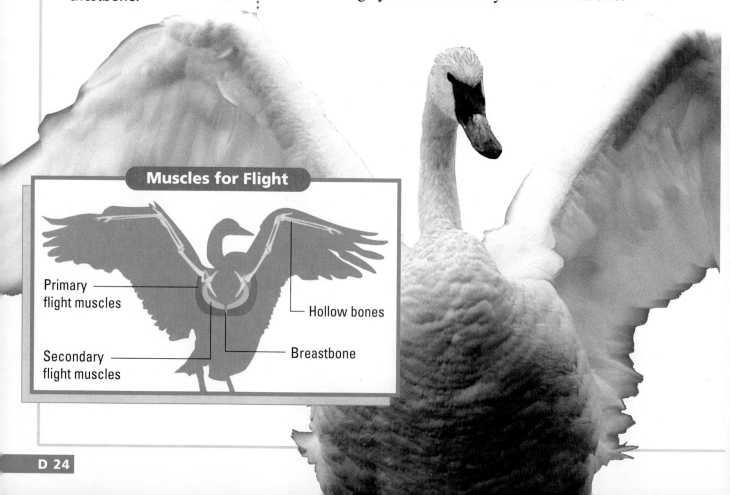

Flapping Onward

Swans are about as tall as a ten-year-old person. But swans' wings are nearly twice as long as their bodies. If your arms were that long, you would hardly be able to lift them, much less flap them up and down. Yet swans can flap their wings up and down with ease. How can they do that? The answer is in their chest muscles.

If you touch the middle of your upper chest, you can feel your breastbone, called your sternum. Your chest, or pectoral, muscles begin at your sternum. They stretch across your ribs and attach to your upper arm bones. By pulling with your pectoral muscles, you can pull your upper arms forward across your body. They're not strong enough to flap the size wings you'd need to fly as shown above.

▼ *Largest of all swans, the trumpeter powers its wings with huge chest muscles attached to a big chestbone.*

Muscles for Flight

Primary flight muscles

Secondary flight muscles

Hollow bones

Breastbone

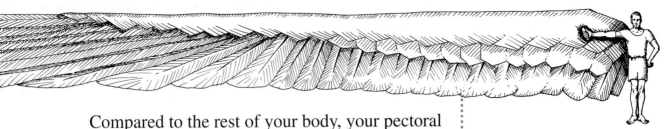

Compared to the rest of your body, your pectoral muscles are thin and light. They make up less than one one-hundredth of your weight. Notice the trumpeter swan's large chest in the picture. The swan's chest is large because of its big, heavy pectoral muscles. They account for about one-fourth of the swan's weight. The swan's pectorals also begin at its sternum and attach to the upper wing bone. But the swan's sternum is much larger than yours; it sticks way out in front of the swan's ribs. If your sternum were that large, you wouldn't be able to see your toes.

The swan's pectoral muscles, or primary flight muscles, pull its wings down. The small picture shows the secondary flight muscles that pull its wings back up. The swan's chest muscles can move the wings for hours at a time. Every year, many swans fly thousands of kilometers, traveling about 50 kilometers an hour.

Swans' chest muscles give swans the power they need to fly. Other muscles give them control. By using the muscles along their shoulders, swans can tilt their wings up or down. By using the muscles inside their wings, swans can twist each flight feather in just the right way. Swans have as much control over the feathers on their wings as you have over the fingers of your hands.

Like all flying birds, swans move through the air thanks to wings and powerful chest muscles. But flying birds also have other adaptations that help them soar through the sky. You'll read about some of these adaptations on the next page.

▲ *An adult human would need wings more than 30 meters long to lift off the ground.*

Nature's Fabulous Flying Machine

Birds have many adaptations for flight.

You have already learned how wings, a large sternum, and large pectoral muscles make flying possible for a bird. But, a bird has many other amazing adaptations for flight. Like a finely tuned machine, a bird's entire body helps it to fly.

Your bones are much heavier than a bird's. What would happen if this red-tailed hawk had bones like yours? Could it fly as easily with a round, fat body? If its legs hung down while it flew, would it be able to fly as quickly? A lightweight skeleton, feathers, and a streamlined body are all adaptations you can learn about as you study these pictures.

Lightweight Skeleton

The less a bird weighs, the easier it is to get off the ground. Hollow bones are an adaptation for flight. The diagram shows the lightweight struts that help support the long, hollow bones of a bird's wings and legs. The skeleton of a frigate bird with a 2-meter wing span weighs less than its feathers weigh!

Bone surface

Supporting strut

Hollow spaces

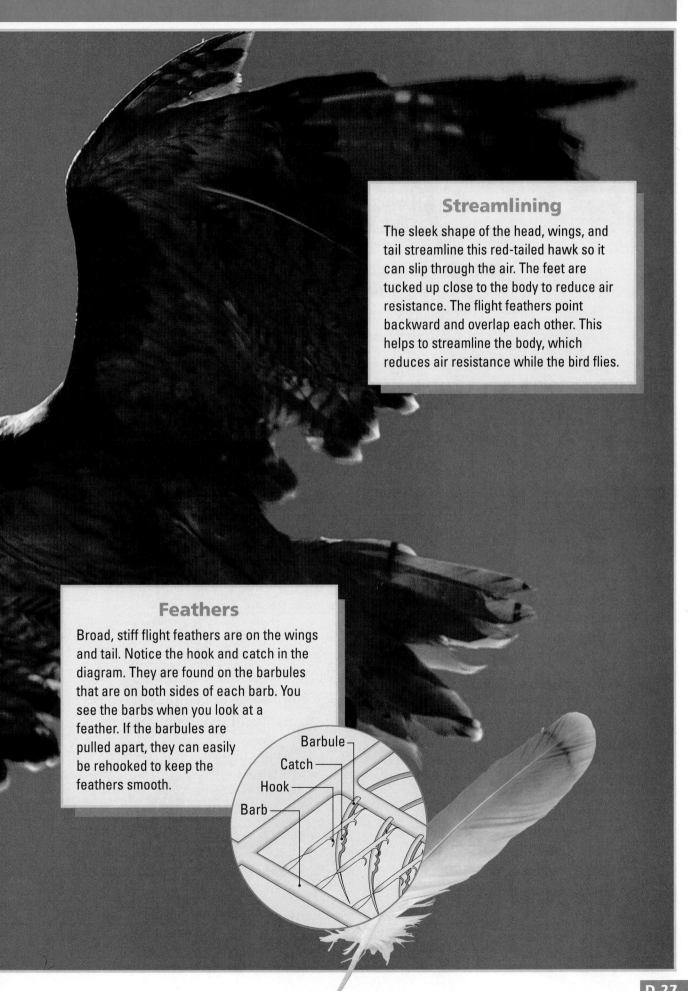

Streamlining

The sleek shape of the head, wings, and tail streamline this red-tailed hawk so it can slip through the air. The feet are tucked up close to the body to reduce air resistance. The flight feathers point backward and overlap each other. This helps to streamline the body, which reduces air resistance while the bird flies.

Feathers

Broad, stiff flight feathers are on the wings and tail. Notice the hook and catch in the diagram. They are found on the barbules that are on both sides of each barb. You see the barbs when you look at a feather. If the barbules are pulled apart, they can easily be rehooked to keep the feathers smooth.

Barbule

Catch

Hook

Barb

Eating Right

With all these adaptations, flying is a breeze—right? Yes and no. Birds need energy to fly—lots of energy. In flight, a bird can use up to 15 times more energy than it does when it's resting. Where do flying birds get all that energy? From the same place you do: food.

Calories are units that tell how much energy an animal can get from a particular kind of food. The more Calories a food contains, the more energy the animal can get out of that food. One gram of barley seeds, for example, has thirty times more Calories than one gram of bean sprouts. In other words, you'd have to eat thirty grams of bean sprouts to get the energy that's in just one gram of barley seeds.

Flying birds need all the Calories they can get, but they don't need extra weight. That's why they eat high-Calorie foods like the seeds in the picture instead of low-Calorie sprouts. They also eat worms instead of grass and insects instead of leaves. If flying birds got their Calories by eating sprouts, grass, or leaves, they'd have to eat so much food that they'd never get off the ground.

Birds stay light by eating high-Calorie foods. But high-Calorie foods don't last forever. Some birds like the flycatcher below, digest and burn food so fast that they need to eat all day long.

▲ For quick energy, birds eat high-Calorie foods like worms, crickets, beetles, and seeds.

▼ Flycatchers, like the one with the bluebottle fly, digest and burn food almost as fast as they can swallow it.

To understand what that means, think about the food you eat in a day: cereal for breakfast, an apple and a sandwich for lunch, chicken and vegetables for dinner. If you put one day's meals on a scale, they might weigh 1 kilogram —less than 4 percent of your weight. By comparison a bird called the Bohemian waxwing can eat three times its weight in a single day! If you ate 1 kilogram of food a day, it would take you about three months to eat three times your weight in food.

Waxwings can eat so many berries because berries are largely water. But even birds that eat more solid food have big appetites. Pigeons eat 7 percent of their weight every day. Starlings eat about 12 percent of their weight. The tiny golden-crowned kinglet eats about 33 percent every day. Smaller birds eat relatively more than larger ones, and they spend more time eating, too. Kinglets eat all day long. Some hawks and eagles can go for several days without any food. But even big flying birds have to eat. If they don't eat, they can't fly; and if they can't fly, they can't survive. One cannot live—or fly—without food.

Checkpoint

1. What is the difference between thrust and lift?
2. How does a tilted wing help a bird?
3. Why are big pectoral muscles needed for flight?
4. How are a bird's bones adapted for flying?
5. What would happen to flying birds if they ate only low-Calorie foods?
6. Take Action! Some birds do not fly. Make a chart that compares their bodies and diets to those of flying birds.

Activity

Blowing in the Wind

Startled birds might take off with a whir of wings and a blur of feathers. In this activity you can observe what makes their flight possible.

Picture A

Picture B

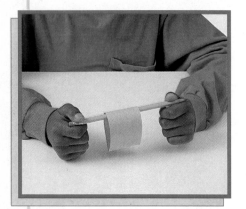

Picture C

Gather These Materials

2 paper cups of the
  same size
masking tape
pencil

long strip of paper
  approximately 15 cm x
  5 cm

Follow This Procedure

1 Make a chart like the one on the next page. Record your observations in your chart.

2 Place one paper cup inside another.

Predict: What will happen to the cup inside if you blow over the rim of the bottom cup?

3 Blow over the rim of the bottom cup as shown in Picture A. Record your results.

4 Fold a long strip of paper in half. Tape the two edges together as shown in Picture B.

5 Put a pencil through the wide part of the paper so that the paper hangs from the pencil as shown in Picture C.

Predict: What will happen to the paper if you blow across the top of the paper?

6 Blow across the top of the paper. Record your results in the chart.

Record Your Results

	Effect of moving air
Two cups	
Paper strip	

State Your Conclusions

1. What force is caused by blowing over the cup?

2. Over which surface of the paper strip is the air pressure lower?

Let's Experiment

Now that you have made an airfoil with paper, find out what shape gives the most amount of lift. Experiment by varying the shape of the paper. You may want to use stiffer paper and try rectangular, triangular, or circular shaped airfoils. Use what you know about scientific methods to find out.

2.2 *Different Wings*

▶ **Do all birds fly the same way?**

Sailors who work aboard ships far out at sea sometimes see a large bird called an albatross, shown in the picture. These huge birds follow ships for months at a time, eating scraps of food that sailors throw overboard.

Wandering albatrosses and other sea birds, such as gulls, have wings that are well-suited to gliding. But many other birds have very different kinds of wings. Over many thousands of years, birds' wings adapted to different environments and diets. Imagine you had to design a wing adapted for a bird that glides over water. What kind of wing do you think that would be?

▼ *The black-browed albatross is adapted to soar for hours above the ocean looking for food. Like the wing of the albatross, the long, narrow wing of the herring gull is suited for gliding.*

Gull Wing Design

Wings for Gliding

Albatrosses and gulls can soar because of their wing design. Notice the long, pointed gull wing in the drawing. Find the long, narrow wings of the albatross in the picture. The wandering albatross has the longest wings of any bird in the world—more than 360 centimeters from wing tip to wing tip. From front to back, however, the wings are less than 30 centimeters at their widest point.

By using its long, narrow wings, the wandering albatross can ride the ocean wind for hours without making a single flap. Wind at the surface of the ocean blows more slowly than wind several meters higher. The albatross uses these differing wind speeds to power its gliding flight. First the bird glides along in the fast upper wind, with the wind at its back. Then it builds up speed by sliding down through the sky while turning its body around. When the wandering albatross reaches the surface of the ocean, it is facing into the slow lower wind. The bird skims along the ocean for a while, grabbing seafood and drinking salt water with its long bill. Then the bird uses its rapid speed and the lifting power of its long wings to soar back up into the sky, where it turns around and prepares for another slide. Albatrosses visit land only to lay eggs and care for their young. In contrast to their graceful flight, the birds are awkward on land. They often crash in a heap when landing on the ground.

Into The Field

Do all birds look alike in flight?

Observe different birds in flight. Write a description of how each type of bird flies. Compare your observations of birds in flight.

Wings for Speed

Gliding over water for hours at a time takes one kind of wing. But chasing after other birds takes a very different kind of wing. The peregrine falcon has a body and wings adapted for speed. As the pictures show, the falcon's long, pointed wings sweep back like the wings of a jet. In normal flight, the falcon zips along at 100 kilometers an hour — twice as fast as most other birds.

The falcon's speed is an adaptation to its environment and its diet of other birds. As the falcon zooms along high above the land, it watches for pigeons, crows, and other birds flying below. When the falcon spots a bird, it stops and seems to hang in the air. Then the falcon folds its wings and dives straight at its meal. Plunging falcons approach speeds of 400 kilometers an hour. The falcon strikes a bird with its talons as it hurtles by; then it picks up the dead bird with its talons. Few birds can escape the speedy falcon.

▼ Like jets, high-speed falcons have swept back wings, cone-shaped heads, and streamlined bodies.

Peregrine Falcon Wing Design

Wings for Hovering

Imagine you could design a bird that hovered like a helicopter while eating nectar from a flower. That bird would have wings like a hummingbird.

The smallest bird in the world, the bee hummingbird is less than 5 centimeters long and weighs only 3 grams. Most hummingbirds are about twice the size of a bee hummingbird. But no matter what their size, they have short, small wings.

Because of the kind of wings they have, hummingbirds can twist their entire wing backward and forward, up and down. You can see these movements in the picture on the right. Thanks to these movements, hummingbirds can fly straight up, straight down, backward, and forward. Hummingbirds can also hover in mid-air. These movements adapt hummingbirds to live among flowers.

As the picture shows, the bird hovers in front of a flower, sticks its long bill inside, and drinks the flower's nectar. Then it backs away and flies to the next blossom. Hummingbirds burn up so much energy flying and hovering that they must eat all day long. Some visit more than 2500 flowers a day.

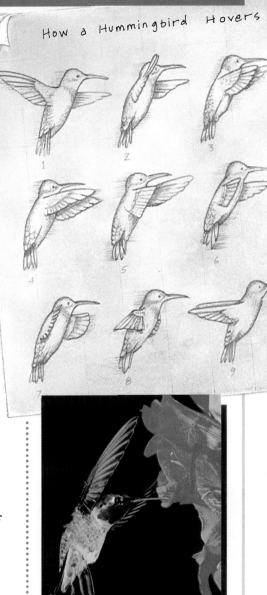

How a Hummingbird Hovers

▲ *As the Anna's hummingbird hovers to drink nectar, its wings flap so fast they make a humming sound.*

Checkpoint

1. How would you describe an albatross wing?
2. How is a peregrine falcon adapted to capture birds?
3. How does the bee hummingbird's ability to hover help it stay alive?
4. Take Action! Design a bird that eats worms and lives in trees. Draw what the bird would look like.

Activity

Birds of a Feather

What helps make the graceful flight of a bird possible? Examine the bones and feathers of a bird to find out.

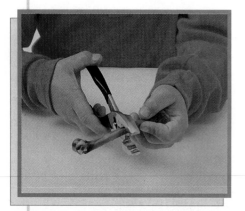

Picture A

Gather These Materials

cover goggles

pair of pliers

chicken bone soaked
 in vinegar

hand lens

bird feather

scissors

Follow This Procedure

1 Make a chart like the one on the next page. Record your observations in your chart.

2 Put on your cover goggles.

3 Use a pair of pliers to break a chicken bone into two pieces. It has been soaked in vinegar to soften it. (Picture A)

> **Predict: *Will the inside of the soaked chicken bone be solid?***

Picture B

4 Use a hand lens to look at the cut ends of the chicken bone. Record what it looks like.

5 Examine a bird feather. Use scissors to carefully cut the feather in half as shown in Picture B.

6 Use the hand lens to examine the cut ends of the feather. Record what the feather looks like inside. (Picture C)

7 Use the hand lens to examine how each of the barbs on the feather fit together. Record what you observe.

Picture C

8 Ruffle the edge of the feather. Observe what happens. Record your observations.

9 Now smooth the feather again and record your observations.

	Observations
Bird bone	
Feather	

State Your Conclusions

1. How is a chicken bone adapted for flight?
2. How is a bird feather well-suited for flight?
3. Suppose you were designing a model plane. How could you use the example of a bird to decide what kind of material to use?

Let's Experiment

Now that you have examined a bird bone and flight feather, examine a down feather from a bird. How is it different from a flight feather?

Identifying Assumptions

Have you ever heard statements like these presented as if they were true?

• When waste material is thrown away, natural forces will clean up pollution.

• People will never travel to Mars.

These statements are assumptions. An **assumption** is a belief that is taken for granted without proof. That is, a person making an assumption believes something is true without testing to make sure it is true.

Thinking It Through

Suppose your friend says, "Because of their weight, larger birds need more energy from the food in their diets than smaller birds do." How can you tell if this is a correct assumption? One way is to decide what your friend is assuming. Then you can judge whether the assumption is true or false.

You can detect assumptions by looking at the evidence and the conclusion, and then figuring out what was assumed. Here are some questions to ask yourself.

What is my friend's evidence?
Large birds weigh more than small birds.
What is my friend's conclusion?
Larger birds use more energy.
What assumption is my friend making?
Large birds fly in the same way as small birds so they have to use more energy.

Your Turn

Read these statements. Write down the evidence, the conclusion, and what is assumed.

1. Birds all have strong pectoral muscles for wing movement, so any animal that can fly must have strong pectoral muscles.

2. A penguin's short wings help it to fly at a fast speed because short wings are best for flying fast.

Chapter Review

Thinking Back

1. In which direction does **thrust** move a bird?

2. How does the shape of a bird's wing help it create **lift?**

3. What gives birds the power to pull their wings up and down?

4. What parts of a bird are adapted for flight?

5. Why do birds eat so much high-Calorie food?

6. How do albatross, falcon, and hummingbird wings help the birds get food?

Connecting Ideas

1. Copy the concept map. Use the terms at the right to complete the map about wing adaptations.

dive   glide

hover

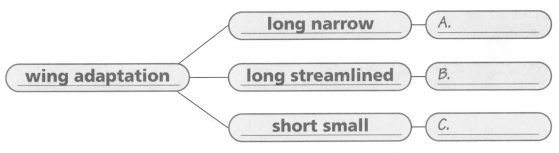

2. Write a sentence or two about the ideas shown in the concept map.

Gathering Evidence

1. In the Activity on page 30, how did you know where the air pressure was lower?

2. In the Activity on page 36, how did you know what helps birds fly?

Doing Science!

1. *Create a display* that shows how different wing shapes relate to the ways birds live.

2. *Design an activity* that shows how different wing shapes produce different kinds of flight.

Learning to Fly

No way! With clay?

Discover Activity

What does it take to fly?

Think about all the things you've seen that can fly. Then design your own flying machine using paper, a straw, a piece of clay, and a paper clip. There's one rule: you must use all materials.

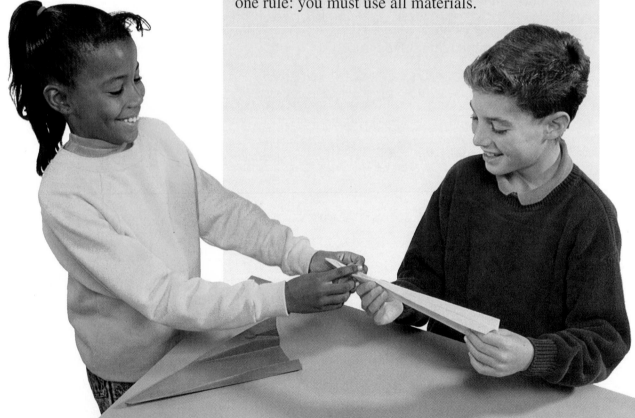

For Discussion

1. *How well did your flying machine fly?*
2. *How can you change your design to make it fly further?*

3.1 *From Balloons to Jets*

▶ *Have you ever wanted to fly like a bird?*

People just like you have always dreamed of soaring through the air. Long before modern times, daredevils strapped artificial wings to their arms and tried to flap like birds. But that didn't work, for reasons you now know. As the years went by, more and more people tried to figure out how birds fly. Joseph and Etienne Montgolfier— two French brothers—finally rose into the sky using a new approach.

Floating in the Air

On September 19, 1783, hundreds of people watched as Etienne lit a fire near the French king's palace. Hot air from the fire rose into a huge balloon made of cotton strips lined with paper. In just four minutes hot air inflated the balloon, and workers fought to hold it to the ground. Do you know why the huge balloon was lifting off? If you said that hot air expanded into the balloon and tried to rise, you'd be right.

In a wicker cage attached to the balloon stood a duck, a rooster, and a sheep. Suddenly, the workers let go. As the picture shows, the balloon lifted off the ground and drifted for eight minutes toward a nearby forest. When the balloon came down, the duck, the rooster, and the sheep escaped. They were the first passengers to survive a flight in a machine built by people.

▲ *Expanding, rising air carried the Montgolfiers' balloon into the sky.*

Otto Lilienthal controlled his glider by swinging his legs from one side to another.

Getting Off the Ground

Soon after this flight, balloons of all sorts carried people into the air. But balloons were poor flyers. They could rise off the ground, but they had no thrust; they needed wind to blow them through the sky. In the late 1700s, birds remained the only true flyers. Amazingly, birds were heavier than air, but they could fly with ease. The search for the keys to flight went on—like your experimenting with a flying machine in the Discover Activity.

A British inventor, Sir George Cayley, thought that birds held the answer to true flight. By studying birds, Cayley learned how a curved wing produces lift. He tested his ideas by designing and flying gliders—planes without engines. Cayley's greatest day came in 1853 when a pilot boarded a new three-wing glider. The glider rolled down a hill, lifted off, and flew 270 meters!

A German glider pilot, Otto Lilienthal, took flight a step further. During the 1890s, Lilienthal made the first controlled flights in gliders. As the picture shows, Lilienthal rested his arms on the glider. To control his flight, he swung his weight to one side or the other. After making more than 2000 flights, Lilienthal died in a glider crash in 1896. But his work paved the way for other inventors. Their challenging puzzle? How to power flight.

Heavier-Than-Air Flight

When two American inventors, Orville and Wilbur Wright, heard of Lilienthal's death, they decided to build a flying machine. The Wrights read every study of flight they could find. They learned about control by watching buzzards twist their wings in flight. They also built gliders to learn even more. Between 1900 and 1902 the Wrights tested their gliders on Kill Devil Hill, a windswept dune off the coast of North Carolina.

Through their test flights, the Wrights learned how to shape the wings. To copy the buzzards, the Wrights hooked wires to the rear edges of their glider's wingtips. In flight, they pulled the wires with levers to get more lift from one wing and less from the other. In that way, the Wrights could keep the glider balanced in gusts of wind. By 1903, the Wrights were ready to solve the problem of thrust.

There were no good propellers in 1903, so the brothers made their own. They also developed a lightweight gasoline engine. On December 17, 1903, they were ready to try the first powered flight in a heavier-than-air machine—*Flyer I*.

As the engine roared to life, Orville climbed aboard and lay on the bottom set of wings. *Flyer I* rolled down a track, and a few seconds later, it flew through the air on its own power! The picture below shows how far it traveled.

▼ *The Wright brothers' first flight covered 37 meters—about half the length of a 70-meter 747 passenger jet.*

An Ancient Dream Come True

How did we learn to soar above the clouds?

Kites and sails were some of the first objects people made that could fly. They were always connected to the ground with poles or with strings.

Balloons and gliders were not connected to the earth. People got the ideas for them by observing sails and kites fly.

The first airplanes had glider wings. They also had engines and propellers to thrust them forward. Engines gave airplanes enough power to lift people off the ground.

It took people many centuries to observe and experiment enough to fly. Since then, people have been able to make many different machines that fly. We can soar at last!

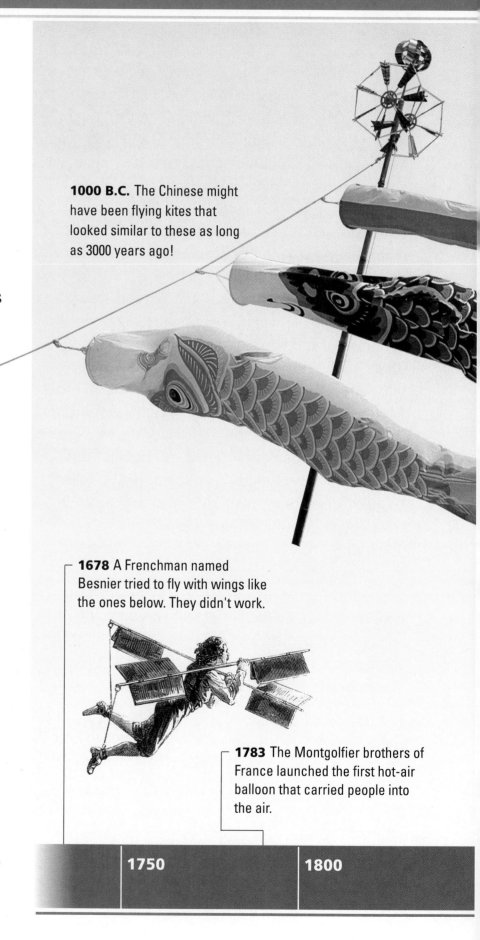

1000 B.C. The Chinese might have been flying kites that looked similar to these as long as 3000 years ago!

1678 A Frenchman named Besnier tried to fly with wings like the ones below. They didn't work.

1783 The Montgolfier brothers of France launched the first hot-air balloon that carried people into the air.

1750

1800

1976 The Concorde, built by Britain and France, provided the first supersonic passenger service flights.

1926 This photograph shows one of the first passenger flights. This plane could only take four passengers at a time between Seattle and Los Angeles.

1903 The first airplane flown by Orville and Wilbur Wright in 1903 had a small engine and propellers.

| 1850 | 1900 | 1950 | 2000 |

Into The Field

How does a balloon move like a rocket?

Blow up a balloon and let it go. Observe and record how the balloon moves. Write all the ways in which it moves like a rocket.

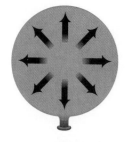

▲ *The balloon flies forward because of jet propulsion.*

Jetting Forward

Human flight leaped forward with the invention of the jet engine. But how does a jet fly? You can understand a jet engine if you think about a balloon. When you blow up a balloon, you force air into it. If you hold the balloon shut, the air pressure inside the balloon will be greater than the air pressure outside. As the picture below shows, the air inside the balloon will also press equally on all parts of the balloon.

But what happens if you open the neck of the balloon? The high-pressure air inside the balloon will rush out. Then, as the other two pictures show, pressure inside the balloon will no longer be equal. No air will be pushing against the balloon at the open neck. But air will still push on the inside of the balloon opposite the opening, causing the balloon to zoom forward.

Simple jet engines are somewhat like balloons. The front of the engine takes outside air in and squeezes it, thereby increasing its pressure. The air pressure inside a jet engine can be almost 30 times greater than the air pressure outside. The middle of the engine creates more pressure by spraying fuel into the air and burning the fuel and air mixture. This burning creates hot gases, which rush out the back of the engine. As gases rush out the back, greater pressure at the front produces **jet propulsion**—forward motion produced by letting high-pressure gas flow in the opposite direction.

Jet engines have changed the way people live, as the picture on page 47 shows. In 1911, Calbraith Rodgers became the first pilot to fly from New York to California. It took him 84 days and many stops to make the 82-hour flight. Millions of passengers now make the same trip nonstop in less than six hours.

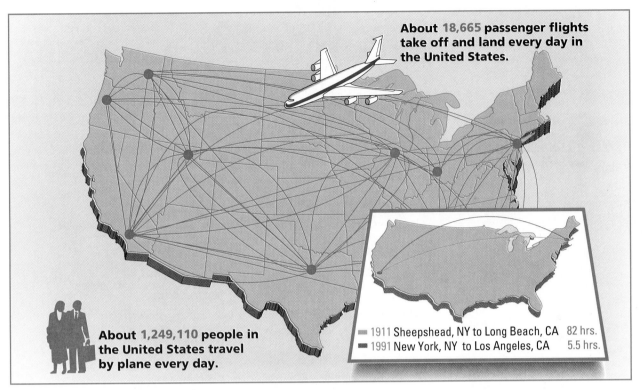

About 18,665 passenger flights take off and land every day in the United States.

About 1,249,110 people in the United States travel by plane every day.

1911 Sheepshead, NY to Long Beach, CA   82 hrs.
1991 New York, NY to Los Angeles, CA   5.5 hrs.

Passenger jets have brought people and places closer together. But they have brought problems as well. Jet engines are noisy and pollute the air. As more people fly, traffic jams increase along with the danger of serious accidents. To help solve these problems, pilots fly at lower speeds near airports to cut down noise and pollution. Scientists and engineers are also building quieter, cleaner jet engines and better air-traffic control systems.

▲ *Just 100 years ago, only birds flew over the United States. Today, passenger planes crisscross the nation day and night.*

Checkpoint

1. What causes hot-air balloons to float?
2. What important fact did George Cayley discover about bird wings?
3. What was unique about *Flyer I*?
4. What was one of the first objects people made that could fly?
5. How does a jet engine work?
6. Take Action! Find out how a squid uses propulsion to move, and make a diagram explaining it.

Activity

Propeller Power

Many things affect the flight of an airplane. Try this activity to build your own propeller plane and experiment with flight.

Picture A

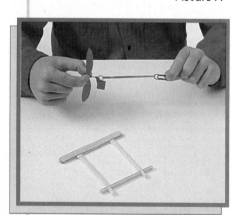

Picture B

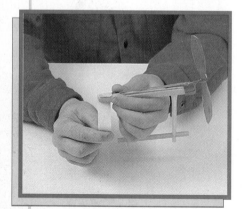

Picture C

Gather These Materials

cover goggles
jumbo straw
scissors
paper hole puncher
regular straw
2 craft sticks
stapler

masking tape
rubber band
paper clip
wooden or plastic
  propeller with hook
5 m of fishing line or
  string

Follow This Procedure

1 Make a chart like the one on the next page. Record your observations in your chart.

2 Put on your cover goggles.

3 Cut the jumbo straw in half. Use the hole puncher to make holes near the top of both pieces of the jumbo straw.

4 Stack two craft sticks on your desk. Sandwich the two jumbo straws between the craft sticks. Staple the sticks together as shown in Picture A.

5 Cut the regular straw to the same length as the craft sticks. Pass the regular straw through the holes in both jumbo straws. (Picture A)

6 Loop a rubber band through a paper clip. Holding the rubber band and paper clip in one hand, twist the rubber band a number of times. Then hook the other end of the rubber band onto the propeller's hook. (Picture B)

7 Attach the propeller on one end of the sticks. Use masking tape to attach the paper clip to the other end of the sticks. (Picture C)

8 Thread fishing line through the top straw. Tie one end of the fishing line to the back of a chair or other support. Pull the line straight and attach the other end to another chair. Your "plane" will fly along the fishing line on propeller power.

Predict: *What will give your propeller its power?*

9 Adjust the twists in the rubber band and let your plane fly.

10 Experiment with the number of twists in the rubber band. Measure how far your plane flies for different numbers of twists. Record your results.

Record Your Results

Number of twists in rubber band			
Distance that propeller plane goes			

State Your Conclusions

1. How can you control how far your plane goes?
2. What important element of flight is your plane not able to perform?

Let's Experiment

Now that you have made your propeller plane fly, what would happen if you increase the weight of your plane by adding more paper clips? Use what you know about scientific methods to find out.

3.2 Into the Future

> ### What kind of planes will you fly in?

Do you ever gaze into the sky and imagine flying in the jumbo jets or private planes you see? These planes will be around in the future. But someday you may fly in planes being designed today—like a passenger plane that flies faster than sound.

Faster Than Sound

Planes that fly faster than sound, or **supersonic** planes, streak through the skies at 1220 kilometers an hour or more. They cross oceans in hours and link people and nations. But supersonic planes have several problems, including noise. If a supersonic jet flew nearby over your house, you'd hear a BOOM! like a bomb. A second later you might hear your windows break. To understand what causes this noise, you need to know more about sound.

When a plane flies, it compresses or squeezes the air directly in front of it. This compressed air is sound that moves as waves away from the plane in all directions. The circles around the plane on the lower left represent compressed air traveling away from the plane at the speed of sound.

▲ The supersonic Concorde carries 128 passengers at twice the speed of sound.

▼ The Concorde passes the speed of sound over water where its sonic boom will not cause damage.

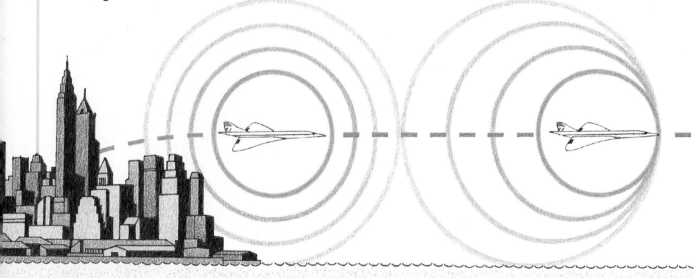

As long as the plane flies slower than the speed of sound, it stays inside the compressed air. But as the plane flies faster and faster, it increases the pressure on the compressed air and approaches the speed of sound in that air. Notice that the plane in the middle picture below is starting to catch up to the compressed air. When the plane flies faster than the speed of sound, like the one in the third picture, it passes through the front of compressed air. The front of compressed air then hits the ground with a powerful *Ka-boom* called a sonic boom.

Today, most passenger planes are subsonic: they fly slower than sound. Only the Concorde is supersonic. The Concorde flies between the United States and Europe in about four hours—half the time of a subsonic flight. But its booms are so loud that 30 countries have rules against the plane. The Concorde is not allowed to fly over the United States. It can fly only to cities on the Atlantic coast.

Besides being noisy, the Concorde guzzles fuel. In fact it uses so much fuel and carries so few people, that a trip on the Concorde costs thousands of dollars. Because the Concorde flies at high altitudes, its exhaust gases may harm the ozone layer. Supersonic jets will grow more important for international trade and travel, but only if these problems can be solved.

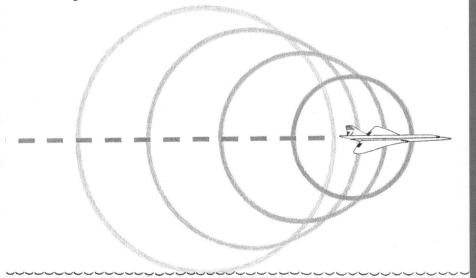

Strength of Sounds

The sonic boom made by the Concorde lasts just seconds but can shatter windows. It is a sound with a very high intensity or strength. The unit that is used to measure the strength of sounds is a decibel.

Sounds just above zero decibels in strength are the weakest sounds the human ear can hear. The chart shows that the sound of conversation is usually about 65 decibels. Decibels of 140 or more produce pain in the ear.

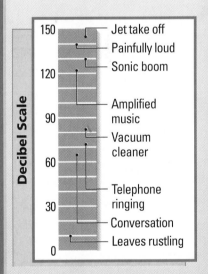

Decibel Scale

150	Jet take off
	Painfully loud
	Sonic boom
120	
	Amplified music
90	
	Vacuum cleaner
60	
	Telephone ringing
30	
	Conversation
0	Leaves rustling

What Did You Find Out?
1. *What makes the sound with the most strength on the chart?*
2. *Does the sound of a phone ringing or a vacuum cleaner have more strength?*

The Promise of the Future

Scientists and engineers around the world are working on a new supersonic plane right now. It will probably look something like the dart-shaped plane in the pictures. If the engineers working on this plane can solve the problems of the Concorde, here's what a future flight might be like.

You settle into your comfortable seat on the new jet as it taxis to a runway at Chicago's O'Hare Airport. The flight will take you to Los Angeles, then on to Tokyo, Japan.

You fill the time before take-off by reading an article about the new plane. You learn that the plane can hold three times as many people as the old Concorde—one reason the fares are lower. But its bigger body and wider wings are also made of new lightweight metals. That means that the plane can go twice as far on a tank of fuel. It can also fly at three times the speed of sound—50 percent faster than the old Concorde.

When your turn for take-off comes, the plane tears down the runway, lifts off, and heads for cruising altitude. The captain announces that you'll be traveling at subsonic speeds to Los Angeles. No one has figured out how to stop sonic booms, so the plane has engines that can fly at both subsonic and supersonic speeds. You'll switch over to supersonic speed for the trip across the Pacific.

▼ The next supersonic plane may look like this one and fly at more than twice the speed of sound.

You fall asleep and wake up just as the plane lifts off from Los Angeles. You rise into the air much higher and faster than before. Soon you're more than 18,000 meters high, just below the ozone layer. Thanks to its new engines, your plane does little damage to the ozone. By mixing fuel and air at different rates, the engines have fewer harmful exhausts than the old Concorde engines.

You're flashing through the sky at nearly 3000 kilometers an hour, but inside, the plane is calm. The nonstop flight to Tokyo will take about four hours—almost eight hours less than a direct subsonic flight.

▲ *This supersonic plane is designed to travel at more than three times the speed of sound.*

As you step off the plane in Tokyo, you look out an airport window and see a flock of birds flying toward the sea. They're flying just as fast as they've always flown: they don't need to go any faster. Why do people have to go faster than the birds? That's a question you'll have to answer for yourself—when you have the time.

Checkpoint

1. Why can't subsonic planes create a sonic boom?
2. Why are lightweight metals and new engines important for the new supersonic plane?
3. **Take Action!** Draw what you believe would be a good design for a new supersonic plane. Explain your design.

Activity

Making Paper Gliders

Did you ever watch pilots do stunts in an air show? Make some paper gliders and put on an air show of your own.

Picture A

Picture B

Picture C

Gather These Materials

cover goggles
3 sheets of paper
ruler

tape
tape measure
timer

Follow This Procedure

1 Make a chart like the one on the next page. Record your observations in your chart.

2 Put on your cover goggles.

3 Use three sheets of paper to make three different paper gliders as shown in the pictures. The diagrams on the next page show how to make one kind of glider. Fold the paper on the dotted lines. Use a ruler to help you make the folds accurately. Use tape where necessary.

4 Take your gliders to an open space to fly them.

CAUTION: Be careful to aim your gliders away from people.

Predict: Which type of glider will travel the farthest?

5 Compare how well each of your designs performs. Use a tape measure and a timer to find out how far they glide and how long they stay in the air.

Record Your Results

	Glider #1	Glider #2	Glider #3
Distance traveled			
Time in the air			
Smoothness of flight			
Accuracy of flight			

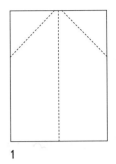

1

6 Try aiming your gliders at one spot. How well can you control them?

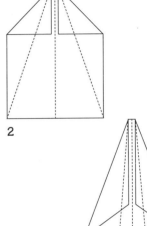

2

State Your Conclusions

1. Which of your designs had the best overall performance?
2. Which wing shape is the best for a paper glider?
3. Why do airplane designs go through a great deal of testing?

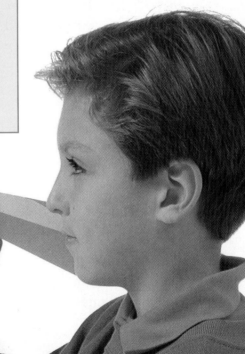

3

Let's Experiment

Now that you have seen how well your gliders perform, experiment with the wing tips. What happens to the flight of the gliders when you bend the wing tips up? What happens when they are bent downward? Use what you know about scientific methods to find out.

Becoming a Bias Detector

Pretend you're a city planner trying to decide whether an airport should be built. The first person you talk to favors the new airport. She says the city must be connected to other cities to grow.

The next person you talk to thinks that the airport is unnecessary. He says planes are noisy and they pollute the environment.

Which person should you believe? Actually, both people may be telling the truth. But each person is only giving the facts that support his or her point of view, or bias. To make informed decisions, it helps to be able to detect someone's bias. Here are some ways to make informed decisions:
• Identify assumptions
• Identify bias
• Identify errors

Thinking It Through
You realize that you need to consider each person's point of view. You begin by thinking about who each person is. The first person is the mayor of the city. The other person owns a home close to where the airport might be built.

You find out that the mayor wants the city to grow and add new businesses because she's proud of the city. You also learn that the mayor feels new businesses will bring new jobs to the city. That will help the unemployed.

The homeowner is afraid that his house will be worth less if it's next to an airport and that the noise and pollution will harm his family.

To make your decision, you will need to talk to many more people. You will have to be a bias detector as you talk to each one.

Your Turn

Ask two adults whether your city or town should build an airport. Ask each person to explain his or her answer. Try to discover each person's bias. Why does she or he hold that bias?

Chapter Review

Thinking Back

1. Why might a hot-air balloon land after a short flight?
2. How is a glider different from an airplane?
3. How did studying buzzards help the Wright brothers learn about flight?
4. What had to be invented before planes could lift people off the ground?
5. How does **jet propulsion** cause a plane to move forward?
6. What are some of the problems caused by jet planes?
7. What causes a **supersonic** plane to make a sonic boom?
8. What is the difference between a subsonic and supersonic plane?
9. What are some of the problems caused by today's supersonic planes?
10. How do designers hope to improve supersonic planes in the future?

Connecting Ideas

1. Copy the concept map. Use the terms at the right to complete the map about how people's machines for flight have changed as they learned about thrust, power, and propulsion.

balloon   **jet**
glider   **plane**

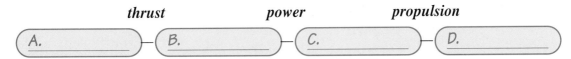

thrust   *power*   *propulsion*

A. ___ — B. ___ — C. ___ — D. ___

2. Write a sentence or two about the ideas shown in the concept map.

Gathering Evidence

1. In the Activity on page 48, how did you know whether your plane would fly a short or long distance?
2. In the Activity on page 54, how did you conclude which design had the best performance?

Doing Science!

1. **Create a news broadcast** that tells about the Wright brothers' first flight.
2. **Design plans** for making a model glider.

Kids Take to the Air

Some kids do things that usually only adults do—like flying an airplane. Here are some stories of some kids who earned their wings.

Seven-year-old Daniel Shanklin flew his way into the record books as the youngest pilot to fly across the country. On May 26, 1991, Daniel, with a flight instructor, took off from San Diego, California. He was so small that he had to sit on a booster seat to see above the dashboard. He did not fly nonstop. Every day for eight days, he flew another section of his route. The final lap of his flight took him to North Carolina. He landed on June 3 in Kill Devil Hills, near Kitty Hawk. This was a historic place to land. Kitty

He was so small that he had to sit on a booster seat to see above the dashboard.

Hawk was the site where the Wright Brothers flew the first airplane, in 1903.

Bibi Stewart and Damien Hernandez seem like average teenagers. But they are also pilots. They are just 2 of 90 students who are members of the Eagle Flight Pilot Training Program in East Orange, New Jersey. The program was begun in 1976 by the Reverend Russell White. He founded the school to give kids ages 11 to 18 a chance to learn how to fly airplanes. To stay in the program, students must obey certain rules and maintain good grades in school. Many graduates of the program later become commercial or military pilots.

Another outstanding pilot is twelve-year-old Bree Meyer-Gilbride. She was concerned about people with AIDS and wanted to help raise money for research. To do this, she decided to take to the sky. With her mom and a flight instructor on board, she flew a single-engine airplane across the country. Her trip helped raise money and made more people aware of her cause. For what she did, Bree has been honored as a "real American hero" and received a special award.

Like any pilot, each of these kids had to learn how to fly before they took the controls of a plane. They studied how a plane works, how to read the instruments, and how to operate the controls. They watched as flight instructors showed them what to do, and they learned the rules of the air. When they finally flew, it was under the watchful eye of a flight instructor.

On Your Own

Daniel, Bibi, Damien, and Bree all had a special dream. They worked to make it come true. Think about your dreams. Write for information about doing something that interests you.

Flying Passenger Jets

William R. Norwood

Occupation: Airline Captain
Words to Remember: "If students want to achieve, it's attainable if they're willing to work at it."

Captain Bill Norwood caught the flying bug when he was in grade school. His principal, Mr. Walker, was an impressive man, a World War II pilot, who loved to talk about flying. "Mr. Walker was so enthusiastic about flying...his face would just light up," Captain Norwood remembers. "So I began to talk more and more to him, and I got interested in flying."

As a youth, Norwood flew model planes. After college, he joined the Air Force and flew huge B52 bombers.

Almost 27 years ago, Norwood joined United Airlines as a passenger jet pilot. He has worked for the airline ever since.

What plane do you like best?
"I fly the Boeing 757 and the Boeing 767, and I like the 757 best. It has a little more power so it climbs faster. The other thing is that it's a smaller airplane, and therefore more responsive."

What is your job as captain?
"As captain, you are in command of the airplane. You are the final decision-maker for whatever happens to and about and around the airplane. You also share flying with the first officer, or co-pilot."

What is trickiest about flying?
"Landing is tricky when you have a wet, slippery runway or a runway with snow that's a little bit slippery. Landing in a strong crosswind on a runway that's not too long is the trickiest thing to do and demands the most skill."

What's the best part of your job?
"I'm doing what I like to do—I like to fly airplanes. I particularly like takeoffs and landings. Most pilots do; that's where you display most of your skills. But part of the fun of flying is also flying the airplane smoothly so passengers don't realize you're in a turn, a climb, or a descent. That's part of being a professional."

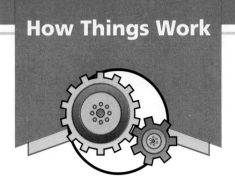

Helicopter: Flying Every Which Way

People can't fly like birds. Instead, for almost 90 years, people have been building machines that can fly. A helicopter is one of those machines.

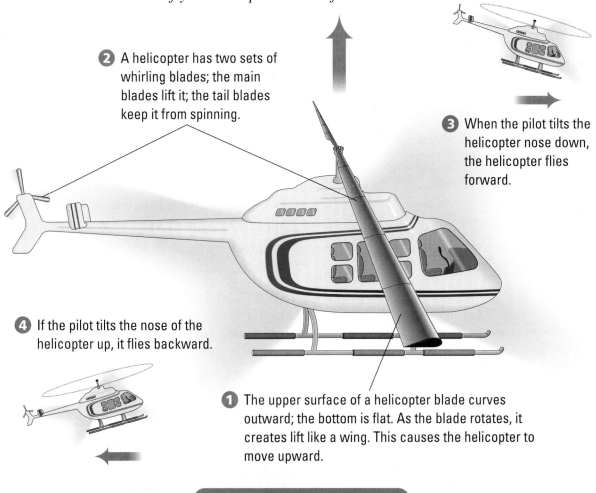

2 A helicopter has two sets of whirling blades; the main blades lift it; the tail blades keep it from spinning.

3 When the pilot tilts the helicopter nose down, the helicopter flies forward.

4 If the pilot tilts the nose of the helicopter up, it flies backward.

1 The upper surface of a helicopter blade curves outward; the bottom is flat. As the blade rotates, it creates lift like a wing. This causes the helicopter to move upward.

Find Out On Your Own

Make a chart in which you compare the way a helicopter and a hummingbird fly. Draw diagrams that show how the two of them are alike.

Module Review

Making Connections

Scale and Structure

1. How does the air help make it possible for birds to fly?
2. Explain how the pressure and density of air cause wind.
3. Why are thrust and lift important in flying?

Evolution

4. How are the wings of different birds adapted for the different environments in which they live?
5. How did aircraft change shape and method of power as people learned more?
6. Describe three problems and three opportunities people face in the future as flying changes.

Using What I Learned

Comparing

1. How is a bird's body adapted for flight as compared to a human?

Predicting

2. You wish to put food out for the birds. Predict which foods birds might choose and explain why.

Communicating

3. Write a paragraph or short story from the viewpoint of a particular bird. As you write, describe how certain parts of your body are adapted to your environment.

Ordering

4. What is the correct order of the historic development of the following types of aircraft: glider, hot-air balloon, supersonic plane, airplane, jet plane?

Relating

5. What causes wind to blow?

Observing

6. Look carefully at each bird to determine which bird is flightless, which has long flights, and which is a hunter. Explain your observations.

A

B

C

Applying What I Learned

Action Project
The natural habitats of birds are affected as new towns and suburbs are developed. Find out what birds are native to your area and what measures are being taken to protect their habitats.

Drawing
Draw a picture that shows how an athlete may use knowledge of wind resistance to increase speed.

Performance Task
Drop these objects from the same height to compare the air resistance of each: a table tennis ball, a plastic foam ball, a sponge, a pencil, a piece of paper, and a tissue.

Science Theater
Prepare a skit that takes you back in time to the invention of one of the aircraft described.

Exhibitions
Make a poster or bulletin board showing the evolution of flight. Explain how new knowledge made each stage possible.

What If
What if local officials proposed using your nearest airport for supersonic aircraft? List reasons for and against this. What would be your reaction?

The Weather Report

The Weather Report

If you're feeling under the weather, why not rise above it? In this module, you'll see the earth from a weather satellite's point of view. You'll find out why weather changes, where climates are located, and how people can predict storms. Don't forget your umbrella!

CHAPTER 1
Changing Weather

This chapter is full of hot air! And cold air too. Changes in the weather come from changes in the earth's atmosphere.

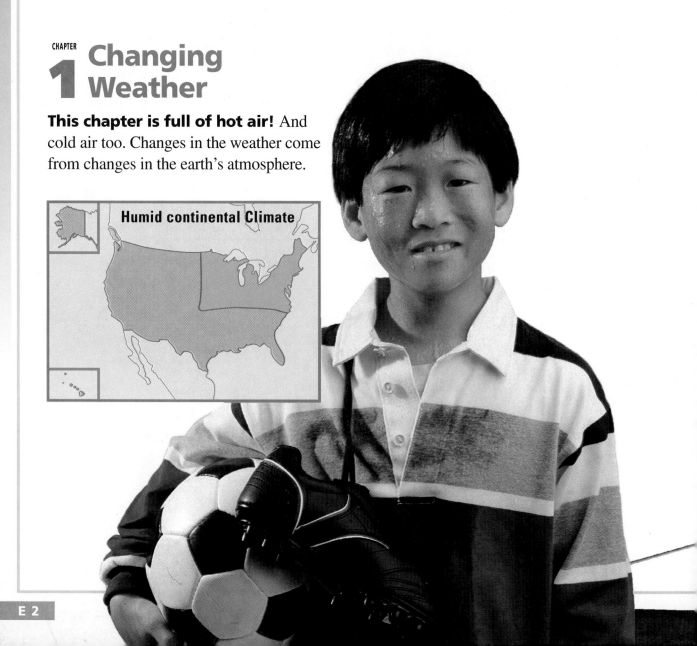

Humid continental Climate

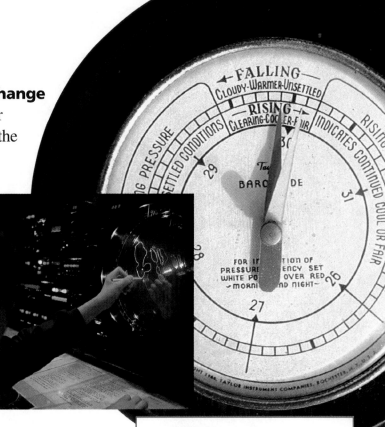

CHAPTER

2 Climate

If you can climb it, it might change the climate. Mountains and other landforms can have a big effect on the earth's climates.

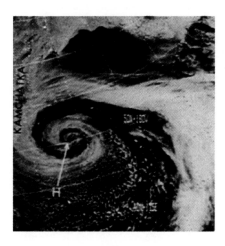

CHAPTER

3 Predicting Weather

Heroic humans hunt hurricanes! Most weather forecasters know enough to stay out of the rain, but some fly right into the earth's most destructive storms.

In this module

At the end of the book

Changing Weather

Wear cover goggles for this activity.

Discover Activity

Can evaporation cool things?

Cover the bulbs of two thermometers with a piece of gauze. Wet the gauze of one thermometer, and then carefully wave both thermometers in the air. Compare the temperatures after two minutes. Using what you know about evaporation and temperature, design and make a cooler.

wet pot

dry pot

For Discussion

1. *Does sunlight help or harm your cooler?*

2. *How can you prove your cooler really works?*

1.1 *Hot and Sticky*

▶ *What makes you so uncomfortable?*

Another goal! Your team is way ahead. You don't know how many times you've run back and forth, kicking that soccer ball. Suddenly the referee blows the whistle. The game is over and it's off to the sidelines. Success!

Like the soccer player in the picture, your shirt is soaked through and perspiration drips down your hot face. You wonder why you didn't seem to sweat like this last week. It seemed like it was a much harder game. This was an easy game so why is the whole team so hot and sweaty now?

You were probably sweating just as much last week, your coach explains. You just didn't notice. This week the air is more humid and so you feel more uncomfortable. A good shower will help you feel better.

But a shower won't answer your question. What does the coach mean by humid? And how could you have been sweating this much last week, and not notice? You will find the answers to these questions in this lesson.

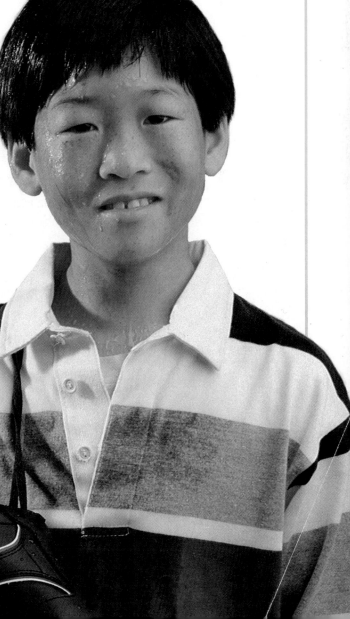

▼ *How hot and sweaty you feel depends on the humidity.*

Humidity: Invisible Water

To understand how humid air can make you feel uncomfortable, you need to know what humidity is. **Humidity** (hyü mid′ə tē) is the amount of water vapor in the air. You can't see water in the air, but it's always there.

How does water vapor get into the air? When water changes from a liquid to a gas, it evaporates. However, evaporation can't happen unless there is energy to start the process. The sun provides the energy that causes the water in the ocean and on land to evaporate.

Sometimes there's more water in the air than at other times. The more water that evaporates into the air, the more humid the air is. When air contains all the water vapor it can possibly hold, it is called **saturated** (sach′ ə rā′ tid) **air**.

When air gets closer to being saturated, evaporation occurs more slowly. That's why you feel so uncomfortable on humid days. Your body always gives off moisture—it sweats. The heat from your body provides the energy for your sweat to evaporate. This helps you feel dry, and also cooler. Remember when you go swimming how cool you feel as the water evaporates from your wet body. If the air is less humid, more water can evaporate and you cool off quickly. But on a day with high humidity, you stay hot and sticky because the air around you already has a lot of water vapor. When you did the Discover Activity, you saw how evaporation causes cooling.

▼ Water vapor has condensed on the cooler mirror.

Clouds: Visible Water

The warmer air is, the more water vapor it can hold before it becomes saturated. But at any one temperature there's only a certain amount of water vapor that air can hold. For example, if saturated air cools down only one degree, the extra water vapor condenses. That means it returns to the liquid state. The girl on page 6 is drawing in the moisture that has condensed on the mirror. When air touches the cold mirror, the air is chilled, and water vapor condenses on the mirror.

The same thing happens when clouds form. When air rises, it cools. Eventually it can cool enough that it reaches its saturation level. The extra moisture condenses into millions of tiny droplets of water, forming a cloud. Even in the summer, temperatures can be below freezing in clouds. So, clouds also contain many tiny ice crystals.

Ice crystals, high in the clouds, grow larger when water vapor freezes on them. When heavy enough, they can fall. As they fall, they bump into other ice crystals and grow. If the air stays cold, they fall as snow. If the air is warm, they melt and fall as rain.

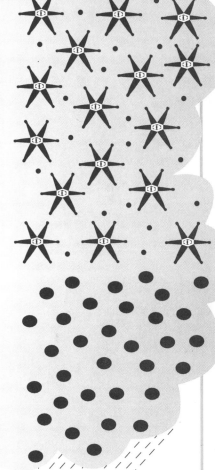

As ice crystals grow, they fall. If temperatures are warm enough, they will melt and reach the ground as raindrops.

Checkpoint

1. Where does the energy come from that evaporates water on the earth?
2. What makes water vapor condense?
3. **Take Action!** What is today's humidity? Check your newspaper, TV, or the radio.

Activity

Making A Rain Gauge

How can you measure rainfall? Try this activity to find out.

Picture A

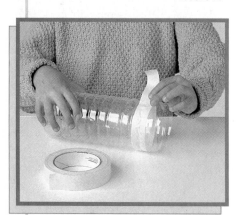

Picture B

Picture C

Gather These Materials

cover goggles

clear, empty plastic
  bottle with a flat
  bottom

scissors

metric ruler

masking tape

waterproof marker

Follow This Procedure

1. Make a chart like the one on the next page. Record your observations in your chart.

2. Put on your cover goggles.

3. Ask an adult to help you cut off the top third of a plastic bottle just below the point where the bottle curves toward the neck. Be extremely careful using the scissors. (Picture A)

4. Turn the top of the bottle upside down to fit the top into the base of the bottle. The top will be a funnel to collect the rain. Tape the edges together with the masking tape. (Picture B)

5. Use your metric ruler and a strip of masking tape to make a measuring scale. Attach the tape down the length of the bottle. Mark off your scale in 0.5 cm segments. (Picture C)

Predict: *How much rain will you collect during a rainfall?*

6 Place your rain gauge outside in an open area where it won't be disturbed. Put the bottle firmly in the ground so it cannot be blown over.

7 Check your rain gauge every day for a week. Record the amount of rain in the bottle each day.

8 Remember to empty the bottle each day after you have taken the measurement and recorded the results.

	Rainfall in cm
Day 1	
Day 2	
Day 3	
Day 4	
Day 5	
Day 6	
Day 7	

State Your Conclusions

1. How did your rain gauge collect rain water?
2. On what day was the amount of rainfall the greatest? the least?
3. Using what you have learned about humidity, explain why there might be water in your bottle even when there has been no rainfall.

Let's Experiment

Explain why you should check your rain gauge and the amount of rainfall you have collected soon after a rainfall (the same day). What would happen to the rain in your gauge if you didn't? Use what you know about scientific methods to find out.

1.2 *Rainy Days*

▶ **What makes weather change?**

Rain, rain, go away. Come again some other day! It would be great if that was all you had to say to make the weather change. Sometimes it seems like bad weather will never end. You'd love to wish it away. At other times, a storm passes by in just a few hours. In this lesson you will learn some of the reasons why storms differ. Then you won't have to wish the weather away—you'll know better what to expect.

Air Masses

Where does weather happen? It happens in the atmosphere—the air around you. And the reason is that air is not all the same. Air can be cold or it can be warm. Air can be dry or it can be humid. A very large body of air that has about the same temperature and humidity all through it is called an **air mass**. Air masses are hundreds of kilometers wide and three to six kilometers high.

When an air mass forms it takes on the temperature and humidity of the area where it is. Just remember two things about air masses and temperature: Air masses that form in tropical areas are warm, and air masses that form in polar areas are cold. And, remember these two things about air masses and humidity: Air masses that form over land are dry and air masses that form over water are humid. Find the polar, dry air mass in the picture. What causes the air in that air mass to be cold and dry air?

▼ *These air masses affect the weather in North America.*

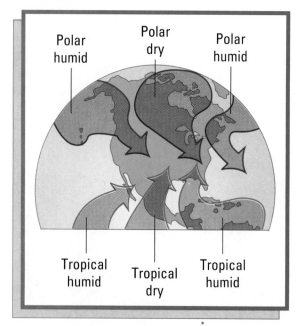

Polar humid

Polar dry

Polar humid

Tropical humid

Tropical dry

Tropical humid

Air masses move. The arrows in the picture on page 10 show which direction different air masses can move. Eventually, different kinds of air masses come into contact with one another.

When two air masses meet, you might expect them to mix together, but that doesn't happen. The area where two different air masses meet is called a **front.** In the picture you can see that the front forms a boundary between the two air masses.

Since there are different kinds of air masses, there are also different kinds of fronts. And naturally you would expect different kinds of fronts to produce different kinds of weather. That's exactly what happens. Understanding air pressure will help you see how different kinds of fronts form and how these fronts cause different kinds of weather.

▼ *The area where two air masses meet is called a front.*

Cold air

Warm air

Front

Low Pressure, High Pressure

Think about all the air that is over you. Air is made of matter and so it has mass, just like all other matter. All that mass is pressing down on the earth's surface—and on you, too! You hardly notice it. But you do notice the effects of high or low air pressure on things around you.

Warm air is lighter than an equal volume of cold air. Its matter, or particles, are farther apart. Because warm air is lighter, it tends to rise from the earth's surface, as you can see below. Because it is rising, warm air presses down on the earth's surface with less force. This is called a low pressure area.

But, remember, warm air can hold more moisture than cold air. As air rises it cools. What do you think will happen? The cooled air can't hold as much water vapor as before. The air's extra moisture condenses, and clouds form. You could find yourself wet from rain or covered in snow because low pressure systems often produce wet weather.

Warm Air

Low Pressure

▼ *Air moves from areas of high pressure to areas of low pressure.*

Cold Air

High Pressure

Unlike warm air, cold air is heavier air. Its matter is more closely packed together. It pushes down harder on the earth's surface, so a cold air mass is called a high pressure area. Since cold air holds less water vapor, it also tends to be drier air. If you're outside, feeling pleasantly dry and cool, chances are you're in a high pressure system.

Wind — High to Low

You've already learned that when air rises, low pressure results. If this is true, something must replace the air that rose, but what? As the surrounding illustration shows, high pressure air flows into an area of low pressure to replace the rising air. Sound mysterious? Don't worry, it's not. Although this process is something you can't see, you've felt it a thousand times before—it's called wind.

Wind is the movement of air from high to low pressure areas. Gentle breezes result when the difference in air pressure between the two pressure areas is small. When the difference between high and low pressure areas is great, watch out! You might be facing a very windy day or changing weather.

When a cold air mass pushes into a warm air mass the warm air rises rapidly. Tall clouds form. Heavy rain or a snow storm can result. Lightning, as shown in the photo on page 15, is often part of a cold front storm.

Cold Front Time

Winds can be clues to big weather changes. Have you ever noticed gentle breezes turn into strong winds? Or did you notice that the wind changed its direction from earlier in the day? If you did, then you were noticing that air was on the move. It could mean that a cold front or a warm front is on its way. But how can you tell the difference?

A cold front is easy to identify. As you can see in the drawing, when cold air pushes into warm air, the warm air rises quickly up out of the way. The rising warm air cools rapidly and produces enormous, towering clouds with dark bottoms called cumulonimbus clouds. There will be heavy precipitation—usually rain or snow, but only in a small area. Since cold fronts move quickly, the rain or snow doesn't last very long. You'll feel a drop in the temperature and notice a change in wind direction. After the storm, the weather is cooler, drier, and sunny.

Cold fronts can also produce thunderstorms. When was the last time you saw—and heard—a thunderstorm? The rapidly moving air in the clouds causes electrical charges to build up. You see lightning when the electricity jumps from one cloud to another, or to the earth. You hear thunder because the air around the lightning flash is heated briefly to a temperature even higher than on the sun. This causes the air to expand explosively, and what you hear is the sound—thunder—from that explosion.

Lightning can be very dangerous. If you are outside during a thunderstorm, seek shelter right away. Try not to be the highest object around, because that is what lightning will often strike first. Since trees are generally the highest objects, stay away from them. If you can't find anywhere to protect yourself, lie down flat or in the lowest spot you can find until the storm passes.

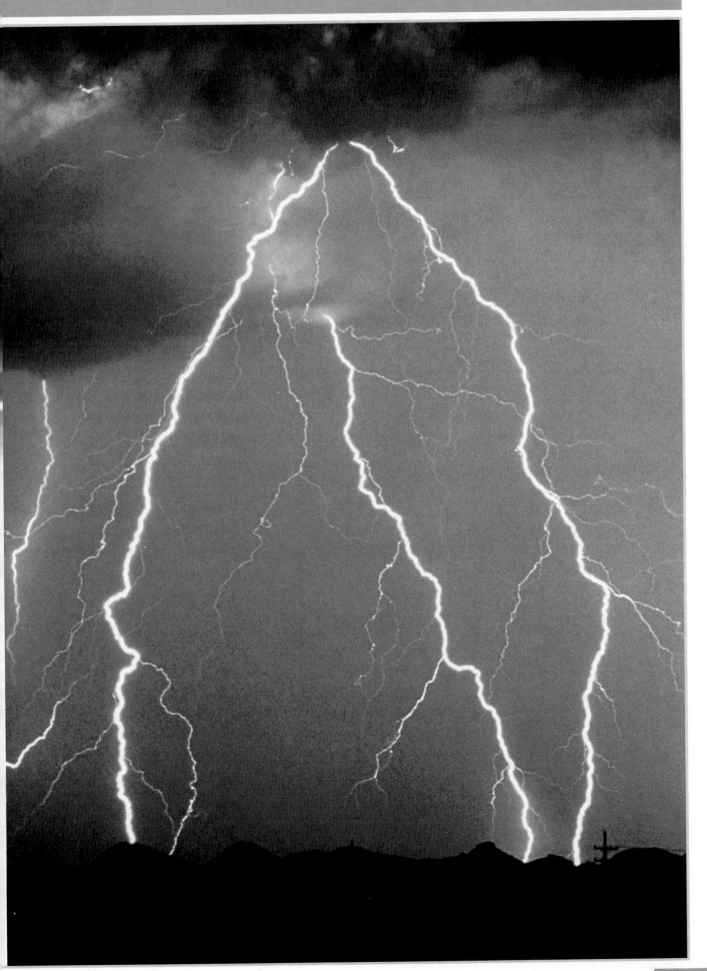

Tornadoes are another type of storm that a cold front can produce. Rapidly rising warm air at a cold front causes more air to move in to replace it. Strong winds are produced. The air may begin to rotate and produce a funnel-shaped cloud that can reach down to the ground. Fortunately, the area that they touch is usually very narrow and they don't last very long.

Warm Front Time

Warm fronts are easy to identify, too. The weather they produce is usually much less exciting. In a warm front, a warm air mass moves toward a cold air mass. You can see in the drawing that warm air doesn't push the cold, heavier air out of the way. Instead, the warm air slides up slowly over the cold air mass. As it gently rises, it also cools and produces clouds. If you see wispy clouds high in the sky followed by lower, thicker clouds it's a clue that a warm front is on the way. The rain or snow produced by a warm front can last for several days. That's because the clouds extend for quite a distance along the front. But it's gentle, light precipitation. When the front passes by, you'll have warmer, milder weather—at least until the next front comes!

▲ When a warm air mass moves into a cold air mass, it slides up over the cold air. Clouds form along the front. Gentle rain, as shown in the photo on page 16, or even snow, can fall.

Checkpoint

1. What influences whether an air mass is hot or cold, wet or dry?
2. What is the difference between high and low pressure air?
3. Why are some winds stronger?
4. What kind of storms often accompany cold fronts?
5. Describe conditions along a warm front.
6. **Take Action!** Make a chart that shows day by day if the air pressure rises or falls in your area. Record the weather each day.

Into The Field

Do clouds move at different speeds?

Observe the clouds outside. Describe how the clouds are moving. Record what you see for at least one week.

High and Low: Measuring Air Pressure

How can you tell when there is a change in air pressure? Find out how you can measure air pressure by making a simple barometer.

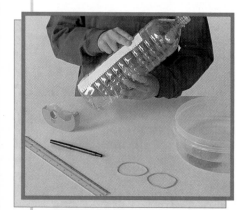

Picture A

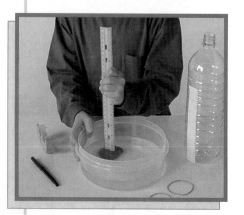

Picture B

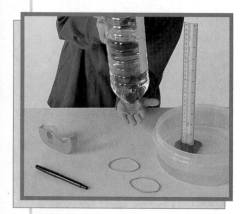

Picture C

Gather These Materials

cover goggles
paper
tape
metric ruler
clear, plastic bottle

modeling clay
plastic bowl
water
2 rubber bands

Follow This Procedure

1 Make a chart like the one on the next page. Record your observations in your chart.

2 Put on your cover goggles.

3 Use a metric ruler to mark a long strip of paper with short lines every 0.5 cm. This will be your measuring scale. Tape the strip along the length of the tall side of the plastic bottle. (Picture A)

4 Put a lump of clay in the bottom of the bowl, near the side. Stand the ruler in the clay. (Picture B)

5 Fill the bowl and the bottle each half full of water.

6 Cover the opening of the bottle with the palm of your hand. Turn the bottle upside down and lower it slowly so that the opening is under the surface of the water in the bowl. (Picture C)

7 Keeping the bottle upright with your other hand, carefully take your hand away from the opening of the bottle. Don't let the bottle tilt. Rest the opening on the bottom of the bowl.

8 Anchor the bottle to the ruler with the two rubber bands. The ruler should help keep the bottle from tipping over.

9 Mark on your paper scale the level of the water in the bottle.

Predict: *What will happen to the level of the water in the bottle?*

9 Keep a record of the water level in the bottle every day for a week. Note whether it goes up or down from where it was at first. The changes will be slight, so check the level carefully.

10 An increase in air pressure outside the bottle will push the water level in the bottle up. A decrease in air pressure will cause the water level in the bottle to go down.

Record Your Results

	Water level	
	up	down
Day 1		
Day 2		
Day 3		
Day 4		
Day 5		
Day 6		
Day 7		

State Your Conclusions

1. How does your barometer show that air pressure is going up or down?
2. Did the weather change at all when the air pressure changed?
3. Using what you have learned, how can you explain the rise or drop in the water level of the bottle?

Let's Experiment

Do you think there could be a relationship between air pressure measurements and weather? Use what you know about scientific methods to find out.

1.3 Moving On

Does weather move in a predictable pattern?

One night in Philadelphia 250 years ago, Benjamin Franklin was waiting for something really special—an eclipse of the moon. Mr. Franklin loved to study the weather. And he usually loved to see a storm develop. But he'd been waiting for this eclipse for weeks. On that very night of the eclipse, a storm developed over Philadelphia. Clouds blocked his view of the sky. What bad luck!

Several days later a newspaper article caught Mr. Franklin's eye. The article described the beautiful view of the eclipse that people in Boston had seen. Then he noticed another article that described a powerful storm that hit Boston the night after the eclipse. Mr. Franklin put down his newspaper and thought about this. Up until this time, most people thought that storms just developed and disappeared right over their heads.

▼ *The same type of weather has moved west to east from Detroit to Philadelphia.*

Monday

Tuesday

DETROIT ✈

Unsettled
turning cloudy, rain developing, high 68, low 56.
Tomorrow: rain ends, breezy, high 74, low 55.

HOUSTON

More he
thunder p
pecially
high 9
Tomo
sunn
high

CLEVELAND

Cool, wet
cloudy with periods of rain, high 67, low 58.
Tomorrow: some sun, chance shower, high 76, low 56.

OLIS

DALLAS-F1

Hot sun
thunderstorm
couple of loca
high 7, low 7
Tomorrow: su
clouds, few stor
high 96, low 74.

WEATHER CLOSE-UP

The 24
and tra
desire
chang

BALTIMORE ✈

ANTA ✈

Some sun
afternoon cl

king good

NEW ORLEANS

Thunderstorms
showers at night, high 89, low 74.
Tomorrow: hot sun,

KANSAS CITY

Lots of sun
warm but dry, fair skies tonight, high 84, low 64.
Tomorrow: sunny, a little more humid, high 88, low 66.

LOS ANGELES

Mainly sunny
morning clouds, otherwise nice, high 83, low 65.
Tomorrow: partly to mostly

While thinking about the newspaper articles he had been reading, Mr. Franklin came up with a different idea. He decided that the storm that had blocked his view of the eclipse in Philadelphia was the same storm that struck Boston the following night. And so that must mean that weather doesn't just sit still like everyone thought. It travels from place to place.

West to East

The idea that weather moves was new 250 years ago. Today, it seems obvious to you. Watch clouds for a few moments and you'll see that even on the calmest days, clouds drift steadily along. But, where are they going?

Look at the diagram of Earth. As Earth rotates the atmosphere moves with it, leading to different weather patterns throughout the world. In the U.S., Earth's rotation usually causes weather to move from west to east. In the newspapers below similar weather is moving across three cities from west to east. Mr. Franklin would not have been surprised!

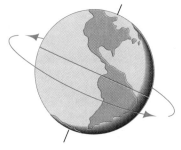

▲ Earth's gravity causes the atmosphere to move with it. Earth's rotation affects global wind patterns.

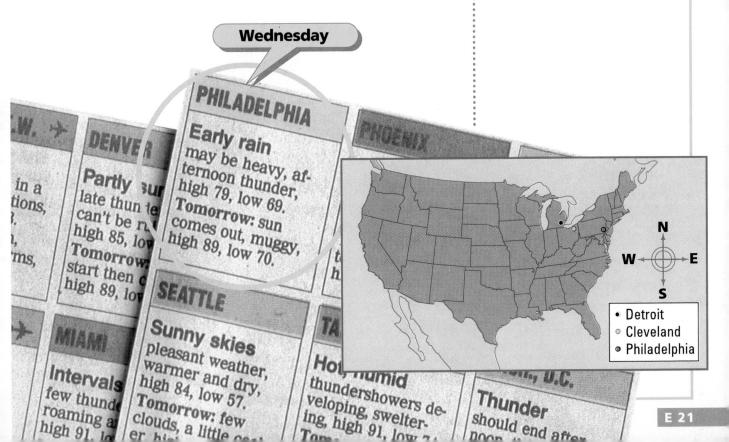

Wednesday

PHILADELPHIA

Early rain
may be heavy, afternoon thunder, high 79, low 69.
Tomorrow: sun comes out, muggy, high 89, low 70.

PHOENIX

DENVER

Partly sun
late thun...
can't be r...
high 85, lo...
Tomorrow...
start then...
high 89, lo...

SEATTLE

Sunny skies
pleasant weather, warmer and dry, high 84, low 57.
Tomorrow: few clouds, a little...

MIAMI

Intervals
few thunde...
roaming a...
high 91, lo...

Hot, humid
thundershowers developing, swelter-ing, high 91, low 7...
Tom...

..., D.C.

Thunder
should end after...

- Detroit
- Cleveland
- Philadelphia

Reading Weather Maps

Is it difficult to read a weather map? It's not hard if you know the language!

With the help of computers, information from satellites and from weather sources all over the world is combined to make weather maps. The symbols on the map make it easier to understand the complex weather systems that the map is showing. Using symbols is easier than explaining all about the weather with words. You can understand the big weather picture by just glancing at a weather map. A key to some of these symbols is shown on the map. Use this weather map and find the warm front. Where is the cold front? According to the map, where is it raining?

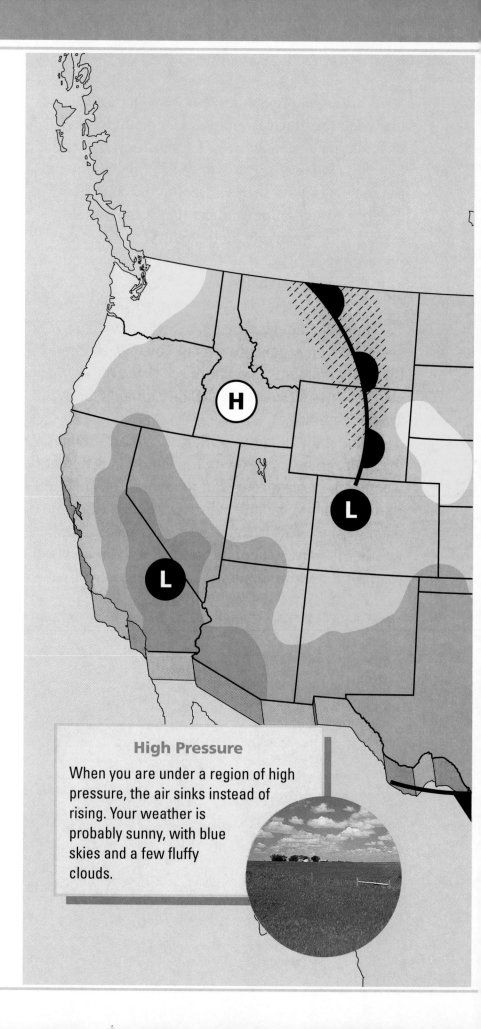

High Pressure

When you are under a region of high pressure, the air sinks instead of rising. Your weather is probably sunny, with blue skies and a few fluffy clouds.

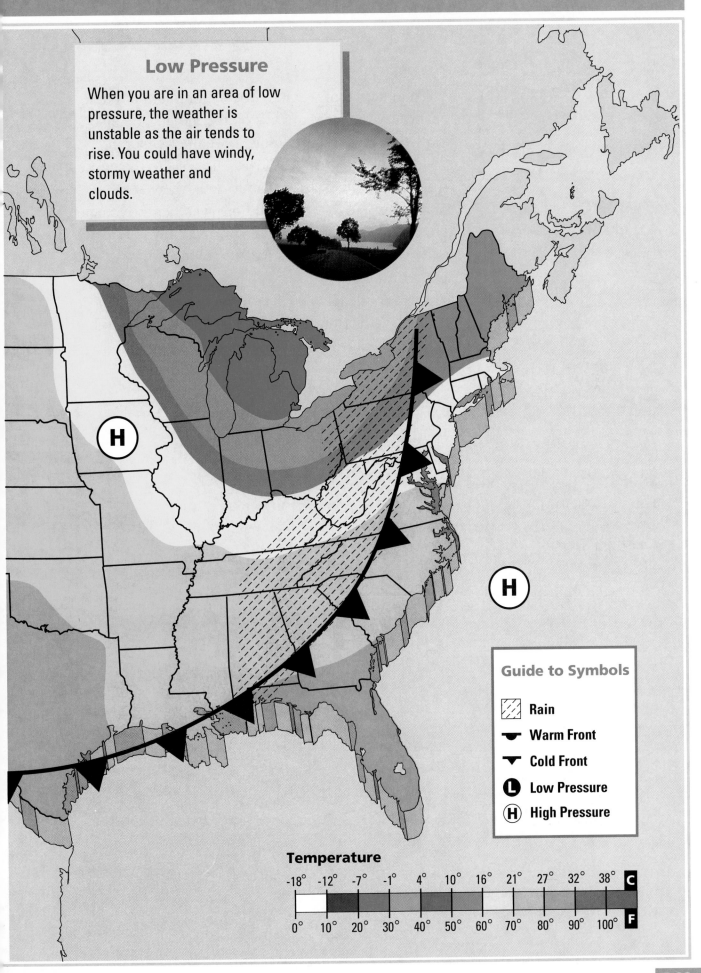

Low Pressure

When you are in an area of low pressure, the weather is unstable as the air tends to rise. You could have windy, stormy weather and clouds.

Guide to Symbols

- ▨ Rain
- ▼ Warm Front
- ▽ Cold Front
- **L** Low Pressure
- **H** High Pressure

Temperature

| -18° | -12° | -7° | -1° | 4° | 10° | 16° | 21° | 27° | 32° | 38° | **C** |

| 0° | 10° | 20° | 30° | 40° | 50° | 60° | 70° | 80° | 90° | 100° | **F** |

Keeping Watch

You know that weather does not remain in one location. Weather is always on the move. You also know that in the United States, weather generally moves across the country from the west to the east, from the Pacific to the Atlantic. But, there are exceptions to every rule, and our weather movement rule is no exception! You can always find someplace in the country where a storm is moving north, or south, or to the northeast or southwest.

Why do we have such a variety in our weather patterns? Mountains, oceans, lakes, deserts, prairies, and other features of our land influence how the weather can move.

▼ *The satellite photos below show a weather system as it moves from west to east.*

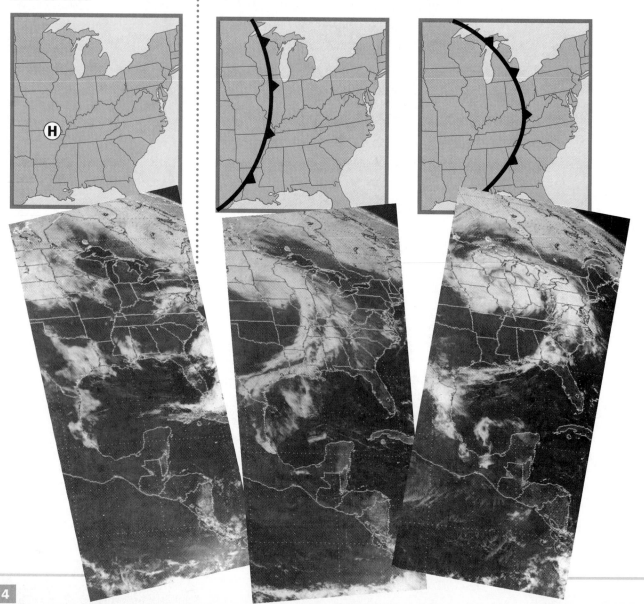

Fronts can suddenly change direction or even stop moving. Different air masses can bump into one another and affect the direction of the air movement in the area. And you probably remember that most of our cold air moves from the north. Tropical air from the south moves northward. But if you look at the big picture, the country as a whole, then overall the weather moves west to east.

By carefully looking at weather maps like the one you just read about, and learning what the symbols mean, you can find out what the weather is like in an area. The next day, you can compare that map with the new one and you can tell where yesterday's fronts have moved. You can also see if there are new ones. Find the satellite pictures on page 24. Information from pictures like these is added to the maps to help show weather changes. The diagrams above the satellite pictures show how they would look on the weather map. New maps on the third day can tell you again what changes have occurred. By then you can probably predict where day four's weather will be. And you should also see, among all the changes and variety in weather across the country, that the weather movement rule holds true—west to east.

Checkpoint

1. In what way does Earth's rotation affect how weather moves?
2. On a weather map, how are cold and warm fronts shown differently?
3. If you live in Illinois and there's a storm over Ohio, will that same storm get you wet in the near future? Why or why not?
4. Take Action! Copy the fronts from a newspaper weather map onto a map for the next day. How have the fronts moved?

Tornado Frequency

Tornadoes are short-lived, powerful windstorms. In the United States they occur mostly in the midwest and the states that border the Gulf of Mexico. Tornadoes often develop where there is a severe thunderstorm. A twisting, funnel-shaped cloud with wind speeds of more than 320 kilometers per hour may extend downward from dark clouds. If the funnel touches the earth, it can cause severe damage.

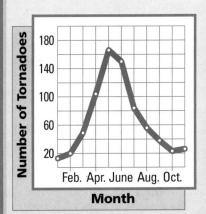

The graph shows the average number of tornadoes per month in the U.S. from 1953–1989.

What Did You Find Out?
1. *In which month is the number greatest?*
2. *In which month is the number fewest?*
3. *In what season do tornadoes occur most often?*

Interpreting Diagrams

Think about the weather maps in the chapter. By reading them, you can find the temperature and weather for your area for the day shown on that map. Weather maps are simply diagrams that help you see what is happening. Interpreting a diagram can help you picture what makes weather happen.

Thinking It Through

This diagram shows a warm front. Use these steps to help you read any diagram.
1. If there is a key, study it to learn what each symbol stands for. The key in this diagram shows which symbol stands for a moving air mass. What symbol helps you find the warm front?
2. Read any labels or other written information on the diagram itself. In this diagram, where is the cold air mass?

Where is the warm air mass?
3. Study how the parts fit together. In this diagram, the arrows mean the warm air mass is moving toward the cold air mass. A warm front is forming.
4. Use what you have learned in this chapter to help you interpret the diagram below. You learned that when a warm air mass moves into a cold air mass, it flows up over the colder air. The result is gentle, long-lasting rains along the warm front. What kind of weather are the people in City C having?

Your Turn

Use the information from the chapter and the steps for reading a diagram. Tell what kind of weather the people in Cities A and B are having.

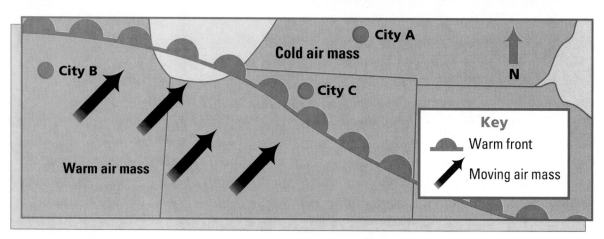

Chapter Review

Thinking Back

1. Why does your body seem to sweat more when **humidity** is high?

2. How does **saturated air** affect evaporation?

3. How does temperature affect the amount of evaporation?

4. What causes condensation droplets to form on the outside of a glass of ice water?

5. Why does most rain start as ice crystals?

6. Describe the temperature, air pressure, and humidity of a warm **air mass**.

7. Explain how a warm **front** can produce gentle, light precipitation that lasts for several days.

8. How do weather maps help you better understand weather patterns?

9. What are some of the factors that determine our weather patterns?

Connecting Ideas

1. Copy the concept map. Use the terms at the right to complete the map about a cold front.

warm air mass   **lightning**
strong winds   **cold air mass**

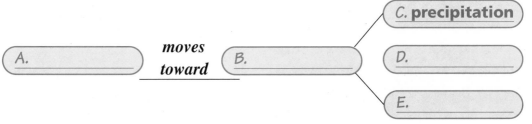

2. Write a sentence or two about the ideas in the concept map.

Gathering Evidence

1. Why might your results from the Activity on page 8 be different from someone else's?

2. How did you know in the Activity on page 18 that there was a change in the air pressure?

Doing Science!

1. **Design an activity** that would demonstrate condensation.

2. **Create a skit** for a weather report. Show the movement of the fronts and high or low pressure areas.

Climate

Turn the lights out.
Let's do a light show!

How bright are direct light rays?

Roll the paper into a tube around the lens of a
flashlight. Tape it in place. Shine the light at
different angles onto a sheet of paper. How do the
brightness and size of the area lit compare to the
angle of the rays of light as they hit the paper?

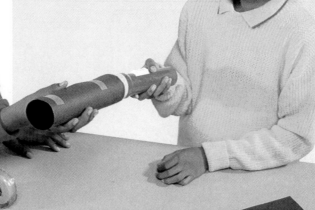

For Discussion

1. Why is sunlight brighter in summer than winter?

*2. How can you prove that direct rays heat things
faster than indirect rays?*

2.1 Starting With The Sun

▶ *Why is it getting dark so much sooner?*

Summer days are great! You can spend hours outside reading or playing with your friends. Gradually, after school starts, you begin to notice a change. It gets darker earlier and earlier. Soon you realize that there is only an hour or two of sunlight left when you get home from school in the afternoon. Why is it getting dark so much sooner?

Shorter Days, Longer Nights

Look at the snowy houses in the picture on the left. The sun is getting ready to set. It is late afternoon on the first day of winter. But, in the picture on the right it is the first day of summer. The sun's light is quite bright. It will be several more hours before the sun sets. Different seasons bring changes in the amount of sunlight—but perhaps you've never known what causes seasons in the first place.

▼ *In winter the sun is ready to set, but in summer it is still bright and sunny at the same time of day.*

There are seasons on Earth because while Earth orbits the sun it is also tilted on its axis. Yes, that's right—tilted! And Earth always tilts in the same direction. Notice in the photos that in some places on Earth, different seasons can bring big changes in the appearance of the land.

Because of that tilt, different parts of Earth point toward the sun and away from the sun during Earth's one year orbit. In the diagram find where Earth's northern half is pointing toward the sun and its bottom half is pointing away. It seems logical that the half of Earth pointing toward the sun receives more sunlight and so has longer days. For that half of Earth it is summer. At the same time, the half of Earth pointing away from the sun is experiencing winter. When you are out in the warm sunshine here in the United States, children in places like Australia and Argentina are zipping up jackets and pulling on mittens.

Six months later, Earth moves in its orbit to the opposite side of the sun. Then, Earth's bottom half points toward the sun and the top half points away. What part of Earth has summer and winter now? Does Earth's tilt on its axis change during its orbit? No, but what changes is the position of Earth in its orbit and the part of Earth pointing toward the sun.

Twice during the year, no matter where it is on Earth, every place receives about twelve hours of darkness and about twelve hours of daylight. This event is called an equinox (ē′ kwə noks). One equinox occurs on about March 21st—the first day of spring. The other is on about September 23rd, the first day of fall.

Spring

Summer

Winter

Fall

▲ In the temperate climate zone, seasons are very different. The photos above, from top to bottom, show winter, spring, summer, and fall.

Twice during the year another event occurs called a solstice (sol′ stis). The winter solstice in the northern half of Earth occurs about December 21st. The winter solstice is called the shortest day of the year because there are fewer hours of sunlight on that day than any other day all year. In places near the North Pole, there is no sunlight at all! For people living in that area, weeks will go by before they see the sun again.

The summer solstice is called the longest day of the year because there are more hours of sunlight on that day than on any other day all year. In the northern half of Earth, the summer solstice occurs about June 21st. What is happening to the hours of sunlight for those people who live on the southern half of Earth?

For people who live near the North Pole, summer brings days when the sun never sets. Weeks go by when even at midnight, the sun continues to shine. In the photo below, special multiple exposure photography was used to photograph the sun's position during one summer day, from 9 p.m. to 4 a.m., in Alaska. For people living in northern Alaska, there is sunlight 24 hours a day!

▼ *In far northern Alaska the sun is visible during the summer even at midnight.*

Toasty Tropical Climates

How would you describe the overall weather where you live? One way is to talk about its climate. A **climate** is the weather conditions which describe an area over many years. These conditions include things like temperature, humidity, and precipitation. Together, they give a general picture of what an area is like. There are three very different types of climates on Earth.

Find the tropical climate zone in the picture. It's on either side of the equator. Air temperatures in the tropical climate zone don't change much during the year. They average above 18°C.

Tropical climates are warm because they receive the sun's direct rays. You noticed in the Discover Activity that the direct rays covered a smaller area than the indirect rays. Since they are not spread out over as large an area, direct rays can produce more heat. What kind of air masses form over tropical climates that receive the sun's direct rays? That's right—warm air masses.

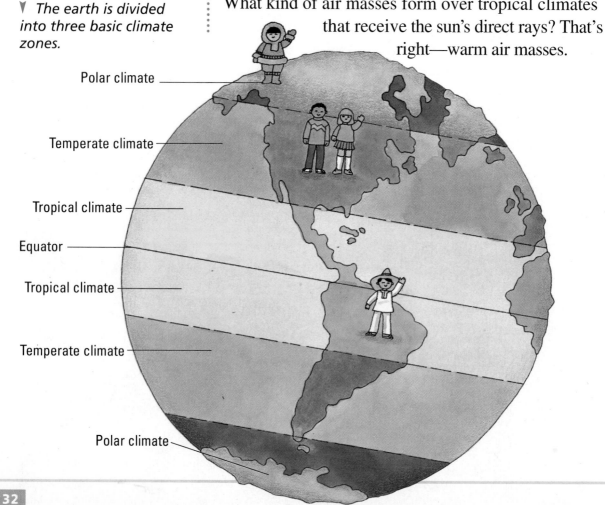

▼ *The earth is divided into three basic climate zones.*

Polar climate

Temperate climate

Tropical climate

Equator

Tropical climate

Temperate climate

Polar climate

Polar Chills

There are two areas on Earth that are called polar climate zones. Find them in the picture on page 32. The average temperature in the polar climate zones is less than 10°C. Why is it so much colder there? There are two reasons. First, in winter when polar areas point away from the sun, they receive no sunlight at all. Second, in the summer, even though the polar zones get sunlight for 24 hours a day, it is indirect sunlight. Indirect rays are spread out over a larger area, and so cannot produce as much heat.

Another reason polar areas are colder is that sunlight passes through a lot more atmosphere before reaching Earth's surface. In fact, the atmosphere blocks many of the indirect rays. What kind of air masses do you think form over polar areas? That's right—cold air masses.

Temperate Climates

Two areas on Earth's surface are called temperate climate zones. Temperate climates have very cold weather in winter and very warm weather in summer. That's because during the summer, temperate climates receive nearly direct rays. But, in winter, temperatures plunge because the sun's rays are indirect. All of the United States except for Alaska and Hawaii lie in the temperate climate zone.

Checkpoint

1. What two things cause seasons?
2. What causes tropical climates to be hot?
3. What causes polar climates to be cold?
4. Where do temperate climate zones lie?
5. **Take Action!** Use a tennis ball as an Earth model. Predict what would happen to the seasons if Earth was not tilted.

Earth Chart

What would a climate chart of the earth look like? Let's investigate and find out.

What To Do
A. Make two charts like the one shown. On the top of the date columns, for the second chart, put Sept. 23 and Dec. 21.
B. Color the bars for each date as follows from top to bottom: 3/21=blue, green, red, green, blue; 6/21=green, red, red, blue, blue; 9/21=blue, green, red, green, blue; 12/21=blue, blue, red, red, green.
C. The colors stand for: blue=cold, green=mild, red=hot.

Record Your Results

	March 21	June 21
Northern Polar		
Northern Temperate		
Tropical		
Southern Temperate		
Southern Polar		

What Did You Find Out?
1. *When it's summer in the north, what's it like in South America? Why?*
2. *Do seasons change near the equator? Explain.*

Activity

The Tilt of the Earth

How does Earth's tilt affect the seasons? Try this activity to observe how sunlight reaches different parts of Earth.

Picture A

Picture B

Picture C

Gather These Materials

plastic foam ball   marker
pencil   flashlight

Follow This Procedure

1 Make a chart like the one on the next page. Record your observations in your chart.

2 Carefully push the pencil (Earth's axis) through the center of the ball (Earth). (Picture A) Ask an adult to help you. Have the eraser end of the pencil pointing up. The eraser end is the axis at the North Pole. The other end is the axis at the South Pole.

3 Use the marker to draw the equator around Earth, halfway between the poles. (Picture B)

4 Hold the North Pole axis so that it tilts toward the front of the room. Have a partner hold a flashlight (sunlight) about 20 cm from Earth, shining the light on the equator. Observe which part of Earth gets more direct sunlight. (Picture C)

Predict: **How does Earth's tilt affect which part of Earth gets more direct sunlight?**

5 Move Earth in a circle around the sun (the flashlight). First, move Earth through one quarter of its orbit of the sun by moving to your right. Repeat step 4.

Record Your Results

Tilt of Earth	Part of Earth getting more direct sunlight
North Pole tilted toward sun	
South Pole tilted toward sun	

6 Move Earth another quarter of the way around the sun in its orbit. Repeat step 4.

7 Move Earth one more time a quarter of the way in its orbit. Again, repeat step 4. Record your observations in your chart.

State Your Conclusions

1. How does Earth's tilt affect how directly sunlight reaches the different parts of Earth?

2. When the North Pole is tilted toward the sun, what season would it be in the United States?

3. Using what you have learned, explain why the countries near the equator do not have seasons.

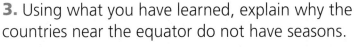

Let's Experiment

Now that you have observed how Earth's tilt affects the seasons, what would happen if Earth was not tilted? Use what you know about scientific methods to find out.

2.2 *Climates, U.S.A.*

> **Does all of the United States have the same climate?**

Most of the United States may be in the temperate climate zone, but that doesn't mean every place in the United States has the same kind of climate. For some people, hot, humid summers and cold, snowy winters may describe where they live. But for others mild, wet winters and mild, dry summers may be more familiar.

What makes our climates so different? Let's jump in a car—imaginary, of course—and take a drive. We'll see some things about the land that cause different parts of the United States to have different kinds of climates. Let's begin in the desert.

Mountains and Climate

Look out your car window—or at the photo on page 37—and you can tell the desert is a place that receives little rain. As the illustration below shows, the American desert has a mountain range on its west side. As moist air moves onto land from the ocean, it bumps into the mountains. As the moist air rises and crosses the mountains, clouds form. Rain falls on the west side of the mountains. By the time this air gets over the mountain and reaches the desert, it has lost a lot of moisture.

▼ Air rises when it meets a mountain. The cooling air produces rain on the west side of the mountain, leaving the east side dry.

From the dry desert, let's drive to the east in our imaginary car. As we climb up the west side of the mountains, we can turn off our car's air conditioner. We are now more comfortable because we've driven to a higher **altitude** (al′tə tüd). Altitude is the height you are above sea level.

High in the mountains the air has expanded and cooled as it has risen. The air has expanded because up high, less air presses down on it from above. As the air expands, it also cools. Remember what happens when air cools? Its water vapor condenses. Look around. Even though the desert lies a few miles away, trees grow here because of the mountain rainfall they receive.

On the next two pages, you can use the map of the United States. It will show you some of the major climate zones in this country. The map will give you a good idea of the great variety of climates in your country.

▲ *Deserts receive very little rain. In high mountain altitudes, rising air cools. Clouds can form and produce rain or snow.*

Climates, U.S.A.

Climates vary across the U.S. because of differences in the amount of rainfall and temperature.

There are no clear boundary lines between climate areas. However, the map gives us a good idea about some of the differences in climates across our country and where some of our climates are found.

Mediterranean climate

Summers in this climate zone are very dry with mild temperatures. Winters are wet with mild temperatures, too.

Grassland climate

This zone gets little rainfall during the year. Polar air brings very cold temperatures and snow in winter. Tropical air brings hot temperatures in the summer.

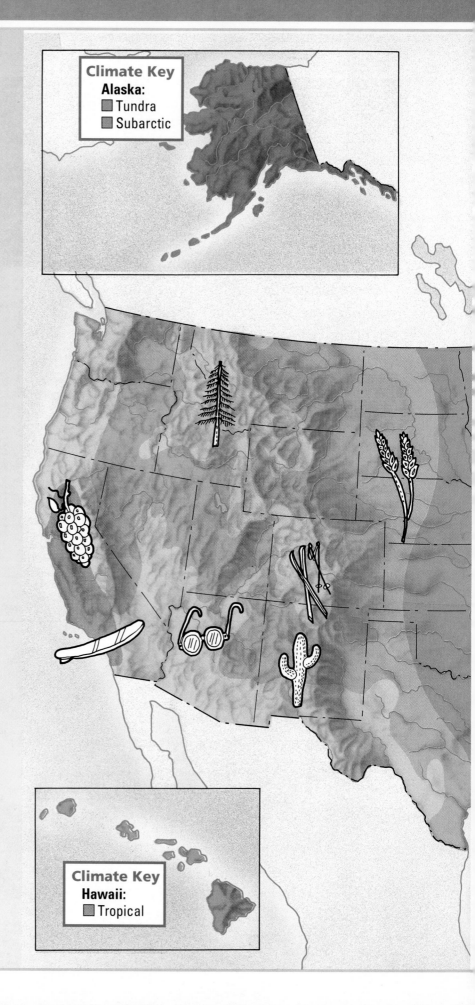

Climate Key
Alaska:
■ Tundra
■ Subarctic

Climate Key
Hawaii:
■ Tropical

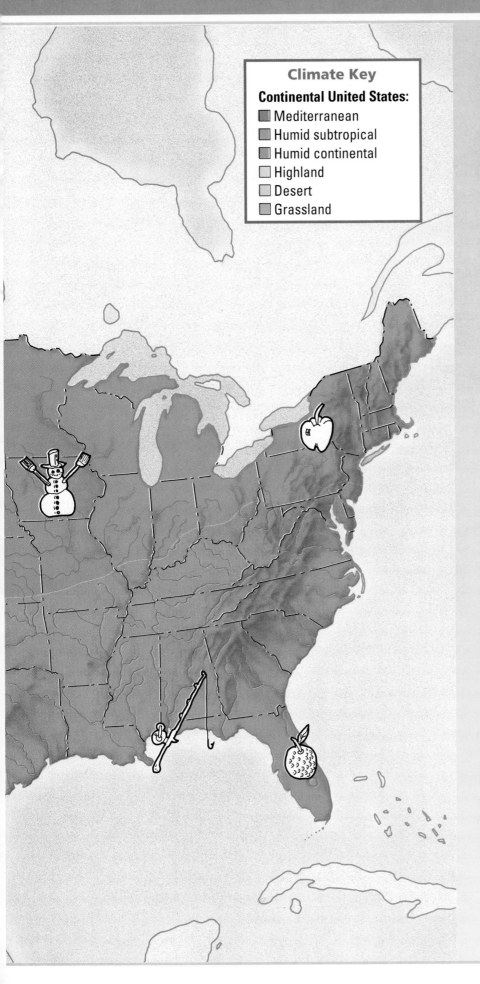

Climate Key

Continental United States:
- Mediterranean
- Humid subtropical
- Humid continental
- Highland
- Desert
- Grassland

Highland climate

These mountain zones have very cold winters and cool summers. The higher the altitude, the cooler the temperatures.

Humid continental climate

This climate has warm summers that are cooler as you go farther north. Winters are very cold with temperatures well below freezing. There is a lot of rain in summer and snow in winter.

Humid subtropical climate

This climate has long, warm and moist summers, followed by mild winters. Freezing temperatures are very rare in the southernmost parts of this area.

Desert climate

This climate receives very little rain during the year. Because there are no clouds to keep the desert insulated, it is usually much hotter during the day than at night.

Warm air

Cooler air

▲ *Cool lake breezes result when warm air over land rises and cooler air over water moves in.*

Bodies of Water and Climates

Let's continue our drive. Where should we go next? The beach, of course! There we can find out how large bodies of water can affect climate.

Whether you are at the ocean or at the Great Lakes shown in the photo above, you probably love beaches. Not only can you jump in the water or bury your friends in the sand, but even on the hottest afternoons, a cool breeze drifts by to cool you. These breezes are no accident!

You learned in Chapter 1 that winds occur when high-pressure air flows toward lower-pressure air. How does that happen at a beach? As the sun rises high into the sky, the land heats up and hot air rises. A low-pressure area forms. But the water in oceans and lakes doesn't heat as quickly as land. The air above them stays cooler. If cool air is next to warm air, what happens? As you can see in the diagram above, the cool air flows toward the warm air, generating a delightful summertime breeze. Unfortunately, these cooling breezes rarely reach more than a few miles inland.

Oceans and lakes give us refreshing breezes, but they do more—a lot more. Large bodies of water heat and cool very slowly. This has a huge effect on the climates of the land nearby.

San Francisco lies only a few miles farther south than Kansas City. Yet, San Francisco enjoys mild summers and winters compared to the hot and cold seasons of Kansas City. Why? It's because the Pacific Ocean just to the west moderates the temperatures of coastal California so that it never gets too hot or too cold. Kansas City doesn't have such a close body of water.

The photo on the right shows another example of water affecting the climates of nearby lands. The Gulf Stream is a current of warm water that flows from the Gulf of Mexico, around the tip of Florida, and all the way through the Atlantic Ocean to England. Without the Gulf Stream, England would experience brutally cold winters. But the Gulf Stream's warm waters keep England's temperatures much milder all through the year.

▼ *The warm Gulf Stream waters travel all the way to England.*

Checkpoint

1. What keeps the American desert from receiving more rainfall?
2. If you had your choice, which climate zone would you prefer to live in?
3. How do bodies of water affect climates?
4. **Take Action!** With an adult, heat a bowl of water and a bowl of sand in an oven for five minutes. Using oven mitts, carefully remove both bowls, and cool for 15 minutes. How do they compare?

Activity

The Heat's On

Which heats up faster in the sun, sand or water? Try this activity to find out.

Picture A

Picture B

Picture C

Gather These Materials

cover goggles
2 aluminum pie pans
2 Celsius thermometers
sand
water

meter stick
2, 100-watt lamps with
  reflectors and stands

Follow This Procedure

1 Make a chart like the one on the next page. Record your observations in your chart.

2 Put on your cover goggles.

3 Fill a pie pan with water. Fill the other pie pan to the same level with sand. (Picture A)

4 Place the pans about one meter apart on a flat surface. Let the pans stand for about 2 hours to be sure the sand and the water are at the same temperature (room temperature).

5 Place a thermometer at the same depth in the middle of each pan. Leave the thermometers for 2 minutes. Then record the temperatures of the water and sand at the 0 in the chart. (Picture B)

6 Carefully place the lamps so that each light is about 40 cm above each pan. Direct each light straight down onto each pan. (Picture C)
CAUTION: The light bulbs in the lamps will be hot.

Predict: *What effect will the lamps have on each pan?*

7 Record the temperature of each pan every 5 minutes for the next 30 minutes.

State Your Conclusions

1. What was the temperature of the sand and water at the beginning?
2. Which heated up faster, sand or water?
3. Using what you have learned so far about weather, how would this difference in absorbing heat affect climate?

Time	Temperature	
	Water	Sand
0		
5		
10		
15		
20		
25		
30		

Let's Experiment

Now that you have compared how fast sand and water heat up, which do you think cools off faster, sand or water? Use what you know about scientific methods to find out.

2.3 *Life in Different Climates*

How is life adapted to different climates?

How are living things able to live in such greatly differing climates? In this lesson we will see how some living things have adapted in ways that help them to find food and water and survive the temperatures in some of the climates of the United States. And the ways they have adapted are as different as apples and oranges.

Warm Oranges

In the southern part of the humid subtropical climate zone, temperatures are almost always above freezing, even in the winter. Because of that, people plant orange trees there. Oranges take a long time from when they flower to when their fruit is ripe. For different types of oranges this can be anywhere from 8 to 20 months. If oranges were planted where temperatures regularly fell well below freezing, the fruit and the growing seeds inside would freeze. The tree itself is so delicate that freezing temperatures could kill the whole tree.

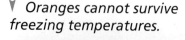
▼ *Oranges cannot survive freezing temperatures.*

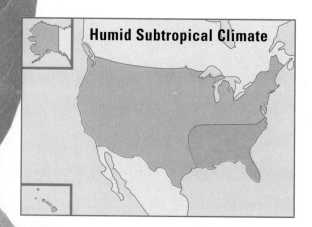
Humid Subtropical Climate

Freezing Apples

Apples are a little tougher. In fact they can't produce fruit and seeds without cold temperatures! You could plant an apple tree next to an orange tree, and all that you would get is a leafy tree—but no apples. Instead, people plant apple trees in climates like the humid continental climate, where there is plenty of rainfall for trees to grow and a period of cold weather. But why would anything require freezing temperatures before it could produce fruit? The reason is because apple trees form their flower buds in the late summer. Then, to survive the cold winter, apple trees, like the one you see in the picture, drop their leaves. The tree goes dormant for the winter. The buds won't open in the spring unless temperatures were freezing during the winter.

In spring, the apple trees' flowers burst open right away, even before their leaves come out. The fruit, with the seeds inside, develops rapidly until ripe. This can take a speedy three to six months, depending on the type of apple. And just as this year's apples are being picked, the tree makes buds again for next year's apple crop.

▼ *Apple trees require a period of cold weather before their buds will open in the spring.*

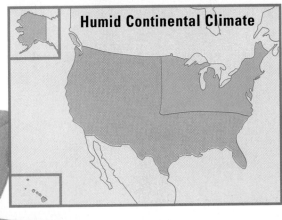

Humid Continental Climate

Trees That Lose Leaves

You've probably noticed that a lot of trees—like apples—lose their leaves in fall and winter. You'll find a lot of trees of this type in the humid continental climate. We call these trees deciduous (di sij′ü əs) trees.

Humid Continental Climate

Deciduous trees have flat leaves that collect lots of sunlight during the long days of spring and summer. But in the fall, they drop their leaves for the winter like the trees in the picture below. This has advantages for the tree. With no leaves, the tree's branches aren't as likely to collect—and be damaged by—heavy snow and ice. In winter, the air is also very dry and water sits frozen on top of the ground where the tree can't use it. Since leaves lose a lot of water, dropping leaves prevents the tree from drying out until spring rains and warmth arrive.

Brightly colored leaves are signals that deciduous trees are preparing for winter. Deciduous trees are great recyclers. Before their leaves fall, the trees take back many of the nutrients (nü′trē ənts) that were in the leaves. Eventually, the leaves fall off. During the winter the nutrients are stored while the tree is dormant. Then in the spring there is a food supply ready to use for the growth of the new leaves.

▲ *Deciduous trees survive dry winter air by losing their leaves.*

Trees That Keep Leaves

Evergreen trees, like the trees in the picture, keep their leaves all through the year. You'll find a lot of evergreens in highland climates where cold weather dominates and the warm season is very brief. Evergreen trees don't have to use energy to grow new leaves every spring like deciduous trees do. They can begin to use the sun's energy to grow right away when warm weather returns. Many evergreens have thin, waxy needles for leaves. Thin needles help prevent water loss and allow cold winter winds to pass without damaging the trees. Snow also slips off the needles easily so branches won't break under heavy snow buildup.

Find the pine cones at the bottom of the page. Many evergreens produce cones like these instead of flowers. There just isn't enough time during the short warm season for the tree to produce flowers and fruit. Instead, seeds develop over a period of two years, safe in their protected cones. This allows evergreen forests to grow in climates where deciduous trees would not be able to produce seeds and survive.

▼ *Evergreen trees have thin needles that help them keep their moisture through dry, winter temperatures.*

Highland Climate

Great Grasslands

Grassland climates receive enough rainfall to support grasses, but not enough for trees to grow. They are scorched by the heat of the summer, and frozen by the howling winds and snowstorms of the winter. Since prairies are mostly flat, nothing stops the winds which race across them. Plants and animals find little shelter above ground. For plants, grazing animals like buffalo and antelope also pose a constant threat. Yet, communities in grasslands thrive. How?

With no mountains or trees to protect them, grasses have adapted to another kind of shelter—the soil. Most of a grass plant grows underground in the roots. The roots spread out in all directions and absorb water and nutrients. The roots also store large amounts of energy for growth. Roots can also extend down deep into the soil, providing a firm anchor for the plant and allowing it to tap deeper water and nutrients.

▼ Only a small part of a grass plant is visible above the ground.

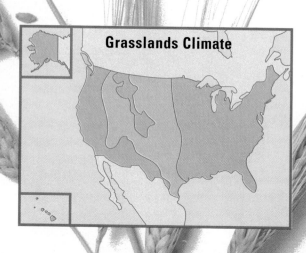

Grasslands Climate

Unlike other plants, grasses grow from their bases, not their tips. That's why grazing animals, like buffalo, can snip off a grass blade without harming the plant. It's also why you can mow your lawn without killing it. Grasses quickly recover from the frequent lightning fires which scorch the prairie. The fires burn the grass blades, but leave the roots unharmed. When new grass blades shoot skyward, their slender forms bend with the wind instead of being torn away by it. The thin shape of grass leaves also keeps them from losing too much water.

Animals like prairie dogs have also found ways to thrive on the plains. Like grasses, prairie dogs find shelter from weather, fire, and predators underground. Prairie dogs dig extensive burrows and live together as a group, or family. Hundreds live together in prairie dog towns and their sharp eyesight helps them alert each other to danger. In the spring, summer, and fall, they eat grasses, mostly in the evenings and mornings when the air is cool.

Into The Field

What adaptations help an organisim survive?
Select a plant or animal that thrives where you live. List the adaptations it has that help it survive.

Checkpoint

1. What is one reason oranges shouldn't freeze?
2. What advantage do apples have by making buds in the fall?
3. What is a benefit of losing leaves in the fall?
4. How can evergreens survive cold, snowy winters without losing their leaves?
5. Could grasses survive if they grew from their tips instead of their bases? Explain.
6. **Take Action!** List the names of trees growing where you live. Place them into two groups: deciduous or evergreens.

Clarifying Generalizations

Sometimes you read a generalization that is hard to explain. Specific examples may clarify the generalization. Finding examples that fit the generalization can help you explain it more clearly.

Thinking It Through

Suppose you want to clarify what climate you would expect in a given place. You see these generalizations:

1. The closer to the Equator you get, the warmer the climate will probably be.

2. The higher the altitude, the cooler the climate will probably be.

3. Areas near large bodies of water tend to have a more moderate climate.

Here are facts about Great Britain:

a. It is 5000 kilometers north of the Equator. This is farther north of the Equator than most of the United States.

b. It has no high mountains.

c. It is an island in a sea.

From statement a, you might expect Great Britain to be cold. From b, you might expect it to be warmer than a country with high mountains. From c, you might expect it to have a moderate climate. Actually, Great Britain has a mild climate, even though it is so far north.

Your Turn

Read the descriptions below of areas of Morocco, in northern Africa. Which descriptions match the numbered generalizations you read?

A. Morocco borders the Mediterranean Sea. Africa lies on the Equator but Morocco's coastal climate is mild.

B. The Atlas Mountains in Morocco have cold, snowy winters.

C. Part of Morocco is in the Sahara Desert. Temperatures there can reach a sizzling 54°C.

Chapter Review

Thinking Back

1. Why do different parts of Earth point toward the sun during the year?
2. What is the difference between the winter solstice and the summer solstice?
3. What are the weather conditions that describe a **climate**?
4. Why is the temperature cool at high **altitudes**?
5. How do mountains affect a climate?
6. What are two things that vary in different climates?
7. What is the Gulf Stream and how does it affect winter temperature?
8. What climatic conditions affect the ability of orange or apple trees to grow in an area?
9. How have prairie dogs adapted to living in grassland climates?

Connecting Ideas

1. Copy the concept map. Use the terms at the right to complete the map about different climates.

polar   tropical
equator   United States

A. **climate**

B. _____
C. _____
D. **temperate**

E. **North Pole**
F. _____
G. _____

2. Write a sentence or two about the ideas in this concept map.

Gathering Evidence

1. In the Activity on page 34, how did you know that different areas would have different climates?
2. In the Activity on page 42, how did you know which heated up faster, sand or water?

Doing Science!

1. *Make a display* of a climate zone. Include high and low temperatures, precipitation, and land or water features that affect the climate.
2. *Design an activity* to show how direct and indirect light rays affect heat produced on a surface.

Predicting Weather

Discover Activity

Are wind and weather related?

Make a simple wind vane like the one shown here. Make sure the arrow can spin freely. Use a compass to position the wind vane so that the "N" points north. Measure and record the wind direction and the weather for two weeks.

For Discussion

1. *Where is the ideal place to put a wind vane?*
2. *Do you see a connection between the weather and the wind direction?*

3.1 Weather Clues Everywhere

▶ What can I tell about the weather?

It's Saturday. You and your friends have big plans to spend the day outside together. Then, you look out the window. Groan! It's raining! What can you do? It would be great if you could make the weather whatever you wanted it to be. Every Saturday could be warm and sunny, if that's what you wanted.

Unfortunately, you can't do much about controlling the weather. But you can prepare for it. Right now you can hear tomorrow's forecast on the radio or TV or read the paper. Those forecasts are based on observations and collecting lots of information using many different instruments. But, you can make observations and collect information too so that you will understand your weather better.

Look around and start asking yourself questions—lots of them! What season is it? Which way is north, south, east, or west? From which direction does the wind blow? Does the wind shift during a storm? Don't forget to look up. What kind of clouds do you see? Learn about clouds and how to find other weather clues on the following pages.

▼ If the arrow on a wind vane points north, the wind is blowing from the north.

Reading Clouds

Clouds come in many shapes and varieties. Recognizing their shapes can tell you a lot about what kind of weather they bring.

Cirrus clouds

Cirrus clouds form high in the sky where it is very cold. They are mostly ice crystals, which gives them a wispy, featherlike look. You can see them floating in patches on clear, sunny, dry days. Cirrus clouds can be a signal that a warm front is on the way.

Stratus Clouds

Stratus means layer. These low, gray clouds cover the sky like sheets. They can be thick enough that they block out most of the sunlight. Stratus clouds often follow cirrus clouds. If they do, you can look for light, steady rain or snow flurries to arrive soon.

Cirrus
- high clouds
- form in patches
- made mostly of ice crystals
- sunny, dry weather

Stratus
- low, gray clouds
- form in layers
- bring continuous rain or snow that can last for days

Cumulus
- fluffy, white clouds
- form in heaps
- bring sunny weather with no rain

Cumulonimbus
- very tall clouds
- form in heaps
- dark bottoms
- bring heavy storms

Cumulus clouds

Cumulus means heap, which is just what these clouds look like! Fair weather cumulus clouds are bright white, fluffy, low clouds with flat bottoms and rounded tops. They float in blue skies in small groups and never produce rain.

Cumulonimbus clouds

Cumulonimbus clouds can grow rapidly. They usually develop on hot summer afternoons or along a cold front. They look like tall, towering cumulus clouds with low, dark gray bottoms. The bottoms are low and dark gray because light can't get through them. The word nimbus means shower and there's a good chance that a heavy shower or even a thunderstorm will follow soon. If the clouds are particularly dark and dense, a tornado could form. Airplanes stay away from these cumulonimbus clouds because of the rapidly moving air within them.

Into The Field

Will tomorrow's weather forecast be correct in your area? *Look at a weather map and the weather prediction printed in today's newspaper. Tomorrow, record if the prediction was correct.*

▼ An easy way to keep track of weather changes is to record them on a chart.

Know Your Clues

People like farmers and sailors spend a lot of time outside. They are usually pretty good at recognizing weather clues. They use these clues to help predict the weather and plan their activities. How do they find these weather clues? The weather clues are all around. It's not too hard for you to find weather clues and learn about the weather patterns where you live.

One of the most important is wind direction. Use the wind vane you made in the Discover Activity to help you tell wind direction. Or, look at how grass is bending or which way flags are blowing.

Once you know wind direction, the Beaufort Scale, like the one on the right, can help you estimate wind speed. Are flags extended all the way out? If so, you have a moderate gale. Checking such conditions with the Beaufort Scale can tell you if you've got a real storm on the way.

Your body can tell you a lot, too. Have you noticed a change in the air temperature? Damp skin or a dry throat can tell you a lot about humidity. The previous pages told you what kind of clouds go with what kind of weather, so be sure to look at the sky.

ime	Temperature	Cloud Description	Type of precipitation
	10°C	Heavy, dark cumulus	Heavy rain
	2°C	Stratus	Light snow
	5°C	None	None
5/ 00 P.M.	8°C	High, cirrus	None

erature	Sky Condition
10°C	Very Cloudy
2°C	Cloudy
°C	Sunny
	Partly cloudy

If a thunderstorm is rumbling outside, you can tell how close it is by watching lightning. When you see a flash, count how many seconds it takes until you hear thunder. Divide the number of seconds by three. The answer will tell you how many kilometers away the lightning struck.

Of course, don't forget to consult weather maps in your local newspaper. Since weather in most of the United States generally moves east, pay special attention to the storms, fronts, and pressure systems to the west.

A good way of following weather changes is to keep records of the weather. Like the boy on page 56, make a chart to record information about the weather. Each day, note the clues you've read about in this lesson. Be sure to record your observations at the same time each day. You might be surprised how quickly you begin to notice the weather patterns of your area. Then, you'll be your own weather expert!

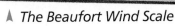

1. Wind does not move flag.
2. Smoke drifts with wind.
3. Leaves and twigs move.
4. Small branches move.
5. Small trees sway.
6. Flag totally extended.
7. Whole trees in motion.
8. Twigs break off trees.
9. Roofs damaged.
10. Trees uprooted.
11. Buildings damaged.
12. Much destruction.

Checkpoint

1. Would you expect rain from a dark layer of cumulonimbus clouds?
2. List four important things to keep track of in your weather journal.
3. Take Action! Use a compass to find out which directions are north, south, east, and west. Record some landmarks where you live that will help you remember the directions.

Activity

Taking the Temperature: Collecting Data

How can you measure temperature accurately? Try this activity to find out how to obtain and compare temperatures.

Picture A

Picture B

Picture C

Gather These Materials

cover goggles

paper

pencil

Celsius thermometer

Follow This Procedure

1 Make a chart like the one on the next page. Record your observations in your chart.

2 Put on your cover goggles.

3 Note the first level on the chart. Choose an exact location at that level (such as the floor level under your desk). Describe this exact location on your chart. (Picture A)

4 Go to the first exact location with the thermometer. Hold the thermometer steady at that spot for 2 minutes. Record the temperature at the end of the 2 minutes on your chart.

Predict: *What kinds of factors might affect the temperature at a particular location?*

5 Record on your chart any factors that might affect the temperature at your first exact location, such as heat from sunlight or a draft from a vent or window.

6 Repeat steps 3, 4, and 5 for each of the other levels on your chart. (Pictures B and C)

Record Your Results

Level	Exact location	°C	Factors of location
Floor level			
Desk top			
Near ceiling			
Corner of room			
Middle of room			
Near window			

State Your Conclusions

1. Which exact location had the coolest temperature? Why do you think it was coolest there?

2. Which exact location had the warmest temperature? Why do you think it was warmest there?

3. Compare your temperature data with those of your classmates. Give 2 reasons why there might be differences in temperature readings for the same exact locations.

Let's Experiment

How important is it to take and record air pressure readings in the same place each day? Use what you know about scientific methods to find out.

3.2 Getting Weather Information

▲ *This early thermometer measures temperature by how high the colored balls in the tubes of liquid move.*

▶ *This early hygrometer measures humidity. When the paper strip running up to the dial shrinks or stretches, it moves the needle on the dial.*

How do meteorologists get their information?

For hundreds of years people had little warning when a hurricane was about to hit. Many lives were lost because there was no time to prepare. Today, **meteorologists** (mē′ tē ə rol′ ə jists)—people who study weather—can tell people where and when a hurricane is expected. But, how do they get this life-saving information?

Simple Weather Tools

The surrounding photos show some of the simpler—and older—instruments that have been used by meteorologists for hundreds of years. Tools like these are still being used today. Meteorologists measure air pressure with a barometer. Scientists and seamen began using barometers in the 1600s. If you did the activity on page 18 you made one kind of barometer. Another kind of barometer contains a metal box with some of the air removed. A spring inside the box connects to a pointer. As air pressure gets higher, it squeezes the box. The box changes shape forcing the pointer to move to a higher number. When pressure drops, the box expands and the pointer moves to a lower number.

Wind vanes measure wind direction and anemometers measure wind speed. Anemometers usually consist of three or four cups which spin around as they catch the wind. As the wind moves faster, the anemometer spins faster.

One of the simplest tools used to study weather is the rain gauge. If you made the rain gauge on page 8, then you know how simple rain gauges are. After a storm, measure the depth of the water in the container. Is the reading from your rain gauge the same as the TV weatherperson's? It may not be. The amount of rainfall can even be different on opposite sides of the same street!

You probably know that thermometers measure temperature. Common thermometers are just sealed glass tubes. They are usually filled with mercury or alcohol. When the temperature rises, the liquid inside expands and moves up the tube.

▼ Barometers and anemometers are used by meteorologists in weather prediction.

Remember the humid air in Chapter 1 that made you feel so uncomfortable? Hygrometers (hī grom′ ə tərz) are used to measure that humidity. A simple hygrometer consists of a human hair which is attached to a pointer. The hair changes length depending on the amount of water vapor in the air. When the air is humid, the hair absorbs water vapor and expands. When the air is dry, the hair becomes shorter.

Modern Instruments

Meteorologists still find the simple tools you just read about very useful. And, now they also have more advanced tools to study weather.

On TV you've probably seen satellite photos of Earth like the one on the right. Satellites send images of Earth and its atmosphere down to weather centers. Meteorologists can look at these images to see how storms and fronts are moving. This helps them predict weather in hard to reach places where other measurements can't be taken.

Very large weather balloons carry thermometers, barometers, and hygrometers into the sky to measure weather conditions far above the earth's surface. These instruments transmit information back to the ground by radio.

Radar reports are very important, too. Radar sends out radio waves. When these waves strike any form of precipitation, they bounce back. By measuring the time the radio waves take to return, radar can pinpoint an object's distance and location. Doppler radar is a newer, slightly different form of radar. Doppler radar can perform like normal radar, but it also detects wind direction and speed inside clouds.

▼ Small weather balloons collect data about the direction of winds.

▲ Instruments that measure temperature and air pressure are protected from the weather.

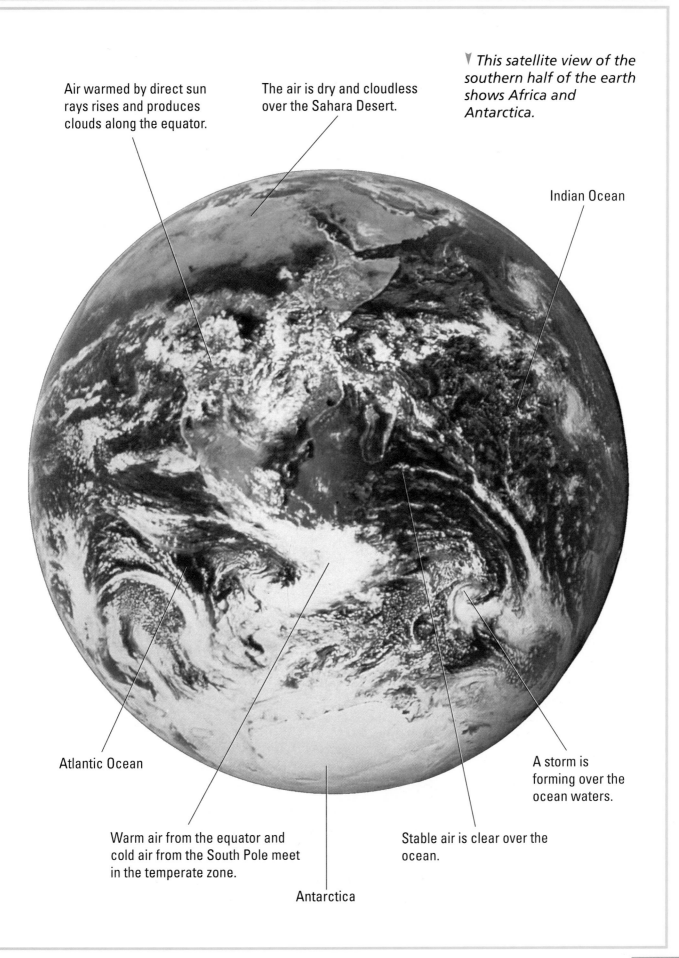

Air warmed by direct sun rays rises and produces clouds along the equator.

The air is dry and cloudless over the Sahara Desert.

▼ *This satellite view of the southern half of the earth shows Africa and Antarctica.*

Indian Ocean

Atlantic Ocean

Warm air from the equator and cold air from the South Pole meet in the temperate zone.

Antarctica

Stable air is clear over the ocean.

A storm is forming over the ocean waters.

Tying It Together

Having a bunch of facts by themselves really doesn't help anyone. Fortunately, weather facts are put to good use—and that's the job of the National Weather Service, headquartered in Washington, D.C.

The National Weather Service puts all these facts together by computer to make weather maps. The weather maps are sent to the 51 Weather Service Forecast Offices (WSFO) around the United States. Find the WSFO for your area on the map on page 65. Next, each WSFO sends the information out to local Weather Service Offices (WSO) nearby.

Each WSO gathers data from its local area. For example, find the WSO in Cincinnati. Each hour it collects temperatures and other readings from nearby places. Then the Cincinnati WSO, like other WSOs, sends out weather forecasts for its local area. All this reaches you when you receive a weather report.

➤ The country's weather information is sent from the National Weather Service to Weather Service Forecast Offices, then to Weather Service Offices, and finally to you.

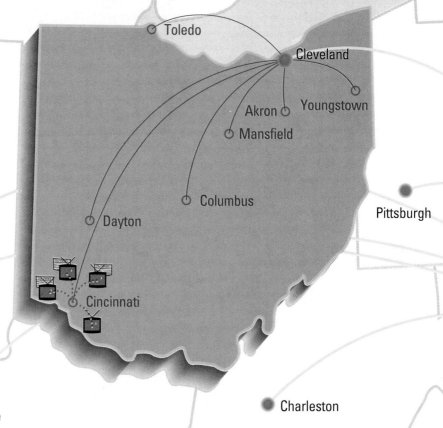

Toledo

Cleveland

Youngstown

Akron

Mansfield

Columbus

Pittsburgh

Dayton

Indianapolis

Cincinnati

Louisville

Charleston

Computers come in handy again when each WSO sends all its local information back to the National Weather Service headquarters. Computers add this information to data from all over the world. Larger weather patterns can then be determined. In addition, computers store many years of weather history. They can quickly compare current weather data to past weather patterns. Because of the use of computers, meteorologists have been able to improve the accuracy of their forecasts.

The National Weather Service issues its forecasts complete with weather maps every few hours. In addition to the computers used for the WSFOs, these forecasts are sent over a special communication line called the National Oceanic and Atmospheric Administration (NOAA) Family of Services. A network of National Weather Service radio stations also broadcasts local forecasts 24 hours a day all over the country. When dangerous weather is developing, emergency warnings are broadcast right away. Some newspapers and television stations get their information directly from the NOAA Family of Services and NOAA Weather Radio.

Portland

Boston

New York

Philadelphia

Washington, D.C.

·WSFO Offices

About 5000 people work for the National Weather Service and their work is extremely important. Predicting storms can save many lives. It also saves billions of dollars for farmers and construction companies. Think of how dangerous flying would be without weather information!

While forecasts have steadily improved over the years, other improvements are on the way. Meteorologists will use computers even more for studying and predicting weather in the future. The computers will perform tasks that people must now do by hand, so that forecasts are generated more quickly. Better satellites, which can actually determine temperatures within storms, will also be launched into space. The National Weather Service will install additional Doppler radar systems to improve weather monitoring.

All of these developments will lead to faster and better forecasts. If you're still not convinced that such forecasts are necessary, read on.

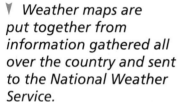

▼ *Weather maps are put together from information gathered all over the country and sent to the National Weather Service.*

Hurricane Watch!

What has wild winds, strong enough to drive a board right through a tree? What can twist and break thick steel cables with ease? What can blow buildings down and bring tons of water in from the sea in minutes? No, it's not Superman, but it is a super storm. The answer is a hurricane—the most destructive storm in the world.

Hurricane season generally lasts between June and November along the Atlantic and Gulf coasts of the United States. This is the time of year when the National Hurricane Center in Miami watches the warming ocean waters carefully for hurricanes.

The National Hurricane Center is responsible for finding out where hurricanes are beginning to develop. They look for groups of heavy cumulus clouds with the help of satellite photos. Many of the cloud groups simply disappear. But some grow larger, and meteorologists watch them closely.

You can see in the satellite photos on the right, that growing storms usually have a swirling shape. The center of the swirl is the storm's eye. Inside the eye, it is calm and cloud free.

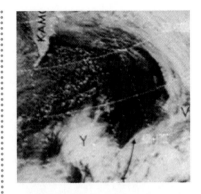

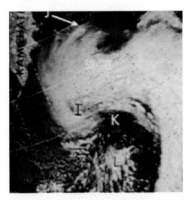

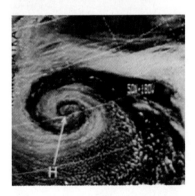

▲ As the storm grows, the winds get stronger. The storm is officially called a hurricane when its winds reach 121 kph.

As a hurricane moves near land, it is watched carefully so that its path can be predicted.

Tremendous, powerful winds whirl around the eye. These are the most destructive winds in the hurricane. These winds are found in the eye wall—a bank of clouds right around the eye. The winds in the eye wall can reach up to 360 kilometers per hour. Along with these winds there are deep cumulonimbus clouds and torrential rains.

As long as the hurricane is over warm water it can continue to grow. As it grows, the entire hurricane moves in a wide, curving path thousands of kilometers over the water. Trace the path of the hurricane as it moves over the water in the illustration on this page.

As meteorologists see the storm building, they get as much information about it as possible. Radar and weather stations provide the National Hurricane Center with some data, but not enough. Specially trained Air Force crews called the Hurricane Hunters fly into the center of hurricanes. Inside the hurricane, they measure wind speed, temperature, humidity, and pressure. They radio this information back to shore. What happens to this information?

Information from the Hurricane Hunters is put into computers that make models of the hurricane. Predictions of a hurricane's strength and direction are based on these computer models. The computers compare this hurricane to past hurricane behavior. Hurricanes like the one in the illustration can—and often do—suddenly change direction. But computer models tell meteorologists what the hurricane's path is most likely to be.

New York City

Washington D.C.

Miami

When a coastal area appears to be in a hurricane's path within the next 24 to 36 hours, the National Hurricane Center issues a Hurricane Watch. Local weather officials instruct people to prepare for the storm by collecting extra supplies like candles, batteries for radios and flashlights, bottled water, and canned food.

The Hurricane Center issues a Hurricane Warning when it expects a hurricane to reach land within 24 hours. This warning means that lives are in danger and people are asked to evacuate (i vak′ yü āt) their homes. These warnings allow people to prepare and have saved thousands of lives.

To improve forecasting in the future, hurricane trackers will rely on a new generation of satellites, radar, and computer models. Still, hurricane forecasting will never be a sure thing and hurricanes will always be dangerous. In 1988, Hurricane Gilbert proved that. Gilbert was the most powerful hurricane in history. Its winds seemed to be over 320 kilometers per hour, killing hundreds of people and devastating cities from Jamaica to Mexico. Storms like Gilbert remind us that while we can't control the weather, we need to keep a watchful eye on it.

Checkpoint

1. Name three simple tools for studying weather.
2. What can Doppler radar do that regular radar can't?
3. How have computers been important in weather forecasting?
4. What signs show that a hurricane is developing?
5. **Take Action!** Write a letter to your favorite TV meteorologist. Find out where the weather information comes from.

How fast are hurricanes?

Hurricanes that may hit the United States start to form in the warm waters of the Gulf of Mexico, the Atlantic Ocean, or the Pacific Ocean. The first hurricane of the season gets a name that begins with A, the second with B, and so on. In the center of the hurricane is the eye. The eye is clear and very calm, especially compared to the whirling winds that surround it. The strongest winds and heaviest rains are in the area called the eye wall. The graph shows the top wind speeds for three hurricanes.

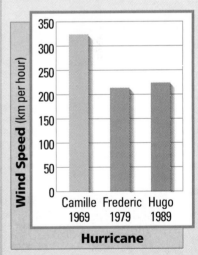

What Did You Find Out?
1. *Which hurricane winds were strongest?*
2. *How much greater were the winds of Frederic than Hugo?*
3. *What is the wind speed total of all three?*

Activity

Wet Bulb, Dry Bulb: Calculating Today's Humidity

How can you determine what the humidity is today? Try this activity to find out.

Picture A

Gather These Materials

cover goggles
2 identical Celsius
  thermometers
strip of gauze, 15-20 cm
2 rubber bands
thread

empty milk carton with
  small hole in the
  middle of one side
water
file card

Follow This Procedure

1 Make a chart like the one on the next page. Record your observations in your chart.

2 Put on your cover goggles.

3 The humidity report you hear on the weather news is called relative humidity. Relative humidity compares the amount of water vapor in the air to the amount of water vapor the air could hold at the same temperature if it was saturated.

4 Wrap the gauze strip around the bulb of one thermometer and tie it on with the thread. Leave a tail of gauze about 5 cm long. (Picture A)

5 Use rubber bands to attach the thermometers to the side of the milk carton with the hole. Push the gauze tail through the hole. (Picture B)

6 Add water to the carton to just below the hole. Be sure the gauze tail extends into the water.

Picture B

Picture C

7 Wait for the gauze to become water soaked. You now have a wet bulb thermometer.

8 Fan the wet bulb thermometer with a file card until the temperature stops going down. (Picture C) Record the temperature on each thermometer.

	Wet bulb	Dry bulb	Difference	Relative humidity %
Morning				
Afternoon				
Evening				

Predict: *Will the 2 bulbs show temperature differences at other times of the day?*

9 Take your thermometers outdoors. Repeat steps 7 and 8 at the other times listed in your chart.

10 Use the Relative Humidity Table in the picture to calculate the humidity at each time of day that you measured. Find the number on the left closest to your dry bulb reading. Then find the number along the top closest to the temperature difference between the 2 thermometers.

11 Follow the dry bulb row across until it meets your temperature difference column. Record this number in your chart.

State Your Conclusions

1. How do the wet bulb thermometer readings vary from the dry bulb readings?
2. How did the humidity at different times of the day compare?

Let's Experiment

Based on what you know, does the humidity change every day? Use what you know about scientific methods to find out.

Relative Humidity Table (in percent)

Dry bulb	Difference between wet and dry, bulb readings in Celsius degrees									
°C	1	2	3	4	5	6	7	8	9	10
18	91	82	73	65	57	49	41	34	27	20
19	91	82	74	65	58	50	43	36	29	22
20	91	83	74	67	59	53	46	39	32	26
21	91	83	75	67	60	53	46	39	32	26
22	92	83	76	68	61	54	47	40	34	28
23	92	84	76	69	62	55	48	42	36	30
24	92	84	77	69	62	56	49	43	37	31
25	92	84	77	70	63	57	50	44	39	33

Organizing Weather Data

When you make an important decision, you usually use more than one piece of data. It may help to organize the data into an easy-to-read form. Here are some ways to show data:

- Bar graphs
- Charts
- Circle graphs
- Line graphs
- Maps
- Tables

Thinking It Through

Suppose your family is thinking of moving to a new city in a different state. You are going to choose between three cities—Denver, Colorado; San Diego, California; and Wilmington, Delaware. Each person is gathering information about the move. Since your family loves the outdoors, your job is to show the number of clear, cloudy, rainy, and snowy days in the three cities. One way to show the different types of days is to put them into a table.

The advantage of a table is that you can read and compare each number for all three cities at one time. A disadvantage is that it's harder to see the difference at a glance.

A bar graph might be a clearer way to present how the numbers for each city compare to each other in general. Look at the bar graph for clear days.

You can quickly see how the weather stacks up in each city. For instance, you can see that San Diego has about twice as many clear days each year as Wilmington does.

A disadvantage of using bar graphs to show this data is that it is hard to show all four types of weather for all three cities in one graph. You probably would have to make four graphs, one for each type of day.

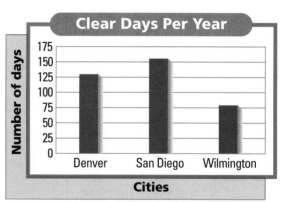

Your Turn

Choose one of the four types of days —clear, cloudy, rainy, or snowy—and find data for where you live. Show the data at least two ways. You may use the way shown on this page or you may choose other ways. Explain which method you prefer and why.

Chapter Review

Thinking Back

1. What weather is associated with the four different cloud types?
2. What are some ways to tell wind direction?
3. How can you tell if a thunderstorm is moving toward or away from you?
4. How do **meteorologists** save lives?
5. How is wind direction identified?

6. How does a weather balloon help meteorologists study the weather?
7. How do satellites provide meteorologists with information about weather?
8. What is the job of the National Weather Service?
9. Why is the job of the National Hurricane Center so important?

Connecting Ideas

1. Copy the concept map. Use the terms at the right to complete the map about the National Weather Service.

**weather maps   local forecast
national information**

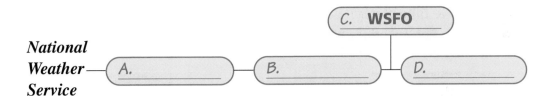

2. Write a sentence or two about the ideas in the concept map.

Gathering Evidence

1. In the Activity on page 58, how did you know which areas of your room were the warmest and coolest?
2. In the Activity on page 70, how did you find out the relative humidity for a given time?

Doing Science!

1. **Design a plan** to show weather patterns developing in your area.
2. **Design an activity** that tracks the local weather for a week. What different elements should you record?

When Should We Plant?

Many people grow flowers and vegetables in their own gardens or in community gardens. Flowers make an area beautiful. They also provide food for bees, butterflies, hummingbirds, and other animals. Vegetables provide food for people and other animals.

The climate in different parts of the country affects when to plant.

Needs and Goals
Vegetable seeds need to be planted early enough so they have time to germinate, grow, and produce the vegetables you eat.

But they can't be planted so early that a frost or freezing temperatures will kill or damage the young plants.

Not all vegetables can be planted at the same time. Some plants are not harmed by freezing temperatures. Other plants can survive very cold but not freezing temperatures. Still other plants are harmed by cool temperatures.

Gathering Information
People in different climates can plant many kinds of vegetables in gardens.

Planting Times

Vegetables	Area A	Area B	Area C	Area D
Beans	April–August	April–June	May–June	May–June
Broccoli	July–October	February–March	March–April	April–May
Carrots	January–December	January–March	March–June	April–June
Celery	July–September	March–May	April–June	March–June
Collards	January–March	February–May	March–June	April–June
Corn	April–June	March–June	May–July	May–July
Cucumbers	April–June	April–June	April–June	May–June
Lettuce	January–December	August–May	March–June	April–June
Okra	April–June	April–June	April–June	May–June
Onions	December–March	December–April	February–May	March–June
Potatoes	September–March	January–March	March–June	April–June
Spinach	January–March	February–October	March–September	April–August

But everyone can't plant vegetables at the same time. The climates in different parts of the country affect when to plant. The key to planting is based on when the last spring frost usually occurs. The map shows different planting times for different areas in the United States. Find out which area on the map has a climate similar to yours.

Possible Alternatives

There are many different kinds of vegetables that people like to plant in their gardens. The table lists some of

these vegetables. Notice that the table also lists when to plant each of them in the different areas. The backs of seed packages also provide information about when to plant.

Evaluating Alternatives

Use the map and table to help you. Think about what vegetables you like to eat. When would you need to plant these vegetables in your area? Is this a time you want to plant your garden?

Making the Best Choice

Choose vegetables that you or someone else in your family likes to eat. Then make sure you can plant these vegetables when they need to be planted. You also can plant seeds indoors earlier in the year and then plant the young plants outdoors at the correct time.

Planting Areas

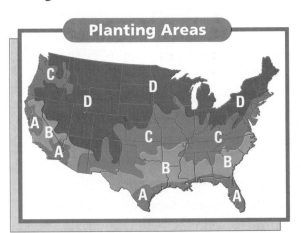

Now You Do It

1. **On Your Own** In your school or local library, look up books on gardening and on vegetable growing. Find some other flowers or vegetables that you would like to grow. When would be a good time to plant them in your area?

2. **Critical Thinking** Many gardeners today use a method called companion planting. They plant flowers and vegetables next to other plants that drive away certain pests. How might companion planting be a better choice than store-bought insect sprays or other pesticides?

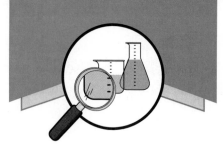

Clouds Make the Weather

Dr. Steve Chin

Occupation: Atmospheric scientist
Hobbies: Volleyball, basketball
Plans for the future: "One day we may be able to control the weather."

The wind roared across the little island, ripping trees from the ground. Clouds darkened the sky as rain pounded the roof. And when it was all over, the people were left with damaged homes, tangled power lines, and flooded streets. Another hurricane had hit. Steve Chin wanted to do something about the hurricanes. How could he keep his home and family safe? He was only a child then. Now Steve Chin is an atmospheric scientist. He studies long-range weather predictions.

How do you study the weather?
"Our main tool is the supercomputer. First we take measurements of cloud systems. Then we use these numbers to make computer models of the clouds. Radar imaging, like the weather maps you see on TV, lets us check whether or not our computer models are correct. Then we can use the computer to find out more information about the clouds— how they move, how much energy they have, and how much moisture they hold. Once we have this information, we can predict how different types of clouds will affect the weather."

How do clouds affect weather?
"So far, scientists have just asked how clouds in general affect the weather. But not all clouds are the same. Think of the weather in Oklahoma. Cloud systems there bring tornadoes and lightning along with their severe storms. Storms in the tropics are different. There you would find tropical storms like the hurricanes that hit Taiwan. One of the main reasons that weather forecasting is not more accurate is that we have not been able to take into account the differences in these types of cloud systems. Our computer models will allow us to make better forecasts."

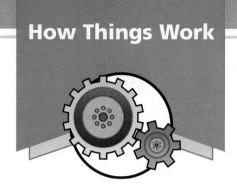

Microbursts and Airplanes

A microburst is a sudden downward blast of air that often happens during storms. When the air reaches the ground, it spreads out in all directions. A microburst can be dangerous for an airplane during takeoff or landing.

1 The microburst rushes down from a rain cloud. This column of wind is about 2 kilometers across and lasts several minutes.

4 As the plane leaves the microburst, winds greatly reduce its airspeed. The pilot pulls the nose up to avoid a crash.

2 A plane enters the microburst and meets the wind head-on. The wind gives the plane greater airspeed and lift, making it climb.

3 Near the center of the microburst, wind pushes the plane down. The pilot pulls the nose up to climb higher.

Find Out On Your Own

Look in books to find out how microbursts can be seen on radar. What instruments help pilots avoid microbursts? Make a poster showing how these instruments work.

Module Review

Making Connections

Systems and Interactions

1. Explain how the meeting of different air masses affects weather.

2. How does the climate of an area affect its plant life?

3. Explain how meteorologists work together to develop national forecasts.

Patterns of Change

4. Why are some air masses warm and others cold, some humid and some dry?

Using What I Learned

Comparing

1. Explain the difference between warm and cold air masses.

2. Explain the difference between deciduous and evergreen trees.

Predicting

3. What would you want to know about an area you were about to visit so that you could take appropriate clothes?

Observing

4. What would be the season in the northern and southern hemispheres, according to the diagram?

Communicating

5. Write a paragraph that compares the weather in two different parts of the world on the same day. Be sure to include factors that will show why the weather in these two places is different.

Ordering

6. From north to south, what is the correct order of the climatic zones: north temperate, south temperate, tropical, north polar, south polar.

Categorizing

7. Name two characteristics of hurricanes.

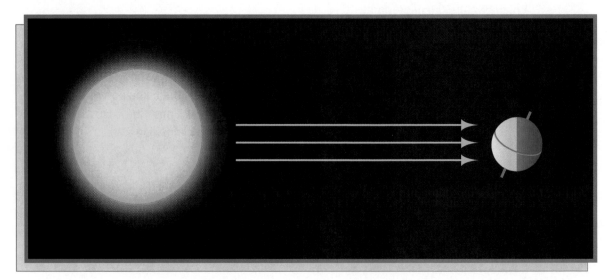

Applying What I Learned

Action Project

Contact your local news station to find out how they measure different elements of the weather and what they do with their information.

Drawing

Draw a picture that shows how the tilt of Earth as it orbits the sun affects the seasons where you live.

Performance Task

Use a protractor, table tennis ball, string, and wooden stick to make a tool that measures wind speed.

Science Theater

Prepare a skit that shows how a local weather person uses forecasting tools to predict your local weather.

Exhibitions

Make a poster or bulletin board showing how the climate varies in different parts of the United States.

What If

What if you were invited to join the crew of a ship going across the ocean? What information would you need to predict the weather before you left?

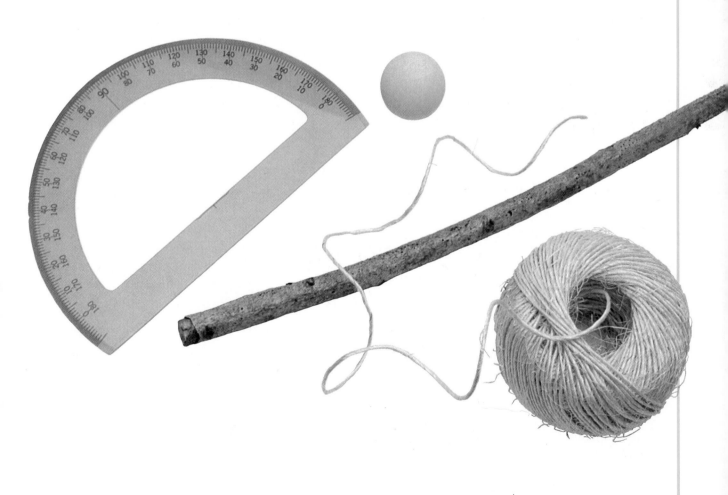

Rainforests

Rainforests

To our smoky and crowded earth, rainforests offer a breath of fresh air. But now the rainforests are disappearing, along with millions of living things that live there. In this module, you'll find out why the rainforests are vanishing and what you can do about it.

CHAPTER 3 Protecting Rainforests

Can the rainforests be saved?

Around the world, adults and children are working together in a race against time.

Life in a Rainforest

Why is it hot at the equator?

Tape a paper cylinder to the lens of a flashlight. While one student holds a globe, stand about two feet back and shine the flashlight directly at the globe. What part of the globe gets the most light? Have the student holding the globe walk around you, copying the revolution of the earth around the sun. Follow the globe with your flashlight.

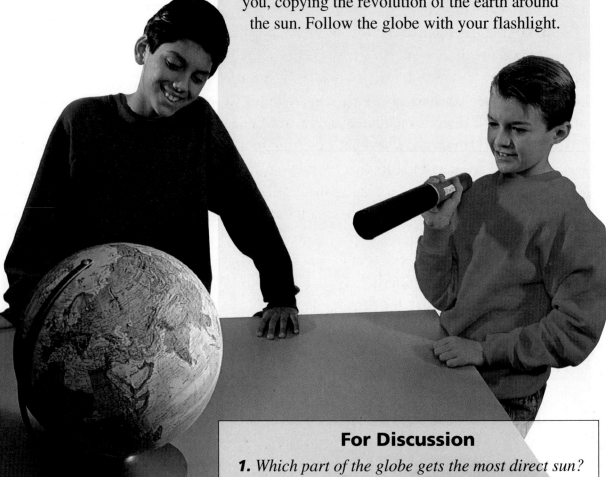

For Discussion

1. Which part of the globe gets the most direct sun?
2. Why is it so hot at the equator all year?

Wet, Hot, and Green

What is the strangest forest in the world?

The air is still and damp. The warm earth smells rich and moist under your feet. Soggy leaves muffle your movements, so you step quietly through the huge forest.

It's dim in this forest, but it's surprisingly easy to walk around. The tallest trees grow so high, you can barely see their tops 30 or 40 meters above your head. The branches of these trees nearly touch one another, all but blocking out the sun. Down here on the forest floor, it's shady. Only scattered plants and smaller trees can survive.

Soon your eyes adjust to the low light. Everywhere you look, you see green—vines, ferns, palms, like the plants in the pictures. Suddenly, you spot flashes of color. Look—an electric blue butterfly and a bird that looks like a leaf! Now, listen closely, and you can hear the sounds of the forest. A monkey howls high in the treetops above. A mosquito buzzes around your ear. When darkness falls, you hear frogs whose calls are sometimes so noisy that you can't hear someone talking right next to you!

Look down. Small leaf bits seem to be walking along the ground! You pick up a leaf and turn it over, only to find an ant carrying the leaf to unknown places. Where are you? Where in the world does this strange forest grow?

▼ *The earth's rainforests are home to thousands of interesting creatures such as the red-eyed leaf frog.*

Tropical Rainforests

Tropical Rainforests Tropic Zone

On the Equator

The strange forest you're visiting is a tropical **rainforest**—a forest that gets at least 200 centimeters of rain a year. Rainforests like the one in the picture at the left grow only in the tropics, which encircle the earth like a giant belt. The tropics lie between 2574 kilometers north and 2574 kilometers south of the equator. Why do tropical rainforests grow only here?

As you already know, one reason is rain. Every year, tropical rainforests get more than five times as much rain as San Francisco. That's a lot!

But there are two other reasons that tropical rainforests grow where they do. Remember from the Discover Activity how the earth tilts on its axis as it revolves around the sun? The sun shines most directly on only one part of the earth all year long—the tropic zone around the equator. That means that in the tropics, the sun shines about 12 hours every single day of the year. The weather stays warm every single day. Look at the diagram to see the amount of light, heat, and water that makes a tropical rainforest possible.

Now see if you can find the tropics on the map at the left. As you trace the equator through the tropics, you see that it passes through three oceans. But notice the pink areas in South America, Africa, and Southeast Asia. Those pink areas are the earth's tropical rainforests.

No other forests in the world are like the tropical rainforests because no other forests grow in such a favorable place. Warm, sunny days and lots of rain are just what most living things need. That's why you find more different kinds of living things in the rainforests than anywhere else. What kinds of living things? To find out, just turn the page.

◄ Dim, green, and wet, rainforests like this one encircle the earth near the equator.

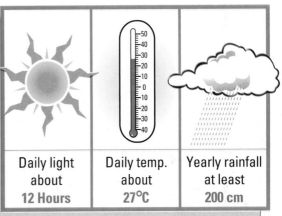

Daily light about **12 Hours**	Daily temp. about **27°C**	Yearly rainfall at least **200 cm**

▲ This mix of light, heat, and rain nurtures the earth's rainforests.

Life and More Life!

Rainforests burst with an abundance of life.

Rainforests cover less than 5 percent of the earth's surface. But they're home to nearly half of the earth's **species**, one kind of living thing. One ten-square-kilometer patch of rainforest supports up to 750 species of trees—from figs and palms to mahogany trees. About 42,000 different species of insects may live in a single hectare!

You find different species of animals in African, American, and Asian rainforests. The traveler's sketchbooks here show just a few of the species found on each continent. Some of the largest rainforest animals live in Africa. By contrast, the rainforests of Central and South America have the most animals that spend their lives high in the trees.

African rainforests have some of the largest animals, such as the gorilla.

Africa

Americas

The Amazon River Basin has the biggest variety of animals.

Asia

Rainforests in Asia have many animals that live on the forest floor—not in the trees.

Rare Life Everywhere

Not all birds would like to make their homes in a wet forest on the side of a volcano. But that's where one species of honeycreeper, the po'o–uli, (pō ō u'lē) likes to live. In fact, it lives only on the side of one volcano on the Hawaiian island of Maui (mou'ē). On the side of that one volcano, you can find the entire world population of po'o–uli birds. All of them live within 2.5 square kilometers.

As you saw, thousands of species of plants and animals make up the rainforests of Africa, Southeast Asia, and South America. But the species you read about were just a few of all the animals and plants that live in those places. Within big forests, a small patch in one place may have different species of plants, birds, snakes, and mammals from a patch in another place. Many of these rainforest plants and animals are very rare. They exist only in one small patch of one rainforest in only one part of the world.

▼ In addition to those species shown, this ten-square-kilometer patch of rainforest might have 750 species of trees, 125 species of mammals, and countless numbers of other species.

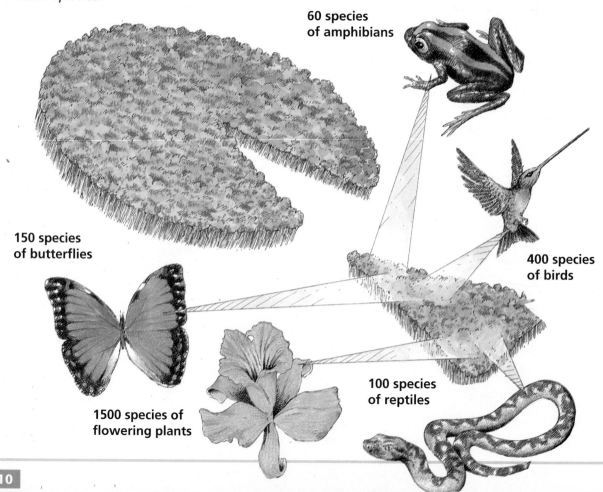

60 species of amphibians

150 species of butterflies

400 species of birds

100 species of reptiles

1500 species of flowering plants

Let's take a look at the huge number of species you might find in a ten-square-kilometer patch of rainforest, shown on page 10. Before we look closer, here's an amazing fact: in this patch of forest, you may find just one member of a species, such as a kind of palm. But you might find millions of members of another species—especially insects.

Our patch of rainforest might be home to 750 species of trees. That means you could walk through this patch of forest surrounded by trees. But you could walk for quite awhile before you saw two trees of the same species. Compare our patch of rainforest to a pine forest in the United States, where almost every tree is a pine. Even forests in the United States with the biggest variety of trees have only 25 species.

Now look at the number of species of birds, reptiles, amphibians, and butterflies in our rainforest patch! No other forest in the world even comes close to this number of different species. The number of insect species in our patch of rainforest is huge. One researcher found 400 different species of insect on *one single* rainforest palm tree! Rainforests are alive with millions of plants and animals. Many live only in their small patch of forest and nowhere else on the earth.

Checkpoint

1. What conditions are needed for a tropical rainforest to grow?
2. How are all rainforests of the world alike?
3. How is a rainforest different from a pine forest?
4. **Take Action!** Plant a small terrarium. Watch how the plants, like rainforest plants, add moisture to the air. Find out how they do it.

Monkeys' Tails

In the rainforests of Central and South America live about 52 species of monkeys. They have what some call a fifth hand—their tails. The monkeys use their tails to swing through the trees, hang from branches, grasp fruits and vines, and to act as a brake as they leap from branch to branch.

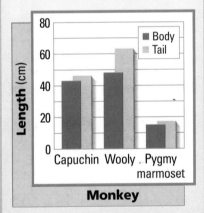

Monkey

The graph shows the body and tail size of three species of rainforest monkeys.

What Did You Find Out?
1. *Which monkey's tail is the longest?*
2. *Which monkey's tail is the shortest?*
3. *How long is the capuchin altogether?*
4. *Compare body length to tail length in the monkeys.*

How Plants "Breathe"

Green plants take in carbon dioxide and water to produce sugar and oxygen. Where are the openings through which carbon dioxide and oxygen pass?

Picture A

Picture B

Picture C

Gather These Materials

potted plant
petroleum jelly

water
paper towels

Follow This Procedure

1 Make a chart like the one on the next page. Record your observations in your chart.

2 Look at the plant and select 4 leaves. These will be the control group. Draw a picture of the plant, showing where your control leaves are.

3 Select 4 other leaves. Cover the underside of each leaf with a thin layer of petroleum jelly. (Picture A) Indicate these leaves on your drawing by marking them with a "u."

4 Select 4 more leaves and cover the tops with a thin layer of petroleum jelly. (Picture B) In your drawing, indicate these leaves with a "t."

5 Wash the petroleum jelly from your hands.

Predict: How do you think the petroleum jelly will affect the leaves?

6 Set the plant in a sunny spot. Water it as needed. (Picture C)

7 Write your observations in your chart.

Record Your Results

Observations			
Date	Control	Undersides covered	Tops covered

State Your Conclusions

1. How do all 3 sets of leaves compare?
2. On which side of a plant's leaves are the openings?
3. Some people like to put wax on the leaves of their houseplants to make them look shiny. Is that a good idea? Why or why not?
4. Clogging the openings to a leaf would be like doing what to an animal?

Let's Experiment

Do you think plants that come from different environments have openings on the same side of their leaves? How could you use this same experimental setup to find out?

LESSON

1.2 Solar-Powered Forest

▼ *Plant-eaters like the flag-footed bug may become meals for meat-eaters like the spider and the emerald tree boa.*

How does a rainforest work?

Insects on the ground, flowers and ferns on the trees, snakes, frogs, birds, and monkeys high in the branches: everywhere you look in the rainforest, there's life and more life. The rainforest is like a big, crowded city with millions of living things looking for food and space. What keeps this amazing forest going?

Life in the Canopy

You can think about a rainforest this way: it's like a big machine powered by the sun. Every single day of the year, when it isn't raining, the sun beats down on the rainforest for about 12 hours. It beats down on the tops of the trees. As the pictures above suggest, the tall trees form a huge, leafy canopy, like a giant umbrella, over the whole forest.

Layers of leaves 6 or more meters deep form the green canopy. The millions of leaves are food-making factories. Each one traps light and combines it with carbon dioxide and water to make sugars. Food, with its energy, passes from the plant's leaves to the stems, flowers, and fruits. In this way, the canopy produces most of the food for the whole rainforest.

As the first picture to the left shows, insects eat plant parts for energy. So do bigger canopy dwellers like sloths and parrots. The second picture shows how plant-eaters sometimes become meals for meat-eaters. In this way, energy passes along a food chain. It moves from plants to plant-eating animals to animal-eating animals. The food chain is a key part of the rainforest **ecosystem**—the community of plants and animals that live in a certain environment.

Rich Life, Poor Soil

The rainforest is so full of lush plants that it makes sense to think they grow in rich, fertile soil. Yet rainforest soil is some of the poorest on the earth. Heavy rains wash minerals and other nutrients out of the soil. How can poor soil support these huge forests?

You find the answer in the rainforest itself. With few nutrients in the soil, plants must get nutrients from somewhere else. Those nutrients come from fallen leaves, fruit peels—even dead animals. The plants must get nutrients from these materials before the rain washes them away.

The rainforest trees have wide, shallow roots with thick mats of hairs, shown below. These roots of the trees absorb nutrients from the top layer of the rainforest soil.

▼ *The roots of rainforest trees grow near the surface of the soil where they can absorb water and nutrients.*

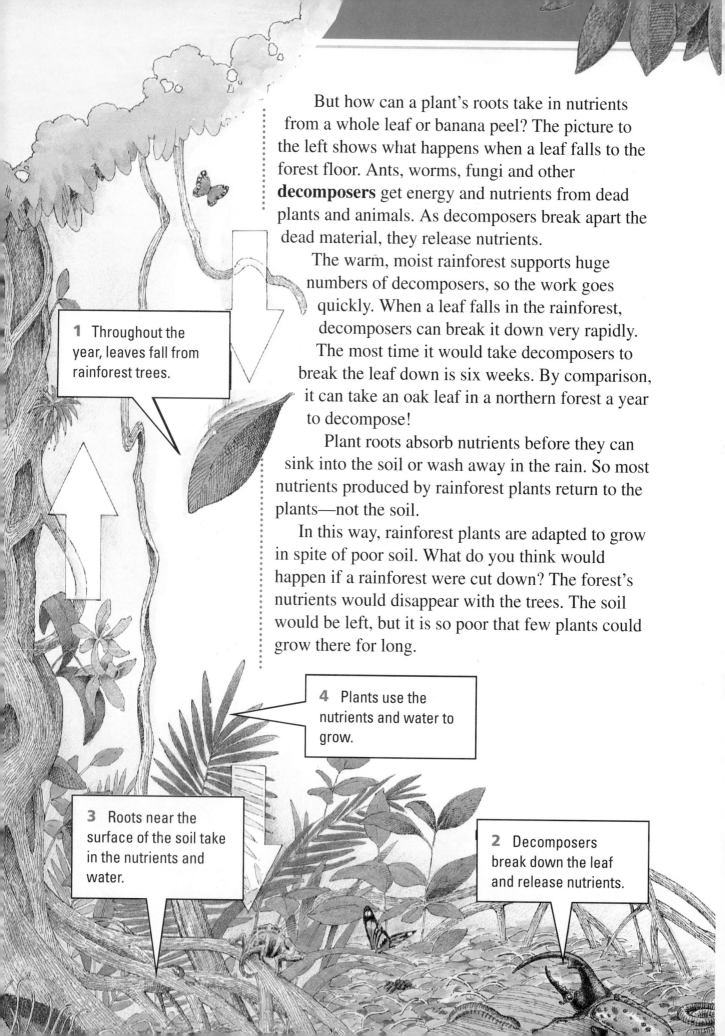

But how can a plant's roots take in nutrients from a whole leaf or banana peel? The picture to the left shows what happens when a leaf falls to the forest floor. Ants, worms, fungi and other **decomposers** get energy and nutrients from dead plants and animals. As decomposers break apart the dead material, they release nutrients.

The warm, moist rainforest supports huge numbers of decomposers, so the work goes quickly. When a leaf falls in the rainforest, decomposers can break it down very rapidly.

The most time it would take decomposers to break the leaf down is six weeks. By comparison, it can take an oak leaf in a northern forest a year to decompose!

Plant roots absorb nutrients before they can sink into the soil or wash away in the rain. So most nutrients produced by rainforest plants return to the plants—not the soil.

In this way, rainforest plants are adapted to grow in spite of poor soil. What do you think would happen if a rainforest were cut down? The forest's nutrients would disappear with the trees. The soil would be left, but it is so poor that few plants could grow there for long.

1 Throughout the year, leaves fall from rainforest trees.

4 Plants use the nutrients and water to grow.

3 Roots near the surface of the soil take in the nutrients and water.

2 Decomposers break down the leaf and release nutrients.

Animals That Help Plants

The butterfly in the picture sits on that flower for a very good reason. The flower's sweet nectar is one of its many sources of food. As you read earlier, plants are the first link in the food chain. The butterfly, like every other animal on earth, would eventually starve if there were no plants.

Would the plants be able to survive without animals? No way! Plants depend on animals just as animals depend on plants. You've already seen one way that plants depend on animals: without certain decomposers, rainforest plants would die from lack of nutrients.

But that's just the beginning. In the rainforest, plants and animals have developed all kinds of partnerships. Why? Life in the rainforest is tough. Every day millions of species compete for light, food, and space. Partnerships give plants and animals a better chance of surviving.

Let's look at rainforest trees, for example. Many of them need animals for **pollination,** in which pollen grains are carried from one plant to another. After pollination occurs, a plant can make seeds. Bumblebees pick up and deliver pollen grains from flowers as they gather nectar. In the rainforest, butterflies, bees, birds, and even bats pollinate plants as they move about collecting food.

◄ In the rainforest, nutrients from decomposed leaves return to the trees, not the soil.

▼ This butterfly from a Central American rainforest helps pollinate plants.

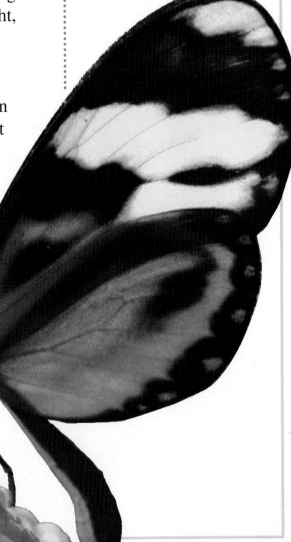

Into The Field

How do living things help each other?
Go outdoors. Find an example of two living things that help each other live. Describe the situation.

▼ After the quetzal eats this wild avocado, it will drop the seed far from the parent plant.

Once the seeds are fully grown, they fall from the trees. But the seeds may not grow if they drop to the forest floor at the base of the parent tree. The light there may be too dim. The parent plant may take too many nutrients and water for the seedling to grow.

In many parts of the world, the wind blows seeds away from the parent plant to places where they can grow. But in the rainforest, the wind reaches only the tallest trees. Inside the protected canopy, the air is still. How do seeds get to a new location? Animals carry them on their bodies or in their stomachs. Some seeds stick to an animal's fur, then drop off far from the parent plant. Many rainforest trees produce brightly colored fruits that help spread their seeds. Animals and birds, like the quetzal (ket säl′) in the picture, eat these juicy fruits. The seeds pass through the animals and fall to the ground far from the parent plant.

Ants and pretty flowers called orchids have another kind of partnership. Some orchid seeds sprout in ant nests high in the canopy. Nutrients from the ants' nest help the orchid grow. As the orchid's roots grow larger, the size of the ants' home grows larger, too. The ants get a big, safe home while the orchid gets nutrients from the nest. The ants also protect the orchid from plant-eating pests.

Leaf-cutting ants have yet another kind of relationship. The pictures on the next page show how leaf-cutters chew off big pieces of leaves high in the trees. Then the ants haul the leaf bits back to their underground nests, as you see in the two smaller pictures.

▲ *Leaf-cutting ants gather food for the fungus in their nests.*

But strangely enough, the ants don't eat the leaves. They chew the leaves to make a nutrient-rich material, which they feed to a fungus growing in their nests. The ants eat only this fungus. Without it, the ants would starve. The fungus cannot survive without food from the ants. The ants and the fungus depend on each other.

In the rainforest many animals and plants depend upon one another. Thousands of partnerships help keep the rainforest ecosystem going. A similar thing is true of the rainforests and the earth's biosphere. Rainforests contribute to the well-being of living things everywhere. You may never visit a rainforest, but it can affect you nonetheless.

Checkpoint

1. Why are green leaves so important in the food chain?
2. Why are the roots of rainforest trees wide and shallow?
3. Why are plant and animal partnerships helpful in the rainforest?
4. Take Action! Find out what part of the rainforest most rainforest animals live in.

Activity

To Rot or Not to Rot

Did you ever forget about a piece of fruit and leave it out for a long time?
It probably began to rot, or decompose. Test some items to see if they rot or not.

Picture A

Gather These Materials

cover goggles	fruit peel
scissors	plastic wrap
1-liter plastic bottle	cloth
shallow bowl	aluminum foil
spoon	piece of bread
soil	piece of popped popcorn
piece of paper	water

Follow This Procedure

1 Make a chart like the one on the next page. Record your observations in your chart.

2 Put on your cover goggles.

3 Use scissors to cut off the neck of a 1-liter bottle. Poke a few small holes in the bottom. Place the bottle in a shallow bowl.

4 Use a spoon to scoop some soil into the bottle until there is a 5-cm layer at the bottom. (Picture A)

5 Place the piece of paper in the bottle, next to the side. You want to be able to see the paper after it is covered. Cover the paper with soil.

6 Add the fruit peel so you can see it near the side of the bottle. Cover it with soil.

7 Continue adding test items and soil until the bottle is full. (Picture B) The last layer should be soil.

Picture C

Picture B

Record Your Results

Observations							
Date	Paper	Fruit peel	Plastic wrap	Cloth	Aluminum foil	Bread	Popcorn

8 Make a drawing of the bottle to keep track of what you "planted" where.

9 Add water to moisten the soil. Cover the bottle with plastic wrap to keep the soil moist. (Picture C)

10 Place the bottle in a warm place. Check it each day for about 2 weeks.

Predict: **Which item will decompose first? Which items will not decompose at all?**

State Your Conclusions

1. Which of the items that you tested were once living or are made of once-living things? Which are not?
2. Why is this process important to the environment?

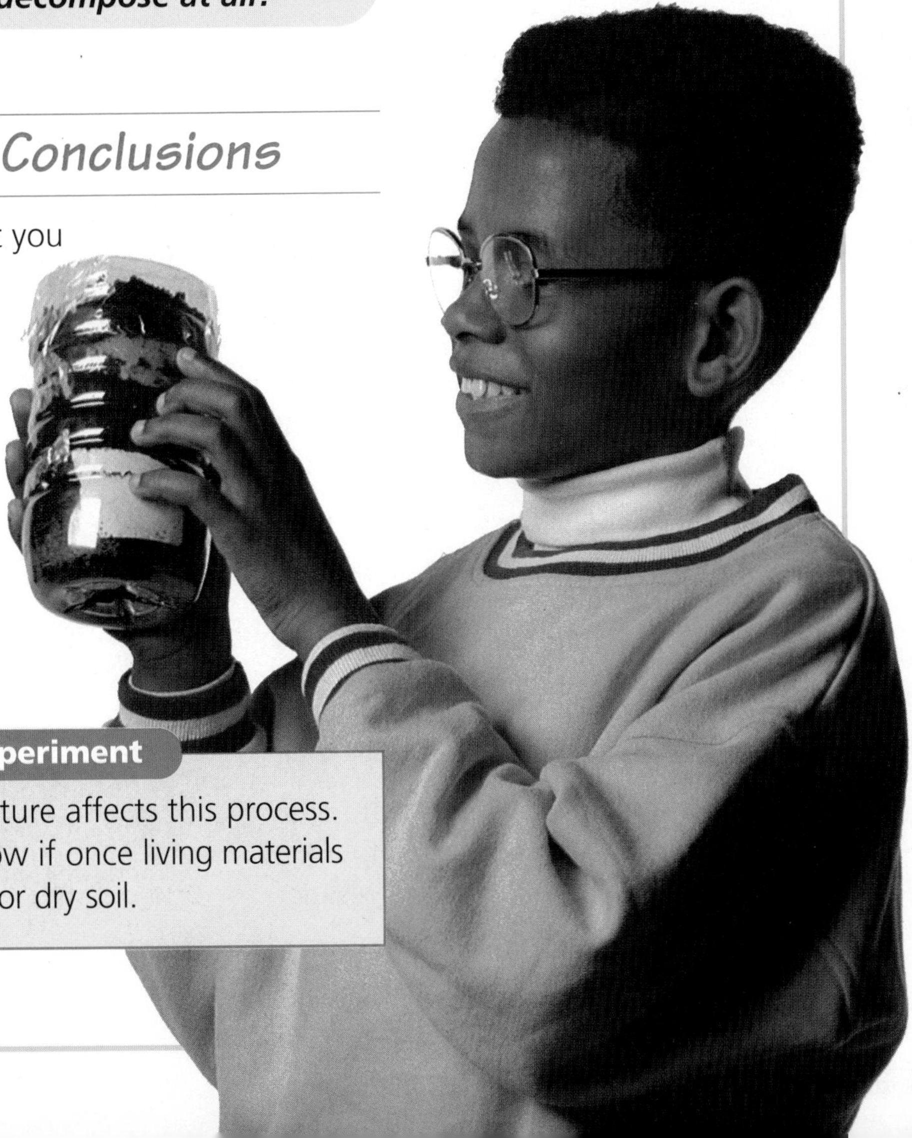

Let's Experiment

Try to find out how moisture affects this process. Do an experiment to show if once living materials decompose faster in wet or dry soil.

Making Diagrams

Sometimes you read a description of an object, place, or relationship and you have trouble understanding the description. What could you do to understand the description better?

You might draw a diagram. A diagram is a simple drawing that helps you to see what something looks like or how it works. The diagram doesn't have to look exactly like what it pictures. It just needs to show the same parts and their relationships.

Thinking It Through

Suppose you read an explanation of how a rainforest has many different levels made up of trees of different heights. Many animals live on the forest floor. But more than half of all animal species live in the trees and almost never set foot on the ground.

The diagram on this page shows the layers of a South American rainforest. As you can see from the diagram, different kinds of animals, such as birds, mammals, and reptiles, live in the different levels of the rainforest. The diagram also gives an idea of the variety of living things found in a rainforest ecosystem. What other ideas does the diagram help you understand?

Layers of a Rainforest

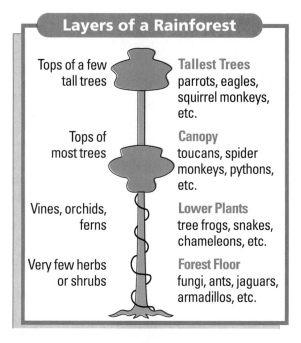

Tops of a few tall trees — **Tallest Trees** parrots, eagles, squirrel monkeys, etc.

Tops of most trees — **Canopy** toucans, spider monkeys, pythons, etc.

Vines, orchids, ferns — **Lower Plants** tree frogs, snakes, chameleons, etc.

Very few herbs or shrubs — **Forest Floor** fungi, ants, jaguars, armadillos, etc.

Your Turn

Make a diagram of a food chain. The sun is the start of the food chain. Green plants produce sugars using energy from sunlight. The plants are the producers. Animals like parrots and monkeys eat, or consume, parts of the plants. They are consumers. Other consumers like snakes, anteaters, and jaguars eat some of the plant consumers. When both plants and animals die, decomposers like bacteria and fungi help break down their bodies.

Chapter Review

Thinking Back

1. Where are tropical **rainforests** located?
2. Why does a rainforest have a greater variety of living things than anywhere else on Earth?
3. What is a **species?**
4. Why is the canopy of a rainforest important?
5. How is the food chain a part of the **ecosystem** of the rainforest?
6. Why is the rainforest soil poor in nutrients?

7. How do **decomposers** help plants get nutrients?
8. Why do you think life is difficult in the canopy?
9. How does **pollination** occur in the rainforest?
10. Describe how leaf-cutting ants and fungi depend upon one another.

Connecting Ideas

1. Copy the concept map. Use the terms at the right to complete the map about the energy in a food chain.

animal eater   **plant**

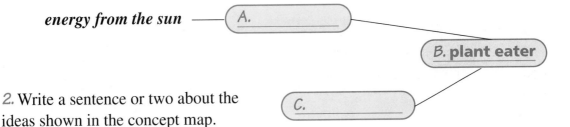

energy from the sun — A. _____

B. **plant eater**

C. _____

2. Write a sentence or two about the ideas shown in the concept map.

Gathering Evidence

1. In the Activity on page 12, how did you conclude where the openings on the plant's leaf were located?
2. In the Activity on page 20, how did you know which items decomposed?

Doing Science!

1. *Create a chart* that shows different ways pollination may occur in a rainforest.
2. *Write a paragraph* that describes a tropical rainforest.

Changing Rainforests

Hey, move over.

What is overcrowding?

Place a 4-meter length of string on the floor in the shape of a circle. Give each of eight students a piece of green paper which represents their own garden. One student should place the "garden" in the circle and find a place to stand inside the circle. Repeat this until all eight students have placed their "garden" and entered the circle.

For Discussion

1. As the circle got crowded, how did you feel?
2. What could you do to fit more students?

2.1 They're Disappearing!

> **Why would anyone harm the rainforests?**

From a distance you can smell smoke and hear the crackling flames. A patch of rainforest is burning, like the patch in the picture. People are burning the trees, vines, and flowers. But why?

Using Rainforests

For thousands of years, people have lived in the rainforests with the plants and animals. Like all of the people on the earth, rainforest people are part of the biosphere. They use the plants, animals, air, and water around them to survive.

But rainforest people know how to live in harmony with their environment. They gather fruits, plants, and roots; build shelters; and make medicines from plants without harming the ecosystem. Sometimes they cut and burn a small patch of trees in order to grow crops. Ashes from the burned plants contain nutrients that farmers mix into the poor soil of the rainforest. That way, they can farm the patch for a few years before the nutrients are used up. Then the people move on to a new plot, leaving the old one untouched for years. Slowly but surely, the small patch of forest grows back.

Today, fires in the forest signal something different. You will find out as you read this chapter.

▲ In many parts of the world, rainforest people clear small patches of land to farm.

Regrowing a Rainforest

The rainforests grow fast, but they can't easily recover from unwise use.

Plants grow rapidly in the warm, wet rainforest, even though the soil is poor and shallow. The spreading roots of rainforest trees and plants protect the soil from sun and wind. They hold the soil in place so it can absorb water like a sponge.

If small patches of forest are cut, the trees can slowly grow back. Find the old clearing in the picture where the forest is starting to reappear. When large patches of forest are cut, however, not enough roots remain to hold the soil. Then the soil washes and blows away. In places, the sun bakes it hard as a brick. When large areas are cleared and not left alone, the forest cannot easily renew itself.

Small clearings are cut for farming, but nearby plants hold the soil and moisture. After a few seasons, farmers move on. They don't return for many years.

10 years after the farmers have left, seedlings of the tallest trees have taken root. In another 90 years, the forest patch will be completely renewed.

1950

1975

2000

▲ *In 1950, rainforests covered about 12 percent of the earth's surface. Some predict that by 2000 more than half of these forests will be gone.*

► *These squares represent the original area of rainforest in different countries. The trees on the squares represent the area of rainforest that remains.*

How Much Is Gone?

As you can see, cutting large chunks of rainforest creates serious problems. The complicated forests took millions of years to develop. Yet half of the world's rainforests have already been cut, as the maps to the left show. Even if people replanted trees, it would take hundreds of years for all the parts of the forest to return.

A fast-growing world population is one reason that forests are being cut. Just 30 years ago, the world had 3 billion people. By 2000, some scientists predict a world population of 6.35 billion.

Forests are an important resource for this exploding population. They provide timber for building homes and wood for heating and cooking. Even though the soil is poor, they provide much-needed farmland and living space.

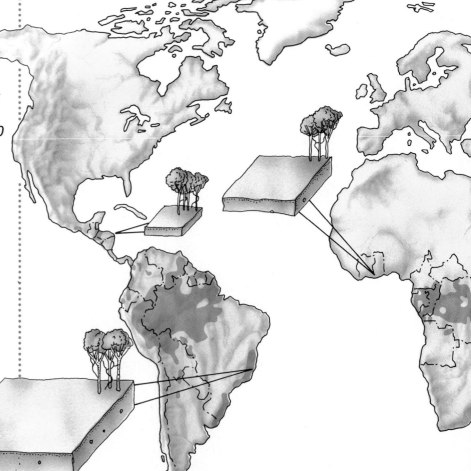

The map below shows the loss of rainforests by 1990. India is one country that has cut nearly all of its rainforests. But it's important to note how fast India's population is growing. In 1975, India had 618 million people. Scientists predict that in just a few years, India's population will top 1 billion. In the Discover Activity, you saw what overcrowding can do to the land.

Haiti, a small island nation in the Caribbean Sea, has also cut nearly all of its forests. Its population is growing too, as are populations in Indonesia, Nigeria, and many other tropical rainforest nations. So the cutting goes on. Between 13 and 15 million hectares of rainforest are cut each year—about 30 hectares of rainforest a minute. Some scientists think that, at this rate of cutting, more than half of the earth's remaining rainforests will be gone by the the year 2000.

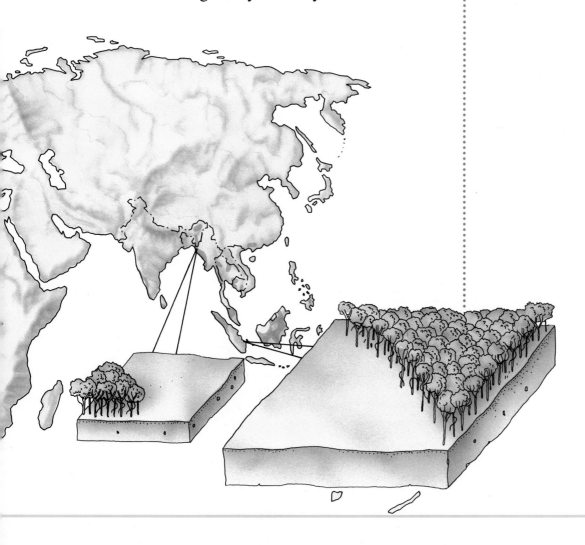

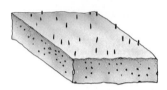

▲ *Raising one cow for beef takes one hectare of land. After a few years, the land cannot support plants.*

Wood, Land, Minerals, and Cattle

Obviously, the destruction of an ecosystem is a serious problem. But solving this problem isn't easy. Many tropical rainforest nations are poor and trying to develop modern ways of life. In their overcrowded cities, millions of people live in poverty, with little food or medical help. These nations need money and organizatons to build housing, schools, factories, and hospitals. To nations struggling with problems like these, the vast rainforests seem to hold the answer.

Brazil is one of many countries that turned to the rainforest to solve its problems. In the 1960s, the government began building highways deep into the forests, like the one pictured below. Then it offered land to settlers living in crowded cities. The government built farms and ranches on rainforest land. At the same time, it encouraged timber companies to log the forests. With loans from other nations, Brazilians built dams to generate electricity and mined for lead, copper, gold, and iron ore. The picture below shows what these developments meant for the rainforests. As you can see, the rainforest has suffered.

➤ *The Trans-Amazon Highway opened up areas deep in the rainforest that could only be reached before by river.*

Rainforest countries like Brazil found buyers for their products in the United States, Japan, and other nations. In the last 40 years, the demand for woods like the teak and rosewood in the picture grew. Many forests in Asia were cut and sold to developed nations for furniture, building materials, and paper.

People in developed nations also bought beef raised on ranches created by clearing rainforests. This beef, much from Central America, was cheaper than beef raised in the United States and Europe.

Timber, minerals, and cattle brought money into many rainforest nations. But as thousands of acres of rainforest were destroyed, the balance of nature was upset. Trees were not replanted in areas that were cleared. Settlers from the cities did not know how to live in the rainforest without destroying it. Without plant cover to slow the runoff of heavy rains, many rivers flooded, killing people and destroying property. Rivers also carried away so much soil that the lakes behind dams in some countries began to fill in. In some places, sun and rain reacted with minerals in the soil and baked it solid. Stretches of eroded land replaced the forests.

Checkpoint

1. How are people a part of the rainforest ecosystem?
2. Why is it better to clear small patches of rainforest land?
3. How has a growing world population affected the rainforests?
4. What can happen when large areas of a rainforest are cut?
5. Take Action! Clip stories from the newspapers about problems caused by cutting rainforests. Put them together in a book and share them with the class.

Washing Soil Away

Is soil lost when a rainforest is cut? Let's investigate and find out.

What To Do
A. Prepare a cut milk carton and grass clump as shown in the diagram.
B. Slowly pour 200 mL of water onto the grass.
C. Pour the water that drains to the lower end into a filter. How much soil has been "washed away?"
D. Repeat steps B and C using a clump of soil with no grass.

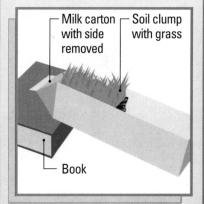

Milk carton with side removed — Soil clump with grass

Book

What Did You Find Out?
1. *Did more soil wash away with or without grass?*
2. *What happens to the soil when the rainforest is cut?*
3. *Explain how the rainforest soil benefits from having trees.*

Model the Greenhouse Effect

Can you create a model that shows how carbon dioxide and water vapor affect the rate at which the earth loses heat? Try this activity to find out.

Picture A

Picture B

Picture C

Gather These Materials

cover goggles
hot water
2 glass jars

2 thermometers
clear plastic wrap

Follow This Procedure

1 Make a chart like the one on the next page. Record your observations in your chart.

2 Put on your cover goggles.

3 Carefully pour hot water into each of the glass jars. Each jar should be about two-thirds full. (Picture A)

4 Put a thermometer into each jar. (Picture B)

5 Quickly cover one of the jars and its thermometer with a sheet of clear plastic wrap. Make sure the jar is well sealed. (Picture C)

6 Record the temperature of each jar on your chart.

Predict: **Which container will keep the water hot longer?**

7 Record the temperature of the water in each jar every 2 minutes for the next 20 minutes.

Record Your Results

Time (min)	Temperature of water in wrapped jar (°C)	Temperature of water in unwrapped jar (°C)
0		
2		
4		
6		
8		
10		
12		
14		
16		
18		
20		

State Your Conclusions

1. Which of the 2 jars of water lost more heat?

2. Why do you think the other jar of water lost less heat?

3. Assume that water vapor and carbon dioxide in the atmosphere are similar to plastic wrap. What effect would they have on Earth's temperatures?

Let's Experiment

What might happen if you doubled the carbon dioxide and water vapor in the atmosphere? How could you demonstrate that effect? Use what you know about scientific methods to find out.

Chondrodendron

▲ *A substance in this vine is used to relax muscles during surgery.*

▼ *A substance from this plant is used to treat malaria, an infectious disease.*

Cinchona

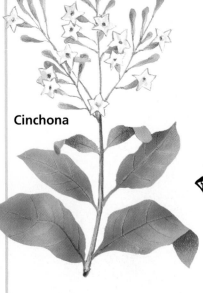

► *A substance from this plant is used as a tranquilizer.*

A Challenge Ahead

▶ *Can the loss of rainforests affect the whole world?*

You bet. Every major ecosystem plays a part in keeping the biosphere healthy. As the ecosystem with the highest number of living things, the rainforests play a special role.

Lost Plants, Lost Animals

As the rainforests disappear, thousands of species of plants and animals disappear with them. Some scientists predict that more than 1 million species will become extinct in the next 25 years. Animals and plants become **extinct** when every member of their species has died.

Natural extinctions occur because the environment is always changing. In nature, these changes are usually slow. But changes in the rainforest have been very sudden. An estimated 50 to 100 species become extinct there *every day*. This is the greatest rate of extinction since dinosaurs and other species died out 65 million years ago.

Rauwolfia

✚Depke
1234 Main
Cleveland, Oh.

Name:

Jane Dolen

Rainforests may contain as many as half of all the species found on earth. If the rainforests are lost, the earth will lose a huge variety of life. That loss could affect the future of remaining life on the earth because species are a resource that cannot be renewed. Once a species is gone, it is gone forever.

Unknown Secrets

Did you know that two drugs that fight cancer came from the rosy periwinkle, the pretty flower in the picture to the right? Did you know that crossing wild plants with farm plants can result in healthier, stronger crops?

Rainforests are wonderful places to look for new medicines and wild species of food plants because so many plant species live there. Scientists have studied fewer than one percent of rainforest plants for medicines. But already about one-fourth of our prescription medicines are based on rainforest plants.

Just as important, many crops are stronger and healthier because they grew from seeds produced by crossing food plants with wild species. For example, scientists discovered one species of wild rice in the Philippines years ago that could resist a deadly rice disease. They crossed other rice plants with it, and today nearly all modern rice plants can survive that disease.

Today, many rainforest species are becoming extinct before scientists can discover and study them. As the rainforests disappear, we may lose the secrets to curing some serious diseases and protecting our food supply.

Rosy periwinkle

▲ *Substances in the leaves of this plant, a native of Madagascar, are used to make drugs that fight leukemia and Hodgkin's disease.*

More Carbon in the Air

Earlier in this module you learned that plants use sunlight to make sugars. In daylight, plants take in carbon dioxide from the air and give off oxygen. People and other animals inhale oxygen and give off carbon dioxide. What a great system! The diagram at the left shows how oxygen and carbon dioxide constantly cycle in the atmosphere, keeping the right levels in the air.

But something in the atmosphere is changing. Right now, there is much more carbon dioxide in the earth's atmosphere than there was 100 years ago. Most of this carbon dioxide comes from power plants, cars, trucks, factories, and planes that burn coal and oil.

But burning rainforests also release carbon dioxide. As the picture below shows, carbon dioxide is released into the air when the rainforests burn. At the same time, the burning of rainforests destroys the living plants that could remove carbon dioxide from the air. That means it's twice as bad for the earth's atmosphere when rainforests burn and are destroyed.

People and other animals breathe out carbon dioxide.

Plants take in carbon dioxide.

People and other animals breathe in oxygen.

Plants give off oxygen.

▲ *Carbon dioxide and oxygen cycle through living things and the atmosphere.*

▼ *Plants take in carbon dioxide. Burning adds carbon dioxide to the air.*

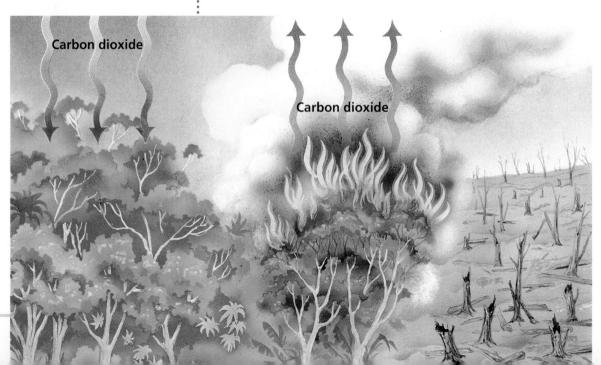

Carbon dioxide

Carbon dioxide

Hotter or Colder?

Some scientists think the extra carbon dioxide in the atmosphere may cause problems. You can perhaps understand why if you compare carbon dioxide to the windows in a greenhouse. Windows let the sunlight into a greenhouse but trap some of the heat that results. The picture to the right shows how carbon dioxide in the earth's atmosphere lets sunlight into the earth and traps some of the warmth. This process is called the **greenhouse effect**.

More carbon dioxide in the atmosphere may trap more heat and cause the earth's average temperature to rise. A rise of just one or two degrees in the earth's average temperature could cause ice at the South Pole to melt. Then sea levels could rise, flooding some coastal cities. In some places heat could cause droughts, killing off major crops.

Some scientists think the opposite might happen. Higher temperatures might cause more water to evaporate, creating a heavy cloud cover. In time, the clouds might block so much sunlight that temperatures might gradually drop.

▲ Energy from sunlight reaches the earth every day and warms it. Some heat escapes, but carbon dioxide traps enough to keep the earth warm.

Checkpoint

1. Why does cutting rainforests cause so many extinctions?
2. How might many extinctions affect life outside the rainforest?
3. How does burning a forest harm the environment?
4. How might a drop in the earth's temperature affect the biosphere?
5. Take Action! Find out how much the earth's average temperature has changed in the last 100 years. Make a chart using that information.

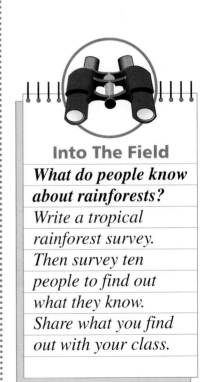

Into The Field

What do people know about rainforests?
Write a tropical rainforest survey. Then survey ten people to find out what they know. Share what you find out with your class.

Activity

Blue, Blue Water

Did you know that an acid can form when you breathe out? This activity will help you see the acid that your breath forms.

Picture A

Picture B

Picture C

Gather These Materials

cover goggles
2 jars
water
bromothymol blue
  solution (BTB)

straw
marker
masking tape
elodea plant

Follow This Procedure

Part I

1 Make a chart like the one on the next page. Record your observations in your chart.

2 Put on your cover goggles.

3 Fill one jar about two-thirds full with water. Add a few drops of bromothymol blue solution (BTB) until the water turns blue. (Picture A)

4 Use a straw to blow into the solution. (Picture B) What happens? Do you know why?

Part II

5 Pour out one-half of the yellow solution into another similar jar. Label the 2 jars A and B using a marker and masking tape. (Picture C).

6 Add an elodea plant to jar A.

7 Set both jars in the sun for 30 minutes.

Record Your Results

	Color at start	Color after 30 minutes	Carbon dioxide present?
Jar A with elodea			
Jar B			

Predict: *What will happen to the color of the solution in both jars?*

8 Observe the solutions after 30 minutes. Record your observations.

State Your Conclusions

1. In which jar was carbon dioxide removed?
2. For what process do plants use carbon dioxide?
3. Would your results be the same if you left the 2 jars out in darkness? Why or why not?

Let's Experiment

Now that you have seen how carbon dioxide is absorbed, change this experiment to show how sunlight affects the amount of carbon dioxide absorbed.

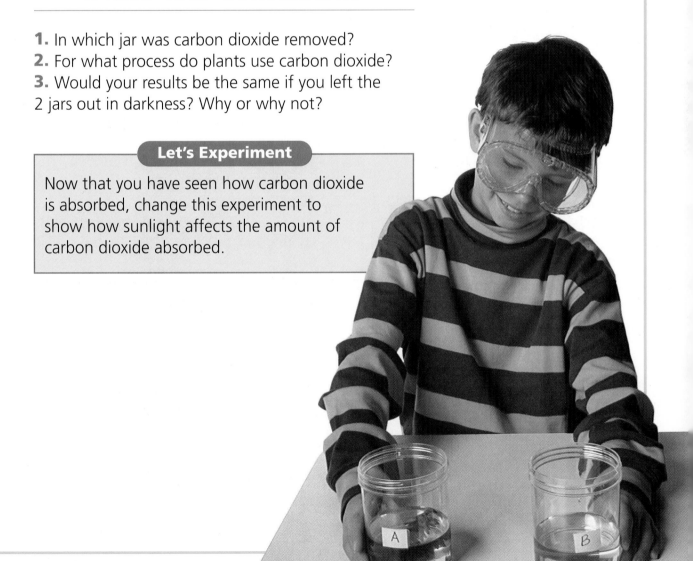

Finding Cause and Effect

"Last night floods destroyed more than 100 homes and businesses in coastal Brazil," the radio announcer says. His statement contained both the cause and the effects.

Can you find the cause and effects in the announcement? A cause is what makes something happen. An effect is the result of that action. Here, the floods are the cause. The destroyed homes and businesses are the effects.

Science is often concerned with cause-and-effect relationships. Often, scientists know a cause and study the effects. Sometimes, they know effects and search for a cause. Other times, scientists study both the cause and effects together.

Thinking It Through

Pretend you are a biologist studying rainforest destruction. You have taken the following notes about a certain area:

• Clearing small patches of land and then abandoning them allows the rainforest to regrow.
• The rainforest is destroyed when too large an area is cleared. Destroying the rainforest causes floods and droughts.

In order to explain how rainforests are being destroyed, identify the cause and effects of the damage. To identify a cause, ask yourself what makes something happen. To identify an effect, ask what the result is.

Clearing just small patches of land and abandoning them is the cause. The effect? The rainforest can regrow.

Clearing too large an area is a cause. The first effect is that the rainforest is destroyed. This causes a second effect: floods and droughts.

Your Turn

1. Write these sentences on a sheet of paper. Underline the cause. Circle the effect.
a. Strong winds knocked over a tree.
b. Some rainforests have been lost because people cleared the land.
2. In this module, find a cause-and-effect relationship that helps rainforests.

Chapter Review

Thinking Back

1. Why does clearing large patches of rainforest land destroy rainforests?
2. Why are rainforests being destroyed?
3. How has Brazil used the rainforest to solve its problems?
4. How does cutting only small patches of land affect the rainforest?
5. How can cutting the rainforest cause a species to become **extinct**?
6. Why is the extinction of plants a serious problem?

7. Since extinctions are part of a natural cycle, why are the extinctions caused by the destruction of the rainforest a problem?
8. How can burning the rainforests affect the atmosphere?
9. How does carbon dioxide in the atmosphere cause the **greenhouse effect**?
10. What problems might be caused by the increase of carbon dioxide in the atmosphere?

Connecting Ideas

1. Copy the concept map. Use the terms at the right to complete the map about the carbon dioxide and oxygen cycle.

animals   **carbon dioxide**
oxygen

B. _____

A. **trees**

C. _____

D. _____

2. Write a sentence or two about the ideas shown in the concept map.

Gathering Evidence

1. In the Activity on page 32, how did you know which jar lost the largest amount of heat?
2. In the Activity on page 38, how did you conclude that the elodea used up the carbon dioxide in the water?

Doing Science!

1. *Make a list* that shows the arguments for destroying a rainforest and those against.
2. *Create an advertisement* that shows how important rainforests are to people in non-rainforest countries.

3 Protecting Rainforests

This poster will let kids know what's happening.

What can you do?

It's important that people know what is happening to the rainforests today. You can share what you've learned about the rainforests. Set aside one week during the year as "Rainforest Awareness Week." Think about things you could do in your school to inform people about rainforests.

For Discussion

1. *What things should people know about the rainforest?*
2. *What's the best way to present this information?*

3.1 *Joining Hands*

How can people save the rainforests?

Leaping lizards! Some people who live in the rainforests are raising lizards called iguanas (i gwä′nəz) for food. That's what student reporter Stephanie Yu of New York found out a few years ago when she visited Costa Rica.

Iguanas live on the rainforest plants. They have long been part of the Central American diet. With a flavor like chicken, iguanas are often cooked in stews. Yet a growing human population has led to the overhunting of iguanas, and so these lizards have become rare in the wild. Today, a small group of farmers in Costa Rica is raising iguanas and releasing them into the nearby rainforest. If the project of the Costa Rican farmers works, more people may be able to earn money raising iguanas. At the same time, they will be saving the delicate rainforests that the iguanas need to survive.

Ideas like these are needed to save the rainforests and other ecosystems. Scientists, leaders, and consumers around the world also need to contribute their efforts. As the cards shown on the right suggest, much has happened since Stephanie visited Costa Rica. In this chapter you'll learn what people are doing to save the rainforests.

▼ *People around the world are working to save the rainforests.*

Rainforest Heroes

People in rainforest countries around the world are working to save their rainforests.

In rainforest countries around the world, people are taking action. These rainforest dwellers are helping to restore their precious rainforests.

In Ghana, Africa, people are planting trees on land once covered by forests. Through the Ghana National Tree Planting Program, farmers have planted more than 3000 hectares of trees every year since 1983.

As the second photo shows, some farmers in Brazil are also replanting trees—mostly fruit trees. Their efforts help save the rainforest and provide them with crops to export. By earning a living from harvesting fruit, the farmers no longer cut the rainforest to farm.

The Awá people in Ecuador have carved a wide *manga*, or strip, around their rainforest land. This 241-kilometer strip marks Awá land to all outsiders who want to clear the forest. But the 9- to 14-meter wide *manga* serves another purpose, too. Here the Awá can plant fruit and nut trees. Then the Awá people can raise, harvest, and export these products to earn much-needed money.

In Java, many families are planting home gardens in rainforest clearings. The home gardens copy the layered structure of the rainforests. Beans and plants used for medicines grow close to the ground. Above them grow banana and papaya trees, then citrus and coffee trees. The tallest trees of all—sugar palms and mangoes—form a kind of canopy. Home gardens help keep the soil in place and the rainforest intact.

Rainforest Parks

As countries realize the value of healthy rainforests, many are taking steps to protect the forests they still have. Brazil, Indonesia, Venezuela, Thailand, Zaïre, and many other countries have created rainforest parks. Costa Rica leads the way: it has protected at least 20 percent of its entire nation. These projects work best when they create new jobs. Instead of cutting down trees, local people can find jobs, such as running hotels and nature centers for tourists.

Creating parks is an important step. But how big must a park be to survive? To find the smallest area of rainforest that can survive, scientists study the *largest* animals. Why? Because the largest animals need the most room to live, hunt, and find mates.

The area must have room for a population of the largest animals. Today, researchers from the Smithsonian Institution in Washington, D.C., are studying how many jaguars, like the one in the picture, are needed for a healthy population. Their current estimate: at least 500 adult jaguars would need to live in an area.

▼ *Jaguars in Central and South American rainforests roam over many miles.*

➤ *Scientists are studying patches of rainforest to learn how big a preserve must be.*

Scientists estimate that 500 adult jaguars need at least 20,000 square kilometers of space—an area almost as big as Massachusetts! Luckily, say the scientists, that much rainforest still stands in South America. Other rainforest areas, especially on islands, don't have such large animals, so their ecosystems can survive in smaller areas.

Using Rainforests Wisely

A worldwide demand for land and timber pushes people to cut the rainforests. Perhaps a worldwide demand for nuts, fruits, and other products will urge people to plant trees and protect them. A recent study showed that harvesting products from living trees could produce two times more money than logging or raising cattle to sell abroad.

People who know how to harvest rainforest products often work the hardest to protect the forests: without the trees, they have no jobs. Besides fruits and nuts, harvesters can take out, or extract, medicinal plants, latex for rubber, oils, and many other products. Harvested properly, these products can be taken from the forest again and again. They can support the people without harming the forest.

Checkpoint

1. How are the Awá people helping to save the rainforest?
2. Why do scientists study the largest animals to determine the smallest size for a rainforest park?
3. How can people earn money from living rainforests?
4. Take Action! Draw a simple rainforest food web that includes jaguars. Then draw the web showing what could happen if the jaguars disappeared.

DATAFILE

SOCIAL STUDIES

Can You Find It?

Conservationists and rainforest people are working together to plan and develop biosphere reserves. These reserves preserve the rainforest while meeting the needs of the nearby human communities. Zones are created that enable both the people and the plant and animal species to prosper. Study the map of the biosphere reserve. Look for places where people are allowed.

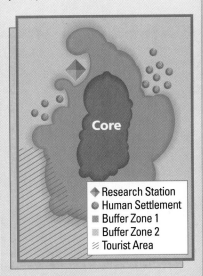

Core

◆ Research Station
● Human Settlement
■ Buffer Zone 1
■ Buffer Zone 2
▨ Tourist Area

What Did You Find Out?
1. *Which zones have housing for people?*
2. *Which zones allow tourists?*
3. *Why do you think Zone 1 and Zone 2 are referred to as buffer zones?*

Activity

Sorting It Out

What happens to glass, plastic, and paper when they get to a recycling plant? The first step is to separate the materials. See how challenging a job that can be.

Picture A

Gather These Materials

cover goggles	4 rubber bands
scissors	window screen with
1 plastic straw	edges taped
1 paper towel	masking tape
a small square of foil	magnet
5 metal paper clips	balloon, blown up
4 pennies	pan of water
4 marbles	

Follow This Procedure

1. Make a chart like the one on the next page. Record your observations in your chart.

2. Put on your cover goggles.

3. Cut the plastic straw up into 5 pieces. Tear the paper towel into 4 or 5 pieces. Roll the pieces into balls. Tear the foil into 5 flat pieces.

4. Place the straw, marbles, paper clips, pennies, foil, paper, and rubber bands on the screen. (Picture A)

Predict: *Which objects will the magnet attract? What property will they share?*

5. Use the magnet to pick up some of the objects off the screen. (Picture B) Place them in a pile. Make a list of those objects in your chart.

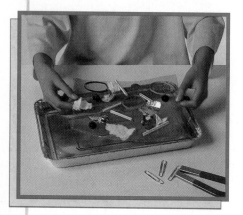

Picture B

Picture C

6 Rub the balloon against your clothing to create an electric charge. One by one, take the objects left on the screen and place them on the balloon. Which ones stick to it? Place these objects in a second pile. Add them to your chart.

7 Fill the pan with water. Place the screen with the remaining objects into the water. (Picture C)

8 Place the objects that float into a third pile. What objects are left?

Record Your Results

	Property	Object
Magnet		
Balloon		
Water		

State Your Conclusions

1. What properties did you use to separate out the materials?

2. Design a big recycling plant. Draw a picture showing how you might separate materials on a large scale.

Let's Experiment

Suppose you were in charge of cleaning and hauling the garbage at a picnic for 100 people. What kind of system would you set up for separating materials at the picnic?

3.2 Kids Save the Rainforests

▶ What can kids do?

You'd be surprised. In just a bit, you'll read about one boy who helped save more than 7000 hectares of rainforest. Like the students in the picture, others are learning about rainforests, teaching adults about the environment, publishing newsletters, and much more. Their efforts are good for us, the rainforests, and the planet. By keeping the green places green, kids may help to keep the planet from overheating. Wouldn't that be cool?

▼ Kids can help save rainforests in many ways—by buying renewable products, recycling, and learning everything they can.

Use Less, Reuse More

You can help save the rainforests by using and wasting fewer products that play a part in their destruction. And guess what! Using and wasting less also solves problems of pollution and overflowing garbage dumps right here at home, while at the same time helping save the world's rainforests.

Conservation means using the earth's resources wisely, not wastefully. **Recycling** means using the same materials over and over again. For instance, a glass bottle can be melted and made into a new bottle. Paper and aluminum cans—products sometimes made from rainforest resources—can be recycled, too.

Many people help by being thoughtful consumers. That means they buy products that are good for the environment and don't buy products that harm it. For example, thoughtful consumers don't buy pets such as tropical birds whose populations may be in danger. Thoughtful consumers also avoid products with wasteful packaging.

Finally, many people don't know why the rainforests are important. You can teach them, as you did in the Discover Activity. Since the rainforests are important to you, learn as much as you can about how rainforests work and help keep our planet healthy. Then tell others what's happening. Let them know they can help by conserving and recycling. These actions can help save rainforests—and other ecosystems, too. Each person can take actions daily that will benefit the rainforest.

Adopt a Forest

In 1987, nine-year-old Roland Tiennsu of Sweden listened to a scientist tell his class that the earth's rainforests are in danger. Roland decided to do something about the problem. With help from his teacher, he started *Barnens Regnskog*, which means the "Children's Rainforest" in Swedish. With his friends, he raised money to help save a stand of rainforest, like the one in the picture. The idea caught on, and now children as far away as the United States and Japan are raising money to buy and protect rainforests in Costa Rica. Today, the Bosque Eterno de los Niños covers about 7000 hectares.

Through the Children's Rainforest and many other organizations, people of all ages are helping to save rainforests and other ecosystems. When they and others conserve and recycle, the whole planet benefits. That's important as more people are born every day. We all need to share more and waste fewer of the earth's precious resources.

Take a moment to think back. In these modules, you've visited blue glaciers and steaming volcanoes, desert canyons and amazing green rainforests—all connected to one another in surprising ways. You've seen how our planet Earth, warmed just enough by the sun, is home to more kinds of life than any part of the universe we know. It's an amazing home, our most beautiful blue planet—a place to care for and enjoy.

◄ *In the United States, Clinton Hill started Kids for Saving Earth. The club helps save rainforests like this one in Costa Rica.*

Into The Field

What can you do to save the rainforests?
Write to an environmental group to find out. Hint: Your library or a telephone book may have a list of groups.

Checkpoint

1. How can conservation help save rainforests?
2. How did Roland Tiensuu's actions help the planet?
3. **Take Action!** Design a poster showing how recycling and consuming products carefully can help save rainforests.

Making Something New From Something Old

Recycling means more than taking back bottles and cans. It also means turning used materials into something new. Make a recycled desk set in this activity.

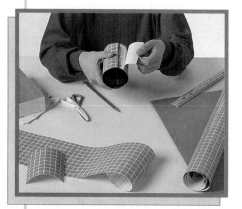

Picture A

Picture B

Picture C

Gather These Materials

cover goggles

scissors

contact paper

cans

cardboard boxes

scrap paper

Follow This Procedure

1 Make a chart like the one on the next page. Record your observations in your chart.

2 Put on your cover goggles.

3 Use scissors to cut a small piece of contact paper to cover a can. This will make a new pencil holder. (Picture A)

4 Cut a large piece of cardboard from a cardboard box. It should be about the size of your desktop. Cover the edges with contact paper. (Picture B) This makes a useful writing mat.

Predict: *What can you do with a lot of old scrap paper?*

5 Cover a small box with contact paper. Cut scraps of paper to put inside. This makes a handy notepaper holder. (Picture C)

6 Put your name on each item in your desk set.

State Your Conclusions

1. How have you cut down on the amount of waste that was produced today?

2. What are some natural resources you conserved by reusing these materials?

Record Your Results

Original Items	New Items

Let's Experiment

Now that you have made a desk set from scrap materials, try making something else. Think of things you could use at home or school or give someone as a present. Make a board game, a model, or a work of art.

Generating Information: Debate

In a **debate**, two people or groups argue opposite sides of an issue. To develop sound arguments, debaters begin by gathering information. Here are some ways to gather information:

- Ask questions
- Discuss
- Observe
- Research

Thinking It Through

Prepare a debate on the best ways to protect rainforests. Consider these:

People can act on their own. They can join conservation groups or raise money to buy rainforest land. They can refuse to buy products made of tropical woods. They can buy products that help. The advantage of this approach is that anyone can do it. The disadvantage is that it takes time. Acting as individuals works slowly, while rainforests are being destroyed at a rapid rate.

World governments can act. The governments in rainforest countries can make strict laws protecting these areas. Governments of richer nations can support new businesses and activities that protect rainforests. This can also help make up for money that is lost when logging and oil drilling companies are kept out of rainforest areas. The advantage is that it could work in large areas quickly. The disadvantage is that it is hard to get governments to act on matters that cost a lot of money.

Think about how to gather information for such a debate. What would your debate be about?

You could have a debate about rainforests. Or you might want to learn how a local nature program works. Who could you talk with or write to with questions? How could you find names of helpful organizations? Where could you find books and magazines for research?

PEOPLE TAKE ACTION!

GOVERNMENT TAKE ACTION!

Your Turn

Divide into two teams. Prepare for your side of the debate. Start talking! Remember, there doesn't have to be a "winning" side. Both sides may come up with helpful ideas and solutions.

Chapter Review

Thinking Back

1. What actions are the people in Java taking to save the rainforests?
2. Why are countries establishing rainforest parks?
3. How can rainforests be "harvested?"
4. What determines the size a patch of rainforest must be in order to be preserved?
5. How does *conservation* help Earth's ecosystems?
6. Describe what *recycling* means.
7. What is a thoughtful consumer?
8. Why would children in Sweden care about a rainforest in Costa Rica?
9. How can you make a difference in protecting the ecosystems of our planet?

Connecting Ideas

1. Copy the concept map. Use the terms at the right to complete the map about protecting the biosphere.

conserving
thoughtful consumer
informing others   recycling

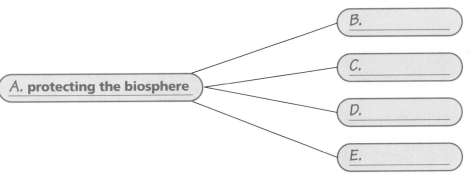

2. Write a sentence or two about the ideas shown in the concept map.

Gathering Evidence

1. In the Activity on page 48, how did you determine the best way to separate different objects?
2. In the Activity on page 54, how did you recycle different objects?

Doing Science!

1. **Create an activity** that compares packaging of two items. Which type of packaging is better for the environment?
2. **Develop a skit** that informs students in your school what they can do to preserve the rainforests.

Kids Saved the Rainforest

What would be your choice for the most beautiful bird in the world? Some say it's the male quetzal. Its back is emerald green, and its belly is ruby red. Its long green tail feathers grow a meter long. Thousands of years ago, Mayan Indians used the quetzal's beautiful feathers to decorate the crowns of their kings.

The quetzal is one of millions of kinds of living creatures preserved in the Children's Rainforest in Costa Rica—the one started by Roland Tiensuu of Sweden. Roland and his friends were able to help save the quetzal and thousands of other rainforest species by hard work. They put on plays, recycled, made and sold T-shirts, asked for donations, and worked at small jobs. They sent the money to a group of scientists in Costa Rica, who bought about 4 hectares of rainforest—

The Children's Rainforest now covers about 7000 hectares.

about the size of 10 football fields. As you know, the Children's Rainforest is much bigger today. With the help of kids from the United States, Great Britain, Japan, and many other countries, the Children's Rainforest now covers about 7000 hectares.

Kids have done even more than this. Recently, a group of students from the Springbrook Nature Center in Minnesota bought more than 12 hectares of rainforest land. They raised money by selling toys made from recycled materials, holding a pancake breakfast, and asking for penny donations. The students gave the money they raised to Kids for Saving Earth. The club arranged to buy rainforest land in the Rio Bravo Reserve in the Central American country of Belize (beh LEEZ).

The Rio Bravo Reserve is home to the quetzal as well as monkeys, snakes, bats, and wild pigs called tapirs. Several kinds of wild cats also live there, among them the jaguar. The beautiful spotted cat is the largest wild cat in the Western Hemisphere.

The jaguar looks a lot like a leopard, but it's heavier. A jaguar can weigh up to 135 kilograms. Jaguars once roamed as far north as Arizona and southern California. But year by year, their habitat has grown smaller. In the Rio Bravo Reserve, however, the jaguars and other animals are safe.

On Your Own

If you want information on what you or a school club can do to help save the rainforests, write to Kids for Saving Earth. You might also find out how to protect wildlife in your own area. Call your local nature center or parks department for suggestions.

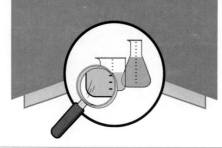

Rainforest Scientist

Occupation: Rainforest scientist

Hobbies: Hiking, reading, swimming, playing guitar

Dr. Diane De Steven

Growing up in a small Ohio town, Diane De Steven found lots to do in her backyard. There were bugs to catch and trees to climb. Nearby were woods to hike and ponds to study. Today Diane still likes to be outdoors. Dr. Diane De Steven studies rainforests.

Why do you study the rainforest?

"Like everyone else, I'm worried that so much of it is being destroyed. Right now I'm working in a protected rainforest. Here no one is allowed to cut down or burn any of the forest."

Why not study endangered forests?

"Other researchers are studying those. In the end, all the facts can be brought together to help solve the problem. But a protected forest shows us how a forest should be working. We can use this information to save endangered forests."

"I study the trees—the backbone of the rainforest. You can tell from the trees that the forest changes on its own. For a period of time, one type of tree is the largest or most common. Then another type takes its place as the forest changes along with the environment around it. The rainforest is very successful. It can support many different kinds of living things. And it may be successful because it can change with its environment."

Can rainforests be saved?

"Right now we're trying to find out how to use the forest without harming it. If large areas of the forest are cut down, they may not come back. But think of the forest as a patchwork quilt. Imagine one patch used for farming, one for grazing, and another for lumber. These patches would be surrounded by uncut forest. After the crops, the grazing, and the lumbering were finished, the forest would slowly move back in."

A Rainforest Partnership

In the rainforest, birds and insects pollinate many flowers. The flowers produce nectar—an important source of food. As they eat the nectar, the birds and insects carry pollen from flower to flower.

1 The bright red petals of the passion flower attract the hummingbird, which is searching for nectar.

2 The flower's female parts are covered with a sticky substance.

3 The male parts of the flower make pollen — tiny grains containing sperm that combine with the flower's eggs to produce seeds. Pollen rubs off on the hummingbird as it feeds on nectar.

4 Pollen grains on the hummingbird's head will stick to the female flower parts. Then the plant can make seeds.

Find Out On Your Own

Use a hand lens to look closely at pollen grains on grass flowers or other flowers. Draw what you see.

Module Review

Making Connections

Systems and Interactions

1. Why do the tilt of Earth on its axis and the sun's rays cause growth of rainforests?

2. How do the producers, consumers, and decomposers within the ecosystem of the rainforest help each other survive?

3. How can the destruction of the trees and other plants of rainforests harm Earth's atmosphere?

4. How are some countries changing their use of the rainforest?

Using What I Learned

Comparing

1. Compare the climate of the rainforest with other climates.

Predicting

2. If efforts are not made to preserve the rainforest, predict what might happen to the atmosphere.

Categorizing

3. Name two things about rainforests that make life in them so abundant.

Communicating

4. Write a letter to your representatives in Congress asking them to explain their ideas about rainforest issues.

Applying

5. Why are people concerned about the extinction of plants in rainforests?

Observing

6. Where on the map are Earth's rainforests located?

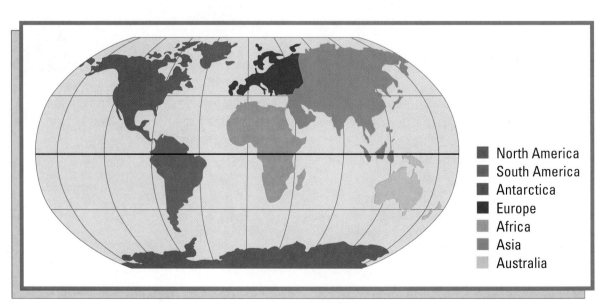

- North America
- South America
- Antarctica
- Europe
- Africa
- Asia
- Australia

Applying What I Learned

Performance Task
Use two plants, two thermometers, and a plastic bag to demonstrate the greenhouse effect.

Action Project
Find out what recycling is being done in your community. What products are accepted? What new products might be added? What percent of your community participates?

Drawing
Make a drawing showing how living things in the ecosystem of the rainforest help each other survive.

Science Theater
Develop a "documentary" that tells your audience about the importance of rainforests, what is currently happening, and what can be done to help preserve rainforests.

Exhibitions
Create a bulletin board or poster that shows how to become a thoughtful consumer. Show examples of products that conserve materials and can be recycled.

What If
What if your community planned to cut down a nearby forest to build a shopping center? What questions might you ask? What arguments might you make against the cutting of the forest? List reasons for and against the plan.

Using Metric

About 1 centimeter

About 1 millimeter

About 1 meter

Water boils (100°C)

Normal body temperature (37°C)

Water freezes (0°C)

1 cm 1 cm
1 cm
1 square centimeter

1 cm 1 cm
1 cm 1 cm
1 cubic centimeter

About 1 kilogram

Degrees Celsius

11 football fields end to end is about 1 kilometer

1 liter of milk

Using Scientific Methods

Scientists ask many questions. No one may know the answers. Then scientists use scientific methods to find answers. Scientific methods include steps like those on the next page. Scientists sometimes use the steps in different order. You can use these steps to do the experiments in this section.

Test Hypothesis If possible, experiments are done to test the hypothesis. Experiments should be repeated to double check the results.

Collect Data The information you gather from the experiment is your data.

Study Data The data collected during an experiment is better understood if it is organized into charts and graphs. Then you can easily see what it all means.

Make Conclusions The conclusion relates to the hypothesis. You might conclude your hypothesis is correct, or that it is incorrect.

Identify Problem The problem is usually in the form of a question such as, "Does a plant need water more than it needs light?"

Make Observations Recorded observations become data and might include the size, color, or shape of something.

State Hypothesis A hypothesis is a likely explanation of the problem. It may turn out to be incorrect; it must be tested.

Safety in Science

Scientists do their experiments safely. You need to be careful when doing experiments too. The next page includes some safety tips to remember.

- Read each experiment carefully.

- Wear cover goggles when needed.

- Clean up spills right away.

- Never taste or smell substances unless directed to do so by your teacher.

- Tape sharp edges of materials.

- Put things away when you finish an experiment.

- Wash your hands after each experiment.

Identifying a Problem

MODULE A

Experimenting with the Size of Splashes

Matt spilled some tomato juice when he poured a glass of juice for his little brother. Some juice landed on the table. More juice fell to the floor. Matt wondered why the splashes on the floor were much bigger than the splashes on the table.

Matt had identified a problem: What causes drops of a liquid to make splashes of different sizes? He knew that gravity was acting on all the drops. Gravity is the force that pulled the drops downward. Also, he believed that all the drops he spilled were about the same size. Matt decided to do an experiment to solve his problem.

Thinking About the Experiment
Matt could think of only one difference between the drops that hit the table and those that hit the floor. The drops that hit the floor had a greater distance to fall.

1. Which tomato juice drops fell from a greater distance?

2. Which tomato juice drops made bigger splashes?

3. What might Matt conclude from these observations?

In science class, Matt had learned that the variable being tested is the part of an experiment that changes. Also, a control is a part of the experiment that does not have the variable being tested.

4. What is the variable being tested in Matt's experiment on the next page?

5. What parts of Matt's experiment do not change?

Try Matt's experiment and see if you come to the same conclusion.

Problem
What causes drops of a liquid to make splashes of different sizes?

Hypothesis
The size of the splash made by a drop is related to the distance the drop falls.

Materials
large sheet of
    white paper
cup
water
food coloring
dropper
meter stick

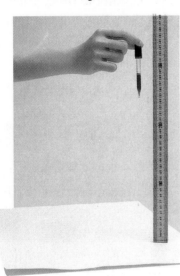

Procedure
1 Fill a cup halfway with water.

2 Add a few drops of food coloring to the water.

3 Lay the paper on the floor.

4 Fill the dropper halfway with colored water.

5 Stand the meter stick up on the paper. Set the stick so it is near one end of the paper. Hold the dropper 25 cm above the paper.

6 Drop 1 drop of colored water on the paper from a height of 25 cm. Write 25 cm on the paper next to the splash.

7 Move the stick a small distance away from the splash.

8 Repeat steps 5 and 6 at heights of 50 cm and 100 cm. After each drop, write the height of the drop next to the splash. Then move the meter stick so there is space on the paper for the next drop.

Data and Observations
Tell what happened to the size of the splash. In a chart like the one below, write: small, bigger, biggest.

Distance	Size of splash
25 cm	
50 cm	
100 cm	

Conclusion
Write your conclusion based on your data and observations.

Practice

Identifying a Problem

1. Suppose you wanted to do an experiment that compared the thickness of liquids to the size of their splashes. Identify the problem you would want to solve in your experiment.

2. How would you change Matt's experiment to solve this problem?

Testing a Hypothesis

MODULE A

Experimenting with Gravity

When the noon bell rang, Tom dropped his apple core into an empty paper cup. On the way out of the lunch room, he pitched the paper cup into a wastebasket. He noticed that the apple core stayed in the cup and landed in the basket—still inside the cup. Tom wondered why the apple core did not fly out of the cup before the cup hit the basket .

Tom had observed many falling objects. He wondered about how the force of gravity affects objects that are falling at the same time. He thought that objects falling together fall at the same rate.

Tom decided to set up an experiment with falling objects. He watched a cup of water fall. Then he poked holes in another cup. He put water into this cup and observed it as it fell.

Thinking About the Experiment

Tom dropped a cup and water to test his hypothesis. He observed the rate at which each fell.

1. What was Tom's hypothesis?

2. What might Tom have observed if the water fell slower than the cup? faster?

Tom observed that water did not flow out of cup 2 when the holes were uncovered and the cup was dropped.

3. What does this tell you about the rate at which the water and cup fell?

4. What does this tell you about Tom's hypothesis?

....

Try It!

Try Tom's experiment and
see if you come to the
same conclusion.

....

Problem

How does the force of gravity affect objects
falling together?

Hypothesis

*Write your own hypothesis for this
experiment.*

Materials

2 paper cups   pencil
   of the same size   tap water
sink or large pail   meter stick

Procedure

1 Label the cups
1 and *2*.

2 Fill cup *1* half
full of water.

3 Hold the cup at
least 1 m above
a sink or pail.
Let go of the
cup and
observe what
happens to it
and the water
as the cup falls.
Record your
observations.

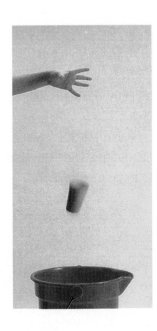

4 Use the point of a pencil to make two
small holes near the center of the bottom
of cup *2*.

5 Cover the holes in the cup with your
fingers. Then fill cup *2* halfway with
water.

6 Hold the cup at least 1 m above a sink
or pail. Take your finger off the holes.
Observe what happens to the water.
Record your observations.

7 Again fill cup *2* half full of water,
holding your fingers over the holes.
Hold the cup over a sink or pail.
Uncover the holes as you let go of the
cup. Observe what happens to the water
and the cup as the cup falls. Record your
observations.

Data and Observations

Situation	Observations
Cup 1 (falling)	
Cup 2 (held)	
Cup 2 (falling)	

Conclusion

Write your conclusion based on your data
and observations.

Practice

Testing a Hypothesis

Suppose you wanted to find out how the
force of gravity affects the water in a cup
with holes on the side.

1. What would your hypothesis be?
2. How could you set up an experiment
to test your hypothesis?
3. What experiment results would
support your hypothesis?

Experiment Skills

Setting Up a Control

Experimenting with Salt Water

Alex was on a vacation with his family. He noticed that it seemed easier to float in the ocean than in the pool back home. Alex knew that ocean water has salt in it. His pool was filled with water from a faucet. This water is fresh water and is not salty.

Alex wondered if things float more easily in salt water than in fresh water. Alex decided to set up an experiment to find out. He filled a cup with salt water. Alex added drops of colored fresh water, vinegar, and rubbing alcohol to the salt water. Alex then watched to see whether the drops floated or sank.

Thinking About the Experiment
Review what Alex wanted to do.

1. What was the problem Alex wanted to solve?

2. Write a hypothesis for the problem.

Alex did not set up his experiment correctly. He did not have a control. The control is the part of the experiment that does not have the variable being tested.

3. Could Alex compare whether the liquids floated more easily in salt water than in fresh water? Explain.

4. What type of water should have been the control?

5. Read Alex's experiment on the next page. How did Alex correct his experiment to have a control?

Try It!

Try Alex's experiment and see if you come to the same conclusion.

Problem

Do things float more easily in salt water than in fresh water?

Hypothesis

Write your own hypothesis for this experiment.

Materials

graduated cylinder
salt
food coloring
water
2 large plastic cups

white vinegar
rubbing alcohol
1 small plastic cup
3 droppers
spoon

Procedure

1. Label one large cup *Fresh water* and the other large cup *Salt water.*

2. Add 200 mL of tap water to each of the large cups.

3. Pour 50 mL of salt into the cup labeled *Salt water.* Stir the salt until it dissolves.

4. Pour 5 mL of fresh water into the small cup. Add several drops of food coloring.

5. Add one or two drops of the colored water to the *Fresh water* cup. Observe what happens to the drops.

6. Now add one or two drops of the colored water to the *Salt water* cup. Observe what happens to the drops. Rinse all the cups.

7. Repeat steps 2 through 6, using colored vinegar instead of colored water in the small cup.

8. Repeat steps 2 through 6, using colored alcohol instead of colored water in the small cup.

Data and Observations

Do the drops mix, float, or sink?

	Fresh water	Salt water
Water		
Alcohol		
Vinegar		

Conclusion

Write your conclusion based on your data and observations.

Practice

Setting Up a Control

You might want to design an experiment to test if solid objects float more easily in water than in other liquids.

1. What would be your control in this experiment?

2. What would be the variable that changes in this experiment?

3. What are some liquids other than water you could use?

Testing a Hypothesis

••••••••••••••••••••••••••••• **MODULE B** •••••••••••••••••••••••••••••

Experimenting with Brine Shrimp

Terry went to a pet store to get some brine shrimp to feed to his fish. He enjoyed looking at all the fish while he was there. Terry noticed that the store owner kept brine shrimp in an aquarium under bright light. He wondered why. He thought of a hypothesis to explain what he noticed: Brine shrimp like light places more than dark places. Terry decided to do an experiment to test his hypothesis.

He bought some brine shrimp and put them in a clear plastic jar. He cut a small hole in a piece of black paper. He wrapped the paper around the jar so that the hole would let light into part of the jar. Then he shined a flashlight through the hole. He took off the paper and observed the brine shrimp.

Thinking About the Experiment

Terry made an observation in the pet store that made him wonder about brine shrimp. Then he thought of a hypothesis.

1. What did Terry notice?

2. What was Terry's hypothesis?

To test his hypothesis, Terry first put the hole in the paper near the bottom of a jar and made observations. Then he moved the hole near the top of the jar and made observations.

3. How did using black paper help Terry test his hypothesis?

4. Why was it important for him to shine the light in two different places?

5. If the brine shrimp had gathered only at the bottom of the jar, would Terry's hypothesis have been correct? Why?

Try Terry's experiment and see if you come to the same conclusion.

Problem

Do brine shrimp like light places or dark places?

Hypothesis

Brine shrimp like light places more than dark places.

Materials

20 brine shrimp	scissors
plastic jar	flashlight
black paper	clock or watch
tape	with second hand

Procedure

1 Put the brine shrimp and salt water in a clear plastic jar.

2 Cut a piece of black paper large enough to wrap around the jar. Cut a small square out of one edge of the paper.

3 Wrap the paper around the jar so that the square hole is near the bottom of the jar. Use tape to hold the paper in place. If the lid of the jar is clear, cover it with black paper.

4 Shine the flashlight through the hole for about 1 minute.

5 Quickly remove the paper and observe where the brine shrimp are. Record your observations in a chart like the one below.

6 Repeat steps 3-5, but position the paper so the square hole is near the top of the jar.

Data and Observations

	Position of Shrimp
Light at bottom	
Light at top	

Conclusion

Write your conclusion based on your data and observations.

Practice

Testing a Hypothesis

1. Suppose you put some warm salt water in the jar. Then you put a funnel in the warm water and pour cold salt water through the funnel. When you remove the funnel, the cold salt water will stay under the warm salt water. You put brine shrimp in the jar and observe their behavior. What is the variable being tested in this new procedure?

2. What hypothesis are you testing?

Setting Up an Experiment

Experimenting with Erosion

Robin lives where winter brings ice and snow. One spring, she saw that some soil had washed away from the hill behind her house. No soil had washed away in her front yard. Her front yard was flat. Robin wondered whether the slope of the land affected the amount of erosion caused by melting ice and snow. She thought it did.

Robin wanted to do an experiment to find out. She needed a way to set up models of flat land and a hill. She decided to use damp sand for soil. She found two lids from shoe boxes to hold the sand. She decided to use ice cubes for melting ice and snow.

Thinking About the Experiment

1. What is the problem that Robin wants to solve?

2. Write a hypothesis for the problem.

The experiment on the next page describes how Robin set up her experiment. She kept every part of the setup the same except for one part. This part is the variable she wanted to test.

3. What parts of the setup are the same for each model?

4. What is the variable Robin's setup tests?

Robin also has a control in her experiment. The control is the part of the setup that shows what happens when ice melts on soil that has no slope.

5. Which part of the setup is the control?

6. What does the part of the setup with the hill of sand test?

Try It!

Try Robin's experiment and see if you come to the same conclusion.

Problem

Does the slope of land affect the amount of erosion caused by melting ice?

Hypothesis

Write your own hypothesis for this experiment.

Materials

2 lids from shoe boxes
aluminum foil
damp sand
2 ice cubes

Procedure

1 Cover the inside of both lids with foil to make them waterproof.

2 Fill each lid with the same amount of damp sand.

3 In 1 lid, shape a steep hill.

4 Smooth out the sand in the other lid so that it is flat.

5 Place 1 ice cube on top of the hill. Place another ice cube in the middle of the flat sand.

6 Watch as the ice melts in each lid. Record your observations in a chart like the one below.

Data and Observations

	Amount of Erosion
Flat land	
Hill	

Conclusion

Write your conclusion based on your data and observations.

Using Models

Experimenting with Properties of Liquids and Solids

Tim's science class was studying earthquakes. He learned that the earth's plates float on partly melted rock, which is located deep inside the earth. This partly melted rock makes up a layer of the earth called the asthenosphere.

Tim read that the asthenosphere is subjected to tremendous pressure and heat. Because of these conditions, rock in the asthenosphere can flow like a very thick liquid.

Tim searched for some ordinary material that shows properties of both a liquid and a solid. He wanted to use this material to make a model of the asthenosphere. He learned that adding water to cornstarch creates a substance with unusual properties. He decided to use cornstarch for his model.

Thinking About the Experiment

In order for a model to be useful, it must show how something looks or works. Scientists use models to describe ideas about nature. They often use a model to represent something, such as the asthenosphere, which they cannot see directly.

1. In the procedure on the next page, describe the point where the mixture best represents the asthenosphere.

2. Would the model be more like a liquid or a solid in step 3? in step 6?

3. What would the nail show?

4. In what part of the procedure could the model be compared to the asthenosphere under pressure?

Try It!

Try Tim's experiment and see if you come to the same conclusion.

Problem

Do some materials have properties of both liquids and solids?

Hypothesis

Some materials have properties of both liquids and solids.

Materials

balance	clear plastic cup
cornstarch, (40 g)	graduated cylinder
nail	spoon
water	

Procedure

1. Pour 15 mL of water into a cup.

2. Mix 10 g of cornstarch in the cup.

3. Place the nail head-first on the surface of the mixture. Observe the consistency of the mixture and whether it can support the nail. Record your observations.

4. Add 5 g more of cornstarch to the bowl and stir until it is mixed. Repeat step 3.

5. Repeat step 4 until the mixture is thick enough to be scooped up and rolled into a small ball. Record your observations.

6. Put the ball of cornstarch mixture in the palm of your hand. Let it warm on your palm for several minutes. Record any changes you see.

7. Remold the mixture into a ball. Apply gentle pressure to the ball for several minutes. Observe and record how the ball responds to pressure.

Data and Observations

Amount of cornstarch	Texture of mixture	Effect on nail
10 g		
15 g		
20 g		
25 g		
30 g		

	Changes in ball shape
In palm	
With pressure	

Conclusion

Write your conclusion based on your data and observations.

Practice

Using Models

Suppose you wanted to find out if a mixture of flour and water has the properties of both a liquid and a solid and can be used to make a model of the asthenosphere.

1. What would be your hypothesis?
2. How would you set up an experiment to test your hypothesis?
3. What would be the model in the experiment?

Setting Up an Experiment

MODULE D

Experimenting with Yeast

Glen was helping his aunt make bread. The recipe called for yeast. His aunt told him that yeast are one-celled organisms. They use an ingredient in the recipe for food. When they use food, they make a gas that causes the bread dough to rise. Glen wondered what ingredient the yeast use for food. The recipe listed flour, sugar, salt, water, eggs, and yeast. Glen wondered if yeast might use sugar for food.

He decided to set up an experiment to find out if yeast use sugar. Since yeast make a gas when they use food, he decided to set up an experiment that would show if gas was given off. By putting balloons over the mouths of jars, Glen can tell if the yeast are using food. The gas they make will help blow up the balloons.

Thinking About the Experiment

1. What is the problem that Glen wants to solve?

2. Write a hypothesis for the problem.

Read Glen's experiment carefully. He kept every part of the setup the same except for one part. This part is the variable he was testing.

3. What did he put in each jar?

4. What parts of the setup are the same for each jar?

5. What is the variable that changes in the setup?

Glen also has a control in his experiment. The control is the part of the setup that shows what happens to the balloon when yeast do not have any food.

6. Which part of the setup is the control?

7. What does the part of the setup with sugar test?

Try It!

Try Glen's experiment and see if you come to the same conclusion.

Problem

What do yeast use for food?

Hypothesis

Write your own hypothesis for this experiment.

Materials

2 identical jars with small mouths
cover goggles
tape
spoonful of sugar

2 spoonfuls of yeast
20 mL warm water
2 balloons

Procedure

1 Put a piece of tape on each of the jars. Write *No food* on 1 piece of tape. Write *Sugar* on another piece of tape.

2 Put a spoonful of sugar in the jar labeled *Sugar.*

3 Put a spoonful of yeast in each jar.

4 Add 10 mL of warm water to each jar.

5 Stretch a balloon over the mouth of each jar.

6 Place the jars in a warm, dark place for the night.

7 The next day observe the balloons. Record the observations in a chart like the one below.

Data and Observations

Descriptions of balloons

	Changes in balloons
Sugar	
No food	

Conclusion

Write your conclusion based on your data and observations.

Practice

Setting Up an Experiment

1. If you wanted to do an experiment to find out if yeast use sugar or corn syrup better as food, what might be your hypothesis?
2. Describe how you would set up the experiment to test your hypothesis.

Testing a Hypothesis

Experimenting with Water

Tina was getting ice cubes from the freezer. She noticed that the water in the tray that had been filled with water was not frozen. The water in the tray that had been only half full was frozen. Tina remembered that during the winter small ponds freeze sooner than larger lakes. In both examples, the water that did not freeze as fast had a larger volume. Tina decided that a larger volume of water cools more slowly than a smaller volume of water.

Tina wanted to test her hypothesis. She decided to use a large and a small jar to stand for a pond and a lake. She used a thermometer to measure how fast warm water cooled in each jar.

Thinking About the Experiment

The experiment on the next page describes how Tina tested her hypothesis.

1. How are the two jars of water alike?

2. How are they different?

3. Tina could have tested her hypothesis using two jars of the same size. Explain how the jars could still have different volumes.

4. Why did Tina begin with warm water?

In an experiment, the part that is different between setups is the variable being tested.

5. What variable is being tested in Tina's experiment?

6. Why did Tina measure the water temperature in both jars at the same time?

Try It!

Try Tina's experiment and see if you come to the same conclusion.

Problem

How does the amount of water affect how fast the water loses heat?

Hypothesis

A larger volume of water cools more slowly than a smaller volume does.

Materials

1 small plastic jar	warm tap water
l large plastic jar	clock or watch
2 thermometers	with second hand

Procedure

1 Fill both jars with warm tap water.

2 Place each jar on a flat surface, about 15 cm apart.

3 Place a thermometer in each jar.

4 Use a clock or watch to time each minute.

5 Read the water temperature in each jar once each minute for the next 10 minutes. Record the temperatures in a chart like the one shown.

Data and Observations

Time in minutes	Temperature in °C	
	Large jar	Small jar
0		
1		
2		
3		
4		
5		
6		
7		
8		
9		
10		

Conclusion

Write your conclusion based on your data and observations.

Practice

Testing a Hypothesis

Another experiment would be needed to find out if large bodies of water warm up faster than smaller ones.

1. Write a hypothesis for this experiment.
2. How could you change the experiment above to test this hypothesis?

Setting Up an Experiment

Experimenting with Evaporation

Julie's science class made salt solutions on Friday. When the bell rang, the students put their jars of solution in a cupboard. Julie left her jar on a sunny windowsill in the classroom.

On Monday, Julie found that only salt crystals were left in her jar. The water had evaporated from her solution. She noticed that the jars in the cupboard still contained solutions. Julie decided that the warm temperature on the windowsill caused her solution to evaporate quickly.

She set up an experiment to see how temperature affects the evaporation of salt water. She left jars of salt water open to air at different temperatures.

Thinking About the Experiment

Julie knew that water slowly disappears if it is left in an open container.

1. What happened to the water in Julie's solution?

2. How could she have kept her solution from evaporating?

3. Could Julie have set up her experiment, shown on the next page, using tap water instead of salt water? Explain.

Julie set up her experiment so that only one thing is different for the jars. The part of the experiment that is different is the variable being tested.

4. What is the same for each jar?

5. What is the variable begin tested in Julie's experiment?

Julie has a control in her experiment. In this experiment, the control is the part of the setup that shows how fast water evaporates in Julie's classroom. Note procedure step 4.

6. Which part of the setup is the control?

Try It!

Try Julie's experiment and see if you come to the same conclusion.

Problem

Does the temperature of the air have an effect on how fast salt water evaporates from an open container?

Hypothesis

Salt water evaporates faster in warm air than in cold air.

Materials

3 jars of same size   water
salt   marker
spoon   200-watt lamp
graduated cylinder   and stand

Procedure

1 Use the marker to label the 3 jars *A*, *B*, and *C*.

2 Prepare a salt solution by dissolving 5 mL of salt in 60 mL of warm water.

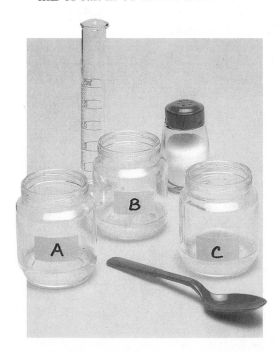

3 Pour 20 mL of the salt solution into each of the 3 jars. Mark the water level on the side of each jar.

4 Set jar *A* under the lighted lamp. Place jar *B* somewhere in the room where it will not be disturbed. Set jar *C* in a cold place. Make sure none of the jars is in a drafty place.

5 Check the jars at the end of each day for 3 days. Record your observations in a chart like the one below.

Data and Observations

Day	Water level		
	A	**B**	**C**
1			
2			
3			

Conclusion

Write your conclusion based on your data and observations.

Practice

Setting Up an Experiment
Suppose you want to find out how air temperature affects the evaporation of a liquid other than salt water.
1. What liquid would you use?
2. What might be your hypothesis?
3. How would you set up an experiment to test your hypothesis?

Making Conclusions

MODULE E

Experimenting with Cotton Thread and Humidity

Jennifer liked to curl her naturally straight hair. She noticed that on dry, cold days her hair stayed curly. On hot, humid days, her curls became looser. Jennifer asked her teacher if human hair shows how much moisture is in the air. The teacher explained that an instrument called a hair hygrometer measures humidity. The hair hygrometer works because hair stretches out when the air becomes humid. The hair absorbs moisture from the air.

Jennifer wondered if she could make a hygrometer from cotton thread. She wondered if the thread would measure relative humidity accurately. She made this hypothesis to answer her question: *A cotton thread hygrometer accurately measures changes in relative humidity.* Jennifer set up an experiment to test her hypothesis.

Thinking About the Experiment
Jennifer collected data in her experiment. She used the data to make a conclusion about the accuracy of her hypothesis. She studied the data to decide if it supported her hypothesis.

1. In the procedure on the next page, what did Jennifer observe to test her hypothesis?

2. On what data would she base her conclusion?

3. What would Jennifer's data and observations have to show in order to support her hypothesis?

The length of the cotton thread did not change. Jennifer concluded that the data she collected did not support her hypothesis.

4. What kind of data would make her conclude that her hypothesis is false?

5. Why did Jennifer need to know the relative humidity of the air?

....

Try It!

Try Jennifer's experiment and
see if you come to the
same conclusion.

....

Problem

Can a cotton thread hygrometer accurately
measure changes in the relative humidity
of air?

Hypothesis

*Recall that Jennifer's hypothesis was
incorrect. Write your own hypothesis for
this experiment.*

Materials

pencil   metric ruler
scissors   shoe box
transparent tape   small nail
cotton thread,   paper, 2 cm x 3 cm
   20 cm long

Procedure

1 Fasten the head
end of the nail to
one end of the
thread with small
pieces of tape.

2 Tape the other end
of the thread to
the inside bottom
of the shoe box.
Tape the thread so
it is centered near
one end of the box.

3 Stand the shoe box on its end so the
thread hangs straight down the middle
of the box.

4 Use the ruler to measure 25 mm on
the edge of the paper. Mark off every
millimeter on the line. Label every
5 mm, starting at 0 mm.

5 Tape the scale to the bottom of the shoe
box, beside the nail. The tip of the nail
should touch the 13 mm mark.

6 Every day for 5 days record the position
of the nail tip on the scale. Try to make
your measurements at the same time of
day. Record your measurements on a
chart like the one shown.

7 Get the actual relative humidity from a
local weather report for each time you
record the nail's position. Record the
actual relative humidity on your chart.

Data and Observations

Date	Position of nail tip	Relative humidity

Conclusion

Write your conclusion based on your data
and observations.

Practice

Making Conclusions

Suppose you wanted to test materials
other than cotton thread for making a
hygrometer.
1. What other materials might you use?
2. If you tested one of those materials
   and found that during high humidity
   the materials sometimes got shorter
   and sometimes got longer, what might
   you conclude?

Making Conclusions

Experimenting with Grape Ivy Leaves

Shannon visited a sunny greenhouse. She bought a grape ivy plant. The woman at the greenhouse told her that this kind of plant grows best when it gets a lot of light.

When Shannon got home, she began to wonder what would happen to the plant's leaves if they did not get enough light. Before she could make any conclusions, she would need to do an experiment. Shannon chose a large healthy branch with six leaves on it. She taped squares of black paper to the front and back of each leaf. She left the plant near a sunny window.

Thinking About the Experiment

1. Why did Shannon cover some of the leaves?

2. Why did Shannon not cover all of the leaves on the plant?

After a week, Shannon removed the paper from the leaves. Three leaves had turned yellow. Two others had yellow spots. The sixth leaf was a pale green.

3. Should Shannon have concluded that her hypothesis was wrong since one covered leaf still looked green? Explain.

4. What part of Shannon's data supported her hypothesis?

5. What conclusion do you think Shannon reached?

Suppose that Shannon had observed no changes in the leaves that were covered for a week.

6. Would that data support her hypothesis? Explain.

7. What conclusion would Shannon have made based on that data?

Problem
What happens to grape ivy leaves when they do not get enough light?

Hypothesis
Leaves of grape ivy plants will not stay green if they do not get enough light.

Materials
2 sheets of black paper
scissors

grape ivy plant
tape
water

Procedure

1 Choose a branch of the plant with 5 or 6 healthy leaves on it.

2 Cut 2 squares of black paper for each leaf on the branch. The squares should be big enough to cover the leaves completely.

3 Tape 2 squares together along 1 edge. Slip a leaf between the 2 squares. Then tape the other edge of the squares together.

4 Put the plant in a sunny place and water it normally.

5 After 1 week, remove the paper from the leaves.

6 Using a chart like the one shown, record how the leaves look.

Data and Observations

	Appearance of leaves
Covered leaves	
Leaves with no color	

Conclusion
Write your conclusion based on your data and observations.

Practice

Making Conclusions

1. If you wanted to experiment to find out if white paper squares block out the same amount of light as black paper squares, how would you change the procedure?

2. If leaves covered with white squares showed no changes, what conclusion would you make?

Glossary

A

adaptation (ad′ap tā′shən), a structure or behavior that helps a living thing live in its surroundings.

adapted (ə dap′tid), made fit to live under certain conditions.

air mass, a large amount of air with the same temperature and humidity.

air pressure (presh′ər), the amount that air presses or pushes on anything.

air resistance (ri zis′təns), a force that slows down the movement of objects through the air.

altitude (al′tə tüd), the height above sea level.

anemometer (an′ə mom′ə tər), a tool that measures wind speed.

asteroid (as′tə roid′), a rocky object orbiting the sun between the planets.

asteroid (as′tə roid′) **belt,** a large group of rocks that orbit the sun between Mars and Jupiter.

atmosphere (at′mə sfir), the layer of gases that surrounds the earth.

atom (at′əm), a basic bit of matter.

axis (ak′sis), an imaginary line through a spinning object.

B

barometer (bə rom′ə tər), an instrument that measures air pressure.

Beaufort (bō′fərt) **scale,** a scale used to estimate wind speed based on observing objects moving in the environment.

biosphere (bī′ə sfir), the region on and surrounding the earth that can support life and that includes the atmosphere, water, and soil.

C

Calorie (kal′ər ē), a specific amount of energy in food.

carbon dioxide (dī ok′sīd), a gas in air that is taken in by plants, exhaled by animals, and given off when fuel is burned.

Celsius (sel′sē əs) **degree,** a unit for measuring temperature.

central vent (sen′trəl vent), a large hole through which magma bursts out of a volcano.

cirrus (sir′əs) **cloud,** a white, feathery cloud made up of tiny pieces of ice.

climate (klī′mit), the average weather conditions of an area over many years.

cold front, the area where a cold air mass moves toward a warm air mass and pushes the warm air up quickly.

colonizer (kol′ə nīz ər), a living thing that comes into an area to eat and live.

comet (kom′it), a frozen chunk of ice and dust that orbits the sun.

compressed (kəm prest′) **air,** air put under extra pressure or squeezed so that it takes up less space.

condense (kən dens′), to change from a gas to a liquid.

conservation (kon′sər vā′shən), protecting from loss or from being used up.

consumer (kən sü′mər), a living thing that depends on producers for food.

contract (kən trakt′), to become smaller in size or to move closer together.

control (kən trol′), the part of an experiment that does not have the variable being tested.

convection (kən vek′shən) **currents,** the circular movement of gases or liquids as a result of differences in temperature.

core (kôr), the center part of the earth.

crust (krust), the top layer of the earth.

cumulonimbus (kyü′myə lō nim′bəs) **cloud,** a cloud that looks like a tall, dark cumulus cloud and often brings thunderstorms.

cumulus (kyü′myə ləs) **cloud,** a white, fluffy cloud that looks like cotton.

D

dark zone, the ocean waters between 1200 and 4000 meters deep where sunlight does not reach.

deciduous (di sij′ü əs) **tree,** one of a group of trees that lose their leaves in the fall.

decomposer (dē′kəm pō′zər), a consumer that puts materials from dead plants and animals back into soil, air, and water.

dissolve (di zolv′), to spread evenly in a liquid and form a solution.

Doppler (dop′lər) **radar,** a type of radar that shows distance and direction of movement.

E

earthquake (ėrth′kwāk), a shaking or sliding of the earth's crust.

ecosystem (ē′kō sis′təm), a community and its nonliving environment.

ellipse (i lips′), the shape of a circle that has been flattened a little.

erosion (i rō′zhən), the moving of weathered rocks and soil by wind, water, or ice.

eruption (i rup′shən), the bursting forth or flowing of lava from a volcano.

evacuate (i vak′yü āt), to withdraw from.

evaporate (i vap′ə rāt′), to change from a liquid to a gas.

evergreen, a plant that stays green all year, including firs and pines.

extinct (ek stingkt′), something that is no longer found living on earth.

F

fault (fôlt), a crack in the earth's crust along which rocks move.

fault-block mountain, a mountain that forms when a big block of rock moves up along a fault.

folded mountain, a mountain that forms when two plates in the earth's crust collide and the edges of the plates crumple.

food chain, the path that energy and nutrients take in a community.

force (fôrs), a push or a pull.

fossil (fos′əl), a trace of a plant or animal that is often found in sedimentary rock.

front, the line where two air masses meet.

G

gas, a state of matter with no definite shape or volume.

geyser (gī′zer), a spring that spouts a fountain or jet of hot water and steam into the air.

glacier (glā′shər), a large mass of ice that moves very slowly.

glider (glī′dər), a motorless aircraft that is kept in the air by rising air currents.

graduated cylinder (graj′ü āt ed sil′ən dər), piece of equipment used for measuring volume.

gravitational force (grav′ə tā′shə nəl fôrs), the pull of gravity that causes all the planets to orbit around the sun.

gravity (grav′ə tē), a force that pulls any two objects together.

greenhouse effect, the trapping of heat by the air around the earth.

H

habitat (hab′ə tat), the place where a living thing lives.

high-pressure area, an area where cool air sinks and pushes down on the earth with more pressure.

Homo sapiens (hō′mō sā′pē enz), the species including all existing races of human beings.

hot spot, a place in the earth's mantle where the mantle melts because of extreme heat.

humidity (hyü mid′ə tē), the amount of water vapor in the air.

hurricane (hėr′ə kān), a huge storm that forms over a warm ocean and has strong winds and heavy rains.

hydrogen (hī′drə jən), a colorless, odorless, gaseous element that burns easily and has less mass than any other element.

hydrosphere (hī′drə sfir), the water portion of the earth.

hygrometer (hī grom′ə tər), an instrument that measures humidity.

hypothesis (hī poth′ə sis), a likely explanation of a problem.

J

jet propulsion (prə pul′shən), a forward motion produced by the reaction of an object to high-pressure gas moving in the opposite direction.

L

lava (lä′və), hot, melted rock that flows from a volcano.

lift (lift), an upward movement.

light zone, the sunlit waters from the ocean surface down to 100 meters.

liquid, a state of matter with a definite volume but no definite shape.

lithosphere (lith′ə sfir), the solid portion of the earth.

low-pressure area, an area where warm air rises and pushes down on the earth with less pressure.

lunar eclipse (lü′nər i klips′), the darkening of the moon as it passes through the earth's shadow.

M

magma (mag′mə), hot, melted rock deep inside the earth.

magma chamber (mag′mə chām′bər), a large, underground lake of magma in the earth's crust.

mantle (man′tl), the earth's middle layer.

mass (mas), the amount of material that an object has in it.

meteor (mē′tē ər), a piece of rock or dust from space burning up in the earth's air.

meteorite (mē′tē ə rīt′), a rock from space that has passed through the air and landed on the ground.

meteorologist (mē′tē ə rol′e jist), a person who studies weather.

mineral (min′ər əl), nonliving solid matter from the earth.

mixture (miks′cher), two or more substances that are placed together but can be easily separated.

molecule (mol′ə kyül), two or more atoms held together.

moraine (mə rān′), a mass or ridge made of rocks, dirt, etc, that were scraped up and deposited by a glacier.

N

nutrient (nü′trē ənt), a material that plants and animals need to live and grow.

O

Oort Cloud, a vast cloud of comets that might exist in space billions of kilometers past the outermost planet.

orbit (ôr′bit), the path of an object around another object.

oxygen (ok′sə jən), a gas that is given off by plants and used by animals.

ozone (ō′zōn) **layer,** the region of concentrated ozone that shields the earth from excessive ultraviolet radiation.

P

pectoral (pek′tər əl) **muscles,** chest muscles.

planet (plan′it), a large body of matter revolving around the sun.

plankton (plangk′tən), the small organisms that float or drift in water, especially at or near the surface.

plate, one of twenty sections of solid rock that make up the earth's crust.

polar climate (pō′lər klī′mit), a major climate zone that receives indirect sunlight all year and that has cold or cool temperatures all year.

pollination (pol′li na′shən), the movement of pollen from a stamen to a pistil.

pollution (pə lü′shən), the addition of harmful substances to land, air, or water.

precipitation (pri sip′ə tā′shən), moisture that falls to the ground from clouds.

pressure (presh′ər), the force exerted on a certain area.

producer (prə dü′sər), a living thing that can use sunlight to make sugars.

property (prop′ər tē), something about an object that can be observed, such as size or shape.

R

rain gauge (gāj), an instrument that measures precipitation.

rainforest, a very dense forest in a region, usually tropical, where rain is very heavy throughout the year.

recycle (rē sī′kəl), to change something so it can be reused.

reef (rēf), narrow ridge of rocks, sand, or coral at or near the surface of the water.

revolution (rev′ə lü′shən), the movement of one object around another object.

rotation (rō tā′shən), one full spin of an object around an axis.

S

saliva (sə lī′və), the fluid in the mouth that makes chewed food wet and begins digestion.

saturated (sach′ə rā′tid) **air,** air that contains all the water vapor it can possibly hold.

season (sē′zn), one of the four periods of the year—spring, summer, fall, or winter.

sedimentary (sed′ə men′tər ē) **rock,** rock made of sediments that have been pressed together.

seismograph (sīz′mə graf), an instrument for recording the direction, strength, and time of earthquakes or other movements of the earth's crust.

solar eclipse (sō′lər i klips′), the blocking of sunlight by the moon as the moon passes between the sun and the earth.

solar system, the sun, the nine planets and their moons, and other objects that orbit the sun.

solid, a state of matter with a definite shape and a definite volume.

solstice (sol′stis), either of the two times in the year when the sun is at its greatest distance from the equator and appears to be farthest north or south in the sky.

solution (sə lü′shən), a mixture in which one substance spreads evenly throughout another substance.

sonic (son′ik) **boom,** a loud noise caused by an airplane crossing through the sound barrier when it travels faster than the speed of sound.

species (spē′shēz), a group of organisms that have the same traits and can produce offspring that can also produce offspring.

star, a ball of hot, glowing gases.

sternum (ster′nəm), breastbone.

stratus (strā′təs) **cloud,** a cloud that forms in layers that spread across the sky.

subduction (səb′dək shən), the sliding of one of the earth's plates under another.

submersible (səb mėr′sə bəl), that which can be put under water.

subsonic (sub son′ik), having to do with speed less than the speed of sound.

supersonic (sü′pər son′ik), capable of moving faster than sound.

system (sis′təm), a group of organs that work together to do a job; a set of things or parts that form a whole and work together or affect one another.

T

temperate climate (tem′pər it klī′mit), a major climate zone that receives indirect sunlight in the winter and more direct sunlight in the summer.

theory (thē′ər ē), one or more related hypotheses supported by data that best explains things or events.

thermometer (thər mom′ə tər), an instrument for measuring temperature.

thrust (thrust), a forward push.

tremor (trem′ər), a weak earthquake.

trench (trench), a long, narrow valley in the floor of the ocean.

tropical climate (trop′ə kəl klī′mit), a major climate zone that receives direct sunlight and has warm temperatures all year.

V

variable (ver′ē ə bəl), anything in an experiment that can be changed.

volcano (vol kā′nō), a mountain with an opening through which lava, ashes, rocks, and other materials come out.

W

warm front, the area where a warm air mass runs into a cold air mass and slides up over the cold air.

water cycle (sī′kəl), the movement of water by evaporation, condensation, and precipitation.

water molecule (mol′ə kyül), the smallest particle of water.

water vapor (wô′tər vā′pər), water in the form of gas.

weathering (weᴛн′ər ing), wearing down or breaking apart rocks.

weight (wāt), force that gravity exerts on a mass.

wind, air that is moving from an area of high pressure to an area of low pressure.

wind vane (vān), a tool that shows wind direction.

Index

O

Obsidian, C36
Ocean floor, C36, C47
Oceans, A51, A53
    climate and, E40-41
    erosion and, B39
    as habitats, B62-71
    pollution of, B76
    See also Beaches; Pacific Ocean
Oort Cloud, A37
Orbit
    of comets, A37
    of Earth, A5, A7, E30, E35-36
    gravity and, A13
    of moon, A10, A18
    of Pluto, A37
    See also Rotation
Orchids, F18
Ore, C61
Oxygen
    in atmosphere, A44, D6, D9, F36
    digestive system and, B50
    in mantle of earth, C6
    plants and, F12-13
Ozone layer, D6-7, D53

P

Pacific Ocean, B65-71
Perspiration (sweat), B51, E5, E6
Pinatubo, Mount, C27
Planet, Earth as a, A5
Planets, A5, A25-40
    names of, A37
    temperature of, A30-31
    See also Solar system
Plankton, A50, A51, B66, B69

Plants
    as colonizers, C33
    extinct, F34-35
    used for medicine, F34, F35
    in rainforest, F10, F15-19
    saltwater, B60
    as survivors, C31
    water and, A49, A50-53, B49, B52-53
    See also Gardening; Seeds; Vegetables
Plates, C12-13
    earthquakes and, C45, C48-55
    mountains and, C44-45, C46-47
    subduction of, C17
Pluto, A25, A34, A36-37
Polar climate, E33
Pollination, F17, F61
Pollution, B24-25, B76
Ponds, A49, B58-59
Prairie dogs, E49
Prairies, E48
Pressure
    of air, D8-9
    earthquakes and, C49
    magma and, C8, C27
Propellers, D43, D45, D48-49
Pumice, C36
Puu Oo, Mount, C9

Q

Quartz, B31
Quetzal, F58-59

R

Radar weather reports, E62, E66, E77
Rain, A47
    air masses and, E12
    amount of, B21
    climate zones and, E38-39
    clouds predicting, E54, E55
    cold fronts and, E14
    erosion and, B34
    formation of, B9, E7
    rocks and, B30-31

Acknowledgments

ScottForesman

Editorial: Terry Flohr, Janet Helenthal, Mary Ann Mortellaro, Kathleen Ludwig, Glen Phelan, Matthew Shimkus

Art and Design: Barbara Schneider, Jacqueline Kolb, George Roth, Cathy Sterrett

Picture Research/Photo Studio: Nina Page, Kelly Mountain, Judy Ladendorf, John Moore

Photo Lab/Keyline: Marilyn Sullivan, Mark Barberis, Gwen Plogman

Production: Barbara Albright, Francine Simon

Marketing: Lesa Scott, Ed Rock

Ligature, Inc.
Pupil Edition interior design and production

Unless otherwise acknowledged, all photographs are the property of ScottForesman. Unless otherwise acknowledged, all computer graphics by Ligature, Inc. Page abbreviations are as follows: **(T)** top, **(C)** center, **(B)** bottom, **(L)** left, **(R)** right, **(INS)** inset.

Module A
Photographs
Front & Back Cover: Background: "Constellations of the Northern Hemisphere" chart © Frank Schaffer Co., Frank Schaffer Publications Inc. Children's Photos: John Moore

Page A2,16,17,22,26,27,28,29,32,33,36,43,59(TL-INS), 60 NASA **A3(T)** Jon Riley/Tony Stone Worldwide **A18,19(T)** A Mount Wilson & Palomar Observatory Photograph **A21(L)** National Optical Astronomy Observatories **A21(R)** National Optical Astronomy Observatories **A44-45(T)** Jon Riley/Tony Stone Worldwide **A44-45(C)** Robin Smith/Tony Stone Worldwide **A44-45(B)** Baron Wolman **A46** Jeff Schultz/Alaska Photo/All Stock **A50(ALL)** William H. Amos **A51** Anne Wertheim/ANIMALS ANIMALS **A53(T)** Don & Pat Valenti/f/Stop Pictures, Inc. **A53(B)** Patrice Ceisel/Tom Stack & Associates **A58** Courtesy of Stuart Elementary School, Patrick County, Virginia **A59** Park Seed Company **A59(TL)** NASA **A62(L)** Don & Pat Valenti/f/Stop Pictures, Inc. **A62(C)** Don and Pat Valenti **A62(R)** Don & Pat Valenti/f/Stop Pictures, Inc.

Illustrations
Page A5 Roberta Polfus **A6-7** Roberta Polfus **A10-11** Roberta Polfus **A18-19** George Kelvin **A34-35** Jacque Auger **A34-35(INS)** Randy Verougstraete **A36** Jacque Auger **A40** Nancy Lee Walter **A44** Roberta Polfus

Module B
Photographs
Front & Back Cover: Background: Paul Berger/Tony Stone Worldwide Children's Photos: John Moore

Page B5 E.R.Degginger **B6-7** Mark Kelly/Alaska Stock Photo **B8(T)** Wolfgang Kaehler **B13(R)** Hermann Eisenbeiss/ Photo Researchers **B16(B)** Wolfgang Kaehler **B24** Robert W. Blickensderfer/Ohio Sea Grant **B25** Robert W.Blickensderfer **B30(R)** Ray Pfortner/Peter Arnold, Inc. **B35(L)** Photo Researchers **B36-37** Francois Gohier/Photo Researchers **B38(R)** Jack Dermid/Photo Researchers **B39(L)** Scott Blackman/ Tom Stack & Associates **B40-41** Robert C. Fields/Earth Scenes **B44-45** Baron Wolman **B48** E.R.Degginger **B51(L)** From BEHOLD MAN/Lennart Nilsson/Bonnier Fakta **B51(R)** Steve Allen/Peter Arnold, Inc. **B54-55** Carl Purcell/Photo Researchers **B58** Visuals Unlimited **B59** Zig Leszczynski/ANIMALS ANIMALS **B62(L)** Andrew J.Martinez **B62(R)** Stephen Frink/Waterhouse **B69** Bruce Robinson **B70(L)** Andrew J. Martinez **B70-71** Fred Bavendam/Peter Arnold, Inc. **B71(INS)** Andrew J.Martinez **B72** Visuals Unlimited **B75** Visuals Unlimited **B76** Will Brown for ScottForesman

Illustrations
Page B22-23 Joe Le Monnier **B35** Charles Thomas **B37** Joe Le Monnier **B38** Walter Stuart **B44** JAK Graphics **B56-57** Walter Stuart **B58-59** Cindy Brodie **B65** Walter Stuart **B67** Walter Stuart **B68** Walter Stuart **B77** George Kelvin

Module C
Photographs
Front & Back Cover: Background: Visuals Unlimited Children's Photos: John Moore

Page C3(TL) Reuters/UPI/Bettmann **C3(B)** Paul Miller/Black Star **C5(T)** Dave Millert/Tom Stack & Associates **C5(B)** Visuals Unlimited **C7(T)** Ron Watts/Black Star **C14** Michael and Patricia Fogden **C19** E.R.Degginger **C22(CR)** Stephen Dalton/Photo Researchers **C25** Gary Braasch **C25(INS)** David Olson/Black Star **C27** Reuters/UPI/Bettmann **C30** Peter Frenzen/U.S.Forestry Service **C31(BL)** Jerry Franklin/U.S.Forestry Service **C32** Gary Braasch **C32(INS)** Gary Braasch **C34-35** David Olson/Black Star **C34(TC)** Thomas Kitchin/Tom Stack & Associates **C34(BC)** Gary Braasch **C35(TC)** Peter K.Ziminski/Visuals Unlimited **C35(BR)** Gary Braasch **C36(C)** Tim Rock/Earth Scenes **C36(B)** Anna E. Zuckerman/ Tom Stack & Associates **C40** William H.Amos **C43** Reprinted Courtesy of H.M.Gousha/ Simon & Schuster **C44** Visuals Unlimited **C45** Visuals Unlimited **C48** David Olson/Black Star **C49** Paul Miller/ Black Star **C49(INS)** Arnold Genthe/Library of Congress **C52(T)** NASA **C58** Alfred Borcover **C60** James E.Stoots, Jr./ Lawrence Livermore National Laboratory

Illustrations

Page C2 Ebet Dudley   **C7** Ebet Dudley   **C8-9** Ebet Dudley
C12-13 Ebet Dudley   **C14-15** Joe Le Monnier   **C16-17** Joe Le Monnier   **C18** Joe Le Monnier   **C18(INS)** Ebet Dudley
C22 Ebet Dudley   **C44-45** Ebet Dudley   **C48** Ebet Dudley
C50-51 Hank Iken   **C56** JAK Graphics   **C59** Rich Lo
C61 Rich Lo

Module D
Photographs
Front & Back Cover: Background: Kim Taylor/Bruce Coleman, Inc.   Children's Photos: John Moore

Page D3(ALL T) Stephen Dalton/Photo Researchers
D3(BL) The Granger Collection, New York   **D5** Michael & Patricia Fogden   **D21** Stephen Dalton/ANIMALS ANIMALS
D22(L) Stephen Dalton/Photo Researchers   **D24(L)** NOAA/NESDIS/NCDC   **D24(R)** T.C.Kelley/Photo Researchers
D26-27 Tom McHugh/Photo Researchers   **D28** Kim Taylor/Bruce Coleman, Inc.   **D32(T)** Frans Lanting/Minden Pictures
D34(L) Wendy Shattil and Bob Rozinski/Tom Stack & Associates
D35(B) Francois Gohier/Photo Researchers   **D38** Pat & Tom Leeson/Photo Researchers   **D40** Richard Legeckis/Nesdid/Rsmas/NOAA/NESDIS/NCDC   **D41** The Granger Collection, New York   **D42(T)** Science Museum, London   **D44(T)** Greg Vaughn/Tom Stack & Associates   **D44(B)** Haward Gallery London, Tetva Associates   **D45(CR)** NASA   **D45(TC)** Library of Congress   **D45(BC)** Library of Congress   **D50(T)** John Covant/Photri, Inc.   **D52** NASA   **D53** NASA
D58(T) AP/Wide World   **D58(B)** M Barrett/H. Armstrong Roberts   **D62(L)** Rod Planck/Tom Stack & Associates
D62(C) Stephen Dalton/ANIMALS ANIMALS
D62(R) Frans Lanting/ALLSTOCK,INC.
D67(ALL) E/NOAA/NESDIS/NCDC

Illustrations
Page D5 Toni Goffe   **D6-7** Francisco Maruca
D8(T) Francisco Maruca   **D8(B)** Toni Goffe   **D24-25** Eric Wright   **D28** Dickson O. Tabe   **D32-33** Kirk Caldwell
D34 Kirk Caldwell   **D35** Kirk Caldwell   **D42-43** Chris Costello   **D50-51** Chris Costello   **D56** JAK Graphics
D58 JAK Graphics

Module E
Photographs
Front Cover: Children's Photos: John Moore

Page E3(TL) NOAA   **E3(TR)** Van Bucher/Photo Researchers
E3(B) Franca Principe, Instituto e Museo di Storra della Scienza, Florence   **E15** Warren Faidley/Weatherstock   **E16** Wolfgang Kaehler   **E22** Michael & Elvan Habicht/Earth Scenes
E23 Elvan Habicht/Peter Arnold, Inc.   **E24(L)** NOAA/NESDIS/NCDC   **E29(L)** G.I.Bernard/Earth Scenes   **E29(R)** G.I.Bernard/Earth Scenes   **E30(T)** James P. Jackson/Photo Researchers
E31 Gary Braasch/Alaska Photo Collection/ALLSTOCK
E37(L) Charlie Ott/Photo Researchers   **E37(R)** E.R.Degginger
E41 ERIM, Ann Arbor, MI   **E45** Richard Kolar/Earth Scenes
E46 Peter B.Kaplan/Photo Researchers   **E47(R)** Peter B.Kaplan/Photo Researchers   **E48(T)** Mickey Gibson/Earth Scenes
E48(B) Peter Arnold, Inc.   **E49** Peter Arnold, Inc.
E50 E.R.Degginger   **E53** E.R.Degginger   **E54(T)** Bob Daemmrich/Stock Boston   **E54(T INS)** Joyce Photographics/Photo Researchers   **E54(B)** Richard Pasley/Stock Boston
E54(B INS) E.R.Degginger   **E55(T)** David Woodward/Tony Stone Worldwide   **E55(T INS)** Gary Brettnacher/Tony Stone Worldwide   **E55(B)** Sam C.Pierson/Photo Researchers

E55(B INS) Tony Freeman/Photo Edit   **E58** E.R.Degginger
E60 Franca Principe, Instituto e Museo di Storia della Scienza, Florence   **E61** Van Bucher/Photo Researchers   **E62(T)** Photo Researchers   **E62(B)** Stephen Frisch/Stock Boston   **E63** Tony Stone Worldwide   **E75** E.R.Degginger

Illustrations
Page E11 Joe Le Monnier   **E12-13** Joe Le Monnier
E14 Joe Le Monnier   **E17** Joe Le Monnier   **E32** Susan Nethery
E36-37 Greg McNair   **E38-39** Joe Le Monnier   **E57** Susan Nethery   **E72** JAK Graphics   **E77** Gary Torrisi

Module F
Photographs
Front & Back Cover: Background: Victor Englebert   Children's Photos: John Moore

Page F2(BR) Michael & Patricia Fogden   **F6** Victor Englebert
F14(T) Michael & Patricia Fogden   **F14(C)** Michael & Patricia Fogden   **F14(B)** Jany Sauvamet/Photo Researchers
F19(L) Gary Retherford/Photo Researchers
F19(C) Jack Swenson/Tom Stack & Associates
F19(R) J.P. Varin/Jacana/Tom Stack & Associates
F24(C) NOAA/NESDIS/NCDC   **F25(L)** Rugerio Reis/Black Star   **F25(R)** Walt Anderson/Visuals Unlimited   **F26** Victor Englebert   **F28** Dan Brennan/Knut Bry   **F30(B)** Loren McIntyre   **F40** John Cancalosi/Peter Arnold, Inc.   **F44(T)** Jane Thomas/Visuals Unlimited   **F44(B)** Loren McIntyre   **F45(T)** Victor Englebert   **F45(B)** George Loun/Visuals Unlimited
F59(T) E.R.Degginger   **F59(B)** Michael Fogden/Bruce Coleman, Inc.   **F60** Courtesy University of Wisconsin

Illustrations
Page F3 John Burgoyne   **F7** Mark Smith   **F8-9** Cindy Brodie
F10 John Burgoyne   **F14-15** John Burgoyne   **F28-29** Joe Le Monnier   **F30** Joe Le Monnier   **F34-35** Wild Onion Studio
F36 Ebet Dudley   **F56** JAK Graphics   **F61** Wild Onion Studio
Leaf Borders throughout module **(F4, 5, 6, 7, 10, 11, 14, 16, 17, 18, 19, 24, 25, 28, 29, 30, 31, 34, 35, 42, 43, 46, 47, 50, 51, 52, 53)** by John Burgoyne